DIVORCE CASUALTIES

DIVORCE CASUALTIES

*Protecting Your Children From
Parental Alienation*

Douglas Darnall, Ph.D.

TAYLOR PUBLISHING COMPANY | DALLAS, TEXAS

Published by Taylor Publishing Company
1550 West Mockingbird Lane
Dallas, Texas 75235

Book design by Mark McGarry
Set in Minion

Library of Congress Cataloguing-in-Publication Data
    Darnall, Douglas.
        Divorce Casualties: Protecting Your Children from Parental Alienation
    / by Douglas Darnall.
        p. cm.
    Includes bibliographical references (p.   ) and index.
    1. Parental alienation syndrome—Prevention. 2. Children of divorced
parents—Mental health—Prevention. 3. Custody of Children—Psychological
aspects. I. Title.
    RJ506.P27D37   1998
    616.85'2—dc21   98–25046
                                                                         CIP

Printed in the United States of America

*To mothers and fathers
for encouraging their children
to have loving and healthy relationships
with their other families*

Contents

Acknowledgments

Divorce Casualties is a culmination of many years of work that would never have been written without families willing to share their story. The love and support from my own friends and family also contributed greatly to its creation. I am grateful to the judges for their time and faith in what I • am trying to accomplish. The late Judge Peter Panagis, Judge John Leskovyansky, Judge Thomas Norton, Judge Richard James, Judge Pamela Rintala, and Referee Alex Savakis all made valuable contributions. Working daily with the destructive influences of alienation have given them an appreciation for the importance of helping families to reduce tensions and prevent parental alienation.

There are many friends who have helped me through the years with editing and offering their suggestions about the contents of the book. I wish to thank Patty Callihan, M.S.; Tony DeRosa, Ph.D.; Arlene McMurrey, Terry Heltzel, Ph.D., Mary Geidner, Jim Maderitz, Janet Frick, Cathy Reppy, Carla Veri-Bowman, Dr. Walter Miller, Jane Spies, Camille Cline, William J. Evans, Ph.D., and of course, my agent and friend, Denise Marcil.

I am grateful to my parents, Paul and Jan Tanner for sharing their wisdom and experiences. Paul, a retired professor at U.C.L.A. has published many books on music and was a member of the Glen Miller Orchestra. Their advice and support has been invaluable.

My family has had to sacrifice a lot with my many late hours working in the den. My wife, Jan and my two daughters, Brianna and Lindsey have been great and have always supported me, helping me when I have felt tired and discouraged. I love them for standing beside me.

Introduction

When parents divorce or separate, their children are often caught in the emotional crossfire. Many couples continue to fight bitterly for years after a divorce, especially over such issues as child support and visitation (referred to as "parenting time" in this book). Yet research has repeatedly shown that the children's adjustment and mental health depend directly on how well their parents get along. In particular, a parent who, consciously or unconsciously, sabotages the children's relationship with the other parent as a means of revenge on their ex-spouse does more lasting damage to the children. This behavior is at the root of parental alienation syndrome.

Perhaps it is ridiculous to think that parents who could not get along in a marriage should be able to get along after the divorce. As challenging as it may sound, parents have to put their personal needs aside and think about what is best for their children. For the children's sake, they must learn to get along with the other parent, resolving disputes without involving the children.

During my fourteen years as a psychologist specializing in custody evaluations, I have worked with over six hundred families going through divorce or custody litigation. I am continually amazed by how many custody or visitation disputes are resolved by simply giving all family members an opportunity to tell their side of the story and then giving them a little education. I work for the court and represent no family member in particular. The parents and children know this, and I think it helps them trust the process. These cases are satisfying to me personally because the families are often able to work out their differences and avoid the costly and emotionally trying experience of a full hearing. I hope the information presented here will help you reach the same goal.

Some parents are deliberate in their desire to alienate. Others alienate without realizing what they are doing. Even if you see your ex-spouse as the primary alienator, your responses to alienating behavior can cause further alienation. Stopping the cycle is difficult, but it must be done for your children. They have the most to gain, so it is worth your hard work.

In writing this book, I became aware of the limitations of our language when I realized that I don't always know who my readers are. Some of you are parents who are divorced or anticipating divorce and are struggling with the relationship with your ex-spouse. Others have children but were never married, and some of you are grandparents worried about your grandchildren. There are grandparents raising grandchildren, single mothers with children from more than one father, blended families with two sets of stepchildren, and teenagers raising babies. Although I do not mean to exclude any of my readers, I have decided to take the easy way out by writing this book as if my readers are two divorced parents. Thus "ex-spouse" is meant to apply in a broader sense to parents who were never married as well as to those who were.

Whatever your circumstances, I hope to show you the following:

- How important it is to avoid alienating your children from their other parent
- How to recognize the symptoms of parental alienation syndrome
- What to do if your ex-spouse is trying to alienate your children from you
- How your behavior may be aggravating alienation
- How to understand your own motivations for alienating your children from the other parent
- Practical methods to minimize the alienation's malignancy
- When and how to seek professional help for yourself or your children
- How to work effectively with attorneys, mediators, and counselors

Throughout the book I have used real-life examples to help you understand the issues more clearly and apply them to your own family.

As you read this book, you may sometimes feel that nothing you do or say is right, and this is a common reaction. It comes from looking closely at how your behavior affects your children and their relationship with their other parent. You will become more aware of the nuances of what you say and your children's reactions to them. You may be surprised to find out what you're doing.

At first, learning to be more sensitive about alienation may feel like it stifles your spontaneity with your children. However, once you become accustomed to it, you will think more carefully about what you are saying to your children, and it will eventually become a natural process. You will judge whether your comments are appropriate, and you will have the insight and the ability to shift gears if necessary.

Don't get discouraged if you do not feel like the perfect parent. No one can make that claim. All you can do is aspire to be a better parent. Perhaps you will learn that much of what you have been doing is right, although there is more you can do to reduce alienation. Parenting is a full-time job that takes a conscious effort on your part. Most of the parents I have worked with do more right than wrong, and I am sure this is true of you, too.

Parents everywhere want the same opportunities: to share in raising their children in peace, to give them the love and protection they deserve, and to revel in their future successes. I sincerely wish you and your children all the best.

DOUGLAS DARNALL, PH.D.
MINERAL RIDGE, OHIO

A Cautionary Note

Going through a divorce is probably one of the most painful and guilt-ridden experiences you will ever encounter. It is an experience you were most likely not prepared to face. Now you are torn between being a loving parent and coping with your fear and hurt from the divorce.

Reading this book will help you learn how to cope with your feelings while continuing to protect your children from the family crisis. You will learn specific ways to strengthen the relationship between you and your children, your children and their other parent, and even you and your ex-spouse.

However, it would is possible to deliberately twist some of the information I have presented and use it maliciously against your ex-spouse. Such vindictiveness is tantamount to child abuse and must be avoided.

If you think you will be tempted to inflict damage on anyone, immediately stop reading. For your children's welfare, you should seek professional help to prevent further harm to your children.

What Is Parental Alienation Syndrome?

"When I'm through telling the judge what you've been up to, you'll be lucky if he lets you say so much as 'hello' to the kids."

Jerri and Jim

Jerri walked into my office hoping to appear confident and determined. Her walk was brisk as she reached out to shake my hand; however, her limp handshake and the tense muscles around her jaw gave her away. She was torn between desperately wanting my help and fearing I would somehow betray her as many others had done in the past. Jerri was not the usual client asking for help from a psychologist. She was sitting before me because the court had ordered her to do so. I had been asked to evaluate her because her ex-husband was trying to get custody of their children away from her.

Sitting on the edge of her seat and armed with her papers, Jerri began telling her story. "Jim and I have been divorced for six years. We have two children—Robert, who's eleven, and Amy, who's seven. I have always had custody. We used to be able to talk to each other until Jim went behind my back. Now he's trying to steal the kids right from under me."

"Why would Jim steal the kids from you?"

"Jim and I started having trouble when I started dating Larry."

"Isn't Larry your present husband?" I asked.

"No, Larry and I are planning on getting married this fall. We have been going together for three years. The kids love Larry, and he's been good to them."

"Well, why did your ex-husband bring you back to court?"

"One night I let Larry spend the night while the kids were home and I thought they were asleep. I know I may have been wrong, but the weather was bad and it was late. Larry had a long drive, so I told him he could stay the night as long as he was out of the house before the kids got up. He left early. I didn't know that the kids knew he was there. They were suppose to be asleep, and they didn't say anything to me about Larry being there. I really think if they were upset, they would have said something. We have a good relationship and have always been able to talk."

Apparently, Amy woke up sometime during the night and went into her mother's room, as she had done many times in the past. Amy was surprised to see Larry sleeping next to her mother. Embarrassed by what she had seen, Amy gingerly backed out of the room, gently closing the door.

Jerri first heard of Amy's discovery a week later when Jim was returning the children from his visit. His hasty walk up to her front door and the expression on his face told Jerri that something was wrong. Seeing the rage in his eyes, Jerri was reminded of their fights before the divorce. Jim, trying to control his anger, demanded to talk with Jerri. Unable to contain his rage, he launched into his assault, telling Jerri about Amy finding her and Larry in bed together. His attack became more vicious, calling her a slut and accusing her of caring only for herself. Jerri was devastated. She wanted to defend herself but could not gather her thoughts fast enough. Like a chicken scurrying her chicks away from danger, she gathered the children and fled into the house. Feeling thwarted, Jim returned home to call his attorney.

Jim would not forgive Jerri. After many weeks, his anger only became more intense. No longer were they able to discuss the children without an argument. He became critical, causing Jerri to react defensively to his allegations. Whatever she did with the children was now under suspicion. Jim started returning the children late from visits and would not return their clothing. He insisted on more frequent phone calls and started having secrets with them. The secrets were the most painful part because Jerri now felt excluded from her children's lives. She could not trust her own children because of what they might say to their father. The cocky and devious looks on their faces when she walked in on their phone calls with him hurt her deeply.

Two years after the initial incident when Amy had seen Larry asleep in her mother's bed, Jim's harassment culminated in a change of custody. Jerri could not believe that her children told the court that they wanted to live with their dad. She did not blame Amy and Robert because she believed that Jim had brainwashed them against her. Instead, she felt furious and betrayed by the court for not seeing what

Jim had done to the children. Jerri felt a terrible emptiness. The house was now so quiet. Neighborhood children who came to the house to play with her children were a reminder of her loss. Jerri knew that she had to adjust for the children's sake, but the pain continued to fester.

Relentless in his pursuit for vindication, Jim brought Jerri back to court yet again one year later. Now he and the children wanted to reduce Jerri's parenting time, or visitation, hours, saying that Amy and Robert were old enough to decide for themselves whether or not they wanted to see their mother. Jerri was now panic stricken by the idea of not seeing her children. Every time she went to court, she cringed when she heard Jim's accusations and lies, and she resented the court's ineffectiveness. She felt powerless and deeply hurt.

Jerri, Amy, and Robert were all victims of Jim's hate and revenge. Sounding self-righteous and beyond moral reproach, Jim began a subtle process of brainwashing the children against their mother. It took him two years to slowly convince them that their mother was "a terrible person whose only concern was for herself." The children became more confused about how to feel. They wanted to both trust their father and love their mother. As time passed, their father's arguments were too convincing for them to resist. The children learned to hate their mother. All Jerri could do was keep her composure and try to rebuild her relationships with the children. She wanted so much for someone to understand how Jim and the court victimized her and the children.

Jim and Jerri's fight is an all-too-common example of how hate, bitterness, and selfishness can destroy families. Both parents can rationalize their behavior, believing they did nothing wrong. You may have drawn your own conclusions about who was right and whether the court was correct in changing custody. Jim may think he triumphed by winning custody, but it was won at the children's expense. Jim may have had a right to be angered by Jerri's behavior, but his deliberate destruction of the children's relationship with her cost them a mutually loving relationship with their mother—an expense the children will bear for many years.

Defining Parental Alienation Syndrome And Parental Alienation

There is a difference between parental alienation and parental alienation syndrome, though the symptoms or what is observed in the children can be similar. The distinction between the two is that parental alienation focuses on how the alienating parent behaves toward the children and the targeted

3

PA – parent behavior
PAS – child behavior

parent. Parental alienation syndrome symptoms describe the child's behaviors and attitudes toward the targeted parent *after* the child has been effectively programmed and severely alienated from the targeted parent.

Parental alienation (PA) is "any constellation of behaviors, whether conscious or unconscious, that could evoke a disturbance in the relationship between a child and the other parent." This definition is different from parental alienation syndrome (PAS) originally coined by Dr. Richard Gardner in 1987: "A disturbance in which children are preoccupied with deprecation and criticism of a parent-denigration that is unjustified and/or exaggerated."

Gardner in his revised book on parental alienation (1998) went on to explain that parental alienation syndrome "arises primarily in the context of child-custody disputes. Its primary manifestation is the child's campaign of denigration against a parent, a campaign that has no justification. It results from the *combination* of a programming (brainwashing) parent's indoctrination and the child's own contributions to the vilification of the target parent. When true parental abuse and/or neglect is present the child's animosity may be justified, and so the parental alienation syndrome explanation for the child's hostility is not applicable."

Dr. Gardner explained that the term is similar in meaning to brainwashing except that the motivation for the alienating parent has both a conscious as well as "a subconscious or unconscious" component. The children themselves may have motivations that make the alienation worse. Their hedonistic outlook for immediate gratification or their desire to avoid discomfort makes them vulnerable allies for siding with the alienating parent. The children become an advocate for the alienating parent by becoming the spokesperson for that parent's hatred. They act as soldiers while the alienating parent is the general directing the action in the background against the targeted parent. Frequently, the children are unaware of how they are being used.

Dr. Gardner's most controversial suggestion for dealing with severe alienation was to remove the children from the alienator's home and place the child with the targeted parent. Later, however, he recanted this recommendation, saying that the children "are likely to run away and do everything possible to return to [the alienating parent's] home." Instead, Dr. Gardner recommended "transitional sites" such as a friend's or family member's house, a community shelter, or a hospital. Each site would have a different level of supervision and resources to help the children and targeted parent. Hospitalization would be used only as a last resort.

Dr. Gardner's definition emphasized the point that the child must be an active participant with the alienating parent in degrading the targeted parent. According to Dr. Gardner, if Amy and Robert had been able to ignore their father's persistent attempts to degrade their mother, then by definition, parental alienation syndrome would not have taken place. Parental alienation (PA) focuses more on the parent's behavior than on the child's role in degrading the victimized parent. Thus, alienation can occur well before the parent's hatred permeates the child's beliefs about the victimized parent. This definition of parental alienation is necessary if parents are to recognize the risk they have for unconsciously falling into a pattern of alienation. By the time the children have come to agree with the alienating parent, it is usually too late to prevent significant damage.

Also, Dr. Gardner's definition states that the criticism of the other parent must be unjustified or exaggerated. I do not believe this is always necessary. One parent can alienate the children against the other simply by harping on faults that are real and provable. Divorced parents should understand that their children need to love both parents if at all possible, even if they themselves have ceased to love their ex-spouse long ago, and they should help the children see the other parent's good points.

It is important to keep in mind that this book isn't about the alienator, or "bad guy," versus the targeted parent, or "good guy." These roles rotate. The same parent can be both the alienator and the targeted parent depending on how he or she is behaving.

You can't assume that the targeted parent is without fault. Targeted parents can become alienators when they retaliate because of their hurt. This puts them in the role of the alienator while the other parent becomes the victim. The roles become blurred because it's difficult to know who is the alienator and who is the targeted parent. Often both parents feel victimized. It is important to remember that alienation is a process, not a person.

Understanding parental alienation and parental alienation syndrome is paramount for a child's welfare and a parent's peace of mind. Divorced parents, grandparents, judges, attorneys, and mental-health workers all need to understand the dynamics of parental alienation and parental alienation syndrome, recognize the symptomatic behavior, and execute tactics for combating this malady.

How Serious Is Parental Alienation?

In 1994 divorces were granted to approximately 2.4 million Americans, including the parents of more than one million children under the age of eighteen. Nearly as many men and women with children will separate. Thanks to sky-high divorce rates and recent increases in the number and viciousness of child custody battles, there has been a marked increase in parental alienation. Children suffer from the split-up of the families because they feel torn, trapped, precariously balanced—as if one wrong move could cost them all their parents' love and acceptance. This can easily lead to disastrous effects on children. Various studies have shown that youngsters exposed to even mildly alienating behaviors may have trouble learning, concentrating, relaxing, or getting along with their peers. They have been known to develop physical symptoms, such as severe headaches, and serious behavior problems.

Alienation will have lasting effects on your children, even into adulthood. Sometimes divorcing parents forget that they not only share a common parenthood but will also share a common grandparenthood. Both parents will have the same grandchildren and maybe even the same great-grandchildren. It is not fair to your children that one day your child and son- or daughter-in-law have to dread asking you and your ex-spouse to come to your grandchild's baptism or graduation because they are afraid that the two of you will fight and ruin the festive affair.

Is Alienation Inevitable?

Yes, some degree of alienation occurs in all but the friendliest divorces. Alienation is usually unconscious and without any malicious intent to harm the relationship between the parent and the children. Though most parents are well meaning, they are often unaware of how their subtle behaviors and comments can hurt the relationship between the children and the targeted parent.

Most parents sincerely believe in the value of their children having a healthy relationship with both parents. During the crisis of a divorce, most parents will consciously work on strengthening this relationship. They will try to build this relationship without degrading the other parent or causing the children to feel a divided loyalty. They encourage visits, talk kindly of the other parent in their children's presence, and set aside their own negative feelings to avoid causing their children distress. They are sensitive to their children's needs and encourage positive feelings toward the other parent. These parents are to be commended for their sacrifice and ability to put their hurt aside for the children's best interest.

Unfortunately, such noble efforts are not always successful and long lasting. At any time before the divorce and even years later, many parents, consciously or unconsciously, begin a divisive campaign to alienate the children from the targeted parent. The campaign can be triggered by any number of events, including the introduction of a new romantic interest, kids getting too busy to visit, envy because of an increase in income, or a desire by one parent to move from the area.

There are times when parents unintentionally cause alienation between either themselves or the ex-spouse and the children. This is done by insinuations and innuendoes. Changes in the tone of your voice, a loss of eye contact, fighting off a teardrop, or a forced smile are all examples of innuendoes that children see and react to. You may understandably try to hide your feelings so you do not upset your children, but this usually does not work. Children are not naïve. They may not know why you feel the way you do, but they will know when you are feeling bad. Not wanting to cause you any more hurt, they may pull away and get quiet.

Factors Contributing to Alienation

Custody litigation creates a competition between parents that is unavoidable to some degree. As long as both of you want custody, you will feel pulled in many directions. You may feel an urgency to align yourself with your children to help ensure your victory. Yet you may still struggle to be fair and resist the temptation to degrade your spouse in your children's presence. Feeling torn between these opposing feelings is a by-product of modern-day divorce, and it sets the stage for alienation.

Alienation will continue to flourish as long as divorces—and custody battles—continue to increase at alarming rates. More fathers are seeking and being granted custody. They are becoming more comfortable in a nurturing and care-taking role, and their belief that they can be a better parent helps to explain why custody litigation is more common. The courts no longer automatically assume that the children are better off living with their mothers. Meanwhile, mothers are realizing that the all-American dream of marriage, a home, and children is not a guarantee of emotional fulfillment. Many women now want an identity in both the workplace and the home. The high costs of living and supporting a family are forcing women to work outside the home even when their children are very young. Consequently, women can no longer argue for custody because of an inherent birthright or because they are available at home to care for the children.

Now that the grounds for divorce in most states are faultless, mothers and fathers find themselves in divorce court fighting to keep what they believe is rightfully theirs. They may have difficulty accepting the idea that they must compete against each other to prove to the court that it is in the children's best interest that they be the custodial parent.

Many other factors will influence your attitudes and perceptions about what happens before and after the divorce, and all of them will make you vulnerable to alienation, either as an alienator or as a targeted parent. In fact, you may find that your role changes—that there are times when you alienate and other times when you feel targeted. Here are some of the factors that contribute to alienation:

- The expectations you and your spouse bring out of the marriage
- How well or poorly the two of you resolve conflict
- The emotional impact made by hearing the words, "I want a divorce," especially when they come without warning or are linked to infidelity
- The adversarial nature of divorce
- The stigma of believing that you have failed as a wife or husband
- Sexist attitudes
- The alienating parent's many possible reasons for resentment
- The betrayed parent's urge to retaliate
- The need to preserve your dignity to avoid humiliation
- Your children's personalities and ability to cope with change
- The judicial system itself, which sets the two parents up as adversaries

The Three Types of Parental Alienators

Parental alienation varies in the degree of severity, as seen in the behaviors and attitudes of both the parents and the children. The severity can be of such little consequence as one parent occasionally calling the other parent a derogatory name; or it could be as overwhelming as Jim's campaign of consciously destroying his children's relationship with their mother. Most children are able to brush off a parent's offhand comment about the other parent that is made in frustration. On the other hand, children may not be able to resist a parent's persistent campaign of hatred and alienation.

Preventing or stopping alienation begins with learning how to recognize the three types of alienators, because the symptoms and strategies for combating each are different. *Naïve alienators* are parents who are generally passive about the children's relationship with the other parent but will

Naïve
Active
obsessed

occasionally do or say something to alienate. *Active alienators* also know better than to alienate, but their intense hurt or anger causes them to impulsively lose control over their behavior or what they say. Later, they may feel guilty about how they behaved. *Obsessed alienators* have a fervent cause: to destroy the targeted parent. Frequently a parent can be a blend between two types of alienators, usually a combination between the naïve and active alienator. Rarely does the obsessed alienator have enough self-control or insight to blend with the other types.

The Naïve Alienator

"Tell your father that he has more money than I do, so let him buy your soccer shoes."

Most divorced parents have moments when they are naïve alienators. These parents mean well and recognize the importance of the children having a healthy relationship with the other parent. They rarely have to return to court because of problems with visits or other issues relating to the children. They encourage the relationship between the children and the other parent and that parent's family. Communication between both parents is usually good, though they will have their disagreements much like they did before the divorce. For the most part, they can work out their differences without bringing the children into it.

Children, whether or not their parents are divorced, know there are times when their parents will argue or disagree. They don't like seeing their parents argue and may feel hurt or frightened by what they hear, but somehow, the children manage to cope, either by talking out their feelings to a receptive parent, ignoring the argument, or trusting that the skirmish will pass and all will heal. What they see and hear between their parents does not typically damage the children of the naïve alienator. They trust their parent's love and protection. The child and the parent have distinct personalities, beliefs, and feelings. Neither is threatened by how the other feels toward the targeted parent.

Naïve alienators usually don't need therapy but will benefit from reading this book because of the insight they will gain about how to keep alienation from escalating into something more severe and damaging for all. These parents know they make mistakes but care enough about their children to make things right. They focus on what is good for the children without regret, blame, or martyrdom.

Cindy and Russ

Cindy received custody of her two daughters. She knew the responsibility would be a challenge since she had had problems with the older, Sue, who was argumentative and frequently fought her mother's attempts to discipline her. Visitation with Sue's father, Russ, had always gone well. So without the children's knowledge, the parents had Sue's custody changed from her mother to her father. The children were split, but they were able to be together every weekend during visits. Sue became angry and hurt when she learned of the change of custody. Feeling betrayed and rejected, she refused to visit her mother. In time, Cindy's hurt and resentment grew because of Sue's refusal to visit. Cindy stopped asking Sue to visit. She rationalized that if Sue wanted to visit, she would call. Sue also refused to ask for a visit because of her belief that "all this is Mom's fault." The time since the last visit grew longer. The impasse became stronger with each believing the other should apologize. In the meantime, Russ did nothing. He rationalized that the problem was between the two of them and he didn't want to interfere.

Russ's passivity heightened the alienation because of his failure to mediate or, at minimum, encourage one of them to break the deadlock. This probably served his self-interest but did nothing to help his daughter. Russ didn't appreciate how much his daughter was hurting and how important it was for her to have a relationship with her mother. Rather than sit back and do nothing, he could have talked to his ex-wife and his daughter, encouraging one of them to start talking to the other. He could have reminded them how much they love each other and their need for the relationship. If this approach did not work, he could have found someone like a grandparent or even a professional to help Sue with her anger.

Characteristics of Naïve Alienators:

- Their ability to separate in their minds the children's needs from their own. They recognize the importance of the children spending time with the other parent so they can build a mutually loving relationship. They avoid making the other parent a target for their hurt and loss.

- Their ability to feel secure with the children's relationship with the other parent's family.
- Their respect for court orders and authority.
- Their ability to let their anger and hurt heal and not interfere with the children's relationship with their other parent.
- Their ability to be flexible and willing to work with the other parent.
- Their ability to feel guilty when they have acted in a way to hurt the children's relationship with their mother or father.
- Their ability to allow the other parent to share in their children's activities.
- Their ability to share medical and school records.

The Active Alienator

"I don't want you to tell your father that I earned this extra money. The miser will take it from his child support check, which will keep us from going to Disney World. You remember he's done this before when we wanted to go to Grandma's for Christmas."

Most parents who return to court over problems with parenting time are active alienators. These parents mean well and believe that the children should have a healthy relationship with the other parent. The problem they have is with controlling their frustration, bitterness, or hurt. When something happens to trigger their painful feelings, active alienators lash out in a way to cause or reinforce alienation against the targeted parent. After regaining control, the parent will usually feel guilty about what they did and back off from their alienating tactics. Vacillating between impulsively alienating and then repairing the damage with the children is the trademark of the active alienator. They mean well, but lose control because the intensity of their feelings overwhelms them.

Active alienators are usually willing to accept professional help when they or the children have a problem that does not go away. They are sincerely concerned about their children's adjustment to the divorce. Harboring old feelings continues to be a struggle, but active alienators hope for a speedy recovery from their pain.

Dori and Mike

Dori is a thirty-two-year-old divorced mother of two boys. Her troubles began when her ex-husband, Mike, learned of her engagement.

"They came home from their visit with an attitude. It's sort of smug, almost sneering. When I said hello to Joey, I caught him in the corner of my eye shooting a disgusted look at Chris, and then I went to hug Chris and caught Joey making retching motions behind my back. I was surprised by their behavior because visits usually go fairly well. I know this must be their dad's doing. He must have had one of his fits and badmouthed me the whole weekend. The other day Joey said that I 'obviously didn't have his best interests at heart.' How would a seven-year-old know to say that unless he heard it from his father first?"

Dori is rightfully suspicious of her children's behavior. They have lost their typical spontaneity and are now secretive and hostile. She suspects her ex-husband's influence on their children. Dori knows there is something desperately wrong but feels powerless to do anything about it. What she sees in her children is characteristic of what parents see when the children are under the powerful influence of an active alienator.

Characteristics of Active Alienators:

- Lashing out at the other parent in front of the children. Their problem has more to do with loss of self-control when they are upset than with a sinister motivation.

- After calming down, active alienators realize that they were wrong. They usually try to repair any damage to the children. When making up, such parents can be comforting and supportive of the child's feelings.

- Like naïve alienators, they are able to differentiate between their needs and those of the children by supporting the children's desire to have a relationship with the other parent.

- Like naïve alienators, active alienators allow the children to have different feelings and beliefs from their own. During the flair ups of anger, however, the delineation between the child and parent's beliefs can become blurry until the parent calms down and regains control. For the most part, older children have their own opinions about both parents based on personal experience rather than what they are told by others. To keep peace, the older child usually learns to keep their opinions to themselves. Younger children become more confused and are more vulnerable to their parents' manipulations.

- Their ability to respect the court's authority and, for the most part, comply with court orders. However, they can sometimes be rigid and uncooperative with the other parent. This is usually a passive attempt to strike back at the other parent for some injustice.

The Obsessed Alienator

"I love my children. If the court can't protect them from their abusive father, I will. Even though he's never abused the children, I know it's a matter of time. The children are frightened of their father. If they don't want to see him, I'm not going to force them. They are old enough to make up their own minds."

The obsessed alienator is a parent, or sometimes a grandparent, with a cause: to align the children to his or her side and together, with the children, campaign to destroy their relationship with the targeted parent. For the campaign to work, the obsessed alienator enmeshes the children's personalities and beliefs into their own. This is a process that takes time, but it is one that the children, especially the young, are completely helpless to combat. It usually begins well before the divorce is final. The obsessed parent is angry, bitter, or feels betrayed by the other parent. The initial reasons for the bitterness may be justified. They could have been verbally and physically abused, betrayed by an affair, or financially cheated. The problem occurs when the feelings don't heal but, instead, become more intense due to the necessary continued relationship with a person they despise because of their common parenthood. Just having to see or talk to the other parent is a reminder of the past and triggers the hate. They are trapped with nowhere to go and heal. Though Clawar and Rivlin (1991) did not specifically discuss the obsessed alienator in their book, they found that five percent of the children in their study were programmed by similar parents "to point of no return," meaning that no interventions were found to be effective in deprogramming these children. These children were emotional and physically lost to the targeted parent. This is the child Gardner (1998) describes as a victim of parenatal alienation syndrome.

There are no validated treatment protocols for either the obsessed alienator or the programmed child. The courts and mental-health professionals are frequently powerless in helping either the obsessed or targeted parents or the children. The best hope for these children is early identification of the symptoms and prevention. After the alienation is entrenched and the children become "true believers" in the parent's cause, the children are usually lost to the other parent for years to come.

The obsessed alienator will probably not finish reading this book because it's contents will only make them feel angrier.

Pam and Bob

Pam and Bob's story represents many of the problems that occur with the obsessed alienator. They had a bitter divorce where allegations of drug abuse and infidelity were thrown about recklessly. After the divorce, Bob married Linda, who had her own children. After years of criminal and domestic court battles, Bob was given custody of his and Pam's two sons, Jake, age twelve, and Jason, age ten. Their daughter, Jessie, age five, stayed with Pam and her husband, Stan.

Bob continued to fight Pam at every turn. He would never allow Pam to change the scheduled visit, though he made frequent requests to have more time with Jessie. Pam usually reacted to Bob's rigidity and curtness by becoming defensive and agitated. She felt frustrated by her inability to "get Bob to bend." To prove her point, Pam taped a phone conversation where she asked Bob to pick up Jessie after a birthday party at 7:30, instead of the usual time of 6:00.

The conversation between Pam and Bob illustrates many aspects of alienation. You will see how both parents get caught up in the frenzied power struggle where Jessie is the unmistakable loser.

Pam: "Hello."
Bob: "Is Jessie there?"
Pam: "Just a minute. Are you picking her up at 7:30 on Friday?"
Bob: "I'll pick her up at six."
Pam: "She not going to be here, Bob."
Bob: "I'll pick her up at six. Have her back from the party early. I'll be there at six."
Pam: "No! No! I have already talked to my attorney."
Bob: "I'll call. Don't worry. I'll be there at six. Put her on. I want to talk to her."

Pam:	"Just a minute. You are not going to make her miss this party." (sounding angry)
Bob:	"Pick her up early. I'll be there at six."
Pam:	"She will be here at 7:30."
Bob:	"She better be there at six."
Pam:	"She's not!"
Bob:	"Put her on the phone. I want to talk to her."
Pam:	"Jessie, telephone."
Jessie:	"Hi Dad."
Bob:	"Hi princess. How are you doing?"
Jessie:	"Good."
Bob:	"Hey, I finally got a hold of you, um, after two weeks."
Jessie:	"I know."
Bob:	"Do you still live down there? Where do you live?"
Jessie:	(soft laugh) "Yeah."
Bob:	"Well, every time Jake or I call you aren't even there. (pause) You know. How is school going?"
Jessie:	"Good."
Bob:	"Did you get a report card yet?"
Jessie:	"No."
Bob:	"You going to come up this weekend?"
Jessie:	"Sure!"
Bob:	"Well, I'm going to pick you up at your mom's at six."
Jessie:	"Okay."
Bob:	"Your mom said 7:30, but I'm going to be there at six, so you tell your mom to be there at six. Otherwise, ah, I don't know how you are going to get up here. But I'm going to pick you up at six."
Jessie:	"Okay."
Bob:	"Leave the party early."
Jessie:	"Okay."
Bob:	"Okay. You'll have, ah, enough time there."
Jessie:	"You know what? I told mom, I, um, said, um, when I leave at six..."(speaking very slow and deliberate, sounding scared)
Bob:	"I'll be there at six..."
Jessie:	"Okay."
Bob:	"And a I'll probably call you and talk to you tomorrow night, but you make sure you get back at your mom's at six 'cause I'll be there at six 'cause we got plans. Okay?"

Jessie:	"Okay."
Bob:	"I'll see you Friday at six."
Jessie:	"Okay. Bye."
Bob:	"Bye. I love you. Bye"
Jessie:	"Bye. See you tomorrow." (playful voice)

After the phone call, Jessie went into the bathroom to take a bath. When Pam entered the bathroom, she found Jessie crying. Jessie said, "Daddy won't let me go to the party." Pam immediately wanted to protect Jessie and felt angry with Bob. While the recorder was still recording, Pam called Bob back, but first Linda (his wife) and then Jake (Pam and Bob's son) would not let her talk to him. In the background, Jessie's voice was heard frantically pleading "Please!" (pause) "Don't tell him I'm afraid!" (Softly crying while gasping for air) "Mummy, don't tell him I'm afraid."

Bob and Pam's argument was tragic for Jessie. Her parents got entangled in a power struggle that neither parent won, over an incident that should have had little consequence for either of them. Bob was the aggressor, though both parents behaved impulsively. He had no concern for Jessie's desire to stay at the party until 7:30. His motivation above all else was to have Pam obey his demand for his usual 6:00 pickup. Pam, thinking that Bob did not believe her, wanted Jessie to tell her father that she wanted to stay at the party.

Jessie was now trapped between her desire to please her mother and having to obey her father. She felt frantic. She did what most children do in the middle of their parents' fight: She lied to one of her parents, her father. Bob, not thinking Jessie would lie, felt vindicated. He immediately saw Pam as someone who was trying to interfere with his relationship with Jessie.

The argument between Bob and Pam could have been avoided. Bob could have asked Pam to explain what was happening with the party rather than demanding that Jessie be home by six. Bob did not understand Jessie's feelings. Pam could have stopped the fight if she had been less insistent about winning the argument. Pam's desire to please Jessie was understandable. She could have given Jessie choices about whether to stay at the party or return home early. Both parents should have tried to help Jessie feel more comfortable by not using her to prove their point.

Bob's behavior is characteristic of an obsessed alienator. He felt self-righteous and was concerned only about what he wanted, with no regard for the consequences. He had no empathy for either Jessie or her mother. Instead, Pam was his target, the enemy to be distrusted.

Characteristics of Obsessed Alienators:

- Their obsession to destroy the children's relationship with the targeted parent.

- Their success in enmeshing the children's personalities and beliefs about the other parent with their own. The children will parrot the obsessed alienator rather than express their own feelings from personal experience with the other parent. The targeted parent, and often the children, cannot tell you the reasons for the obsessed alienator's feelings.

- Their beliefs sometimes becoming delusional and irrational. No one, especially the court, can convince obsessed alienators that they are wrong. Anyone who tries is the enemy.

- Their efforts to seek support from family members, quasi-political groups, and friends to share in their belief that the other parent and the system victimize them. The battle becomes "us against them." The obsessed alienator's supporters are often seen at the court hearings even though they haven't been subpoenaed.

- Their unquenchable anger. They believe they have been victimized by the targeted parent and whatever they do to protect the children is justified.

- Their desire for the court to punish the other parent with court orders that would interfere or block the parent from seeing the children. This would affirm in the obsessed alienator's mind that they were right.

- The court's authority does not intimidate them. The obsessed alienator believes in a higher cause: protecting the children at all cost.

Am I an Alienator?

At this point, you may be asking yourself whether you are an alienator and, if so, which type of alienator you are. Don't despair if you are thinking of yourself as someone who could alienate your children. Remember, to some degree alienation can't be helped. Every parent occasionally communicates an attitude that causes or reinforces alienation between their children and the other parent. There are probably occasions when you act like a naïve alienator and other times you question whether you are an obsessed alienator. It's understandable why you may be confused by the overwhelming feelings you experience during a divorce or custody battle. To help give you some insight into these feelings and the resulting behavior, take a few minutes and complete the Parental Alienation Scale (PAS) in this section. This will help you become better aware of how your behavior can influence your children.

Before completing the Parental Alienation Scale, I must give you a word of caution. This scale has not been normed or validated, though it has been administered to about four hundred parents. Therefore, you must be careful about interpreting the results at the end of the scale. Your score is not meant to be a definitive conclusion about your behavior or parenting but to stimulate your thinking.

There are two versions of the PAS: one for custodial parents and one for noncustodial parents. Fill out the version that applies to you. If you don't have a child between the ages of four and seventeen, the PAS will not be valid because you will have to leave too many items blank. It's important to answer all of the items the best you can.

Rate each item by putting the number in the box that most accurately describes how frequently you behave in the manner described by the item. If you have more than one child, answer each item as to how the item relates to your oldest child. You must answer all items.

5   All the time
4   Most of the time
3   Sometimes
2   Rarely
1   Never

PARENTAL ALIENATION SCALE FOR CUSTODIAL PARENTS

1. I make negative comments to my children about my ex-spouse. ❏
2. I argue with my ex-spouse about the scheduled visitation. ❏
3. I ask my children about my ex-spouse's personal life. ❏
4. For whatever reason, I have denied my ex-spouse visits. ❏
5. I accuse my ex-spouse of abusing alcohol or drugs. ❏
6. I remind my children that we donít have enough money because of the divorce. ❏
7. I refuse my ex-spouse access to school grades or medical records. ❏
8. I do not give my ex-spouse the children's schedule of social activities. ❏
9. I ask the children who they want to live with. ❏

10. I ask my children to keep secrets from my ex-spouse. ❑
11. I schedule secret phone calls with the children. ❑
12. I pick up the children from a visit when they call and complain. ❑
13. I feel uncomfortable when my children visit my ex-spouse's parents. ❑
14. I show the children the divorce papers. ❑
15. I cancel visits. ❑
16. I do not notify my ex-spouse when the children have a medical
    emergency. ❑
17 I cancel visits because the children are too ill to go. ❑
18. I believe my ex-spouse exaggerates the children's medical
    problems. ❑
19. I feel frustrated because my ex-spouse does not listen to what
    I say. ❑
20. I do not talk to my ex-spouse. ❑
21. I have hit my ex-spouse during a fight. ❑
22. I believe my ex-spouse lets the children run wild. ❑
23. I have good reasons for being critical of my ex-spouse. ❑
24. I cringe when the children talk about having a good time with my
    ex-spouse. ❑
25. I feel resentful when my ex-spouse shows up at school functions. ❑
26. I believe my children have good reasons for not wanting to visit. ❑
27. I do not allow the children to go on a visit if my ex-spouse is
    more than 15 minutes late picking them up. ❑
28. I remind my ex-spouse that I will take him or her back to court. ❑
29. I believe the children are too busy to have regular visits. ❑
30. I know what is best for my children. ❑
31. I call my ex-spouse names in front of my children. ❑
32. I allow the children to use their stepfather's last name. ❑
33. I have suggested to the children that their stepfather adopt them. ❑
34. I believe that my ex-spouse does not discipline the children. ❑
35. I believe that my ex-spouse should follow my rules. ❑
36. I give my ex-spouse advice. ❑
37. My children will not hug or kiss me in front of my ex-spouse. ❑
38. My life is private. There are some things that I do not want
    my children to tell my ex-spouse. ❑
39. I listen in on the children's phone calls when they talk to
    my ex-spouse. ❑
40. I ask my children to get me information about my ex-spouse's
    activities. ❑
41. I have trouble keeping promises to the children. ❑
42. I make up my own rules rather than listen to the court. ❑
43. I believe that the court has no right to tell me what to do. ❑
44. I feel angry at my ex-spouse. ❑

45. I wish my ex-spouse would just disappear. ❏
46. I believe that my ex-spouse is a poor parent. ❏
47. I believe my ex-spouse uses the children to get back at me. ❏
48. I believe that the children have good reason for wanting to live with me. ❏
49. I believe that my ex-spouse does not really love our children. ❏

Now total the column _____

PARENTAL ALIENATION SCALE FOR NONCUSTODIAL PARENTS

1. I make negative comments to my children about my ex-spouse. ❏
2. I argue with my ex-spouse about the scheduled visitation. ❏
3. I ask my children about my ex-spouse's personal life. ❏
4. I missed buying my children Christmas or birthday presents. ❏
5. I accuse my ex-spouse of abusing alcohol or drugs. ❏
6. I remind my children that we don't have money because of the divorce. ❏
7. I remind the children that one day they can come and live with me. ❏
8. I have secret rendezvous with the children. ❏
9. I ask the children who they want to live with. ❏
10. I have secrets with the children. ❏
11. I schedule secret phone calls with the children. ❏
12. I feel I have to go and pick up the children when they call and complain about my ex-spouse. ❏
13. I feel uncomfortable when the children visit my ex-spouseís parents. ❏
14. I show the children the divorce papers. ❏
15. I cancel visits. ❏
16. For whatever reason, I have not returned the children's clothes after a visit. ❏
17. I do not go to the children's school activities or sporting events. ❏
18. I believe my ex-spouse exaggerates the children's medical problems. ❏
19. I feel frustrated because my ex-spouse does not listen to what I say. ❏
20. I do not talk to my ex-spouse. ❏
21. I have hit my ex-spouse during a fight. ❏
22 I believe my ex-spouse lets the children run wild. ❏
23. I have good reasons for being critical of my ex-spouse. ❏
24. I cringe when the children talk about having a good time with my ex-spouse. ❏

25. I do not pay child support. ❏
26. I have good reasons for not wanting the children to live with my ex-spouse. ❏
27. I am too busy to visit the children. ❏
28. I remind my ex-spouse that I will take him or her back to court. ❏
29. I return the children late from a visit. ❏
30. I know what is best for my children. ❏
31. I call my ex-spouse names in front of my children. ❏
32. I remind the children that there are things they are not to tell their other parent. ❏
33. I suggest to the children that they tell my ex-spouse they want to live with me. ❏
34. I believe that my ex-spouse does not discipline the children. ❏
35. I believe that my ex-spouse should follow my rules. ❏
36. I give my ex-spouse advice. ❏
37. My children will not hug or kiss me in front of my ex-spouse. ❏
38. My life is private. There are some things that I do not want my children to tell my ex-spouse. ❏
39. I listen in on my children's phone calls when they talk to my ex-spouse. ❏
40. I ask my children to get me information about my ex-spouse's activities. ❏
41. I have trouble keeping promises to the children. ❏
42. I make up my own rules rather than listen to the court. ❏
43. I believe the court has no right to tell me what to do. ❏
44. I feel angry at my ex-spouse. ❏
45. I wish my ex-spouse would just disappear. ❏
46. I believe that my ex-spouse is a poor parent. ❏
47. I believe my ex-spouse uses the children to get back at me. ❏
48. I believe the children have good reason for wanting to live with me. ❏
49. I believe that my ex-spouse does not really love our children. ❏

Now total the column _____

Scoring

The purpose of the Parental Alienation Scale is to give you some insight about how your behavior may, unknowingly, cause alienation between your children and their other parent. Hopefully your score will encourage you to look at yourself and how you are behaving with your children. Add the numbers in the boxes for a total score and compare your score with the interpretation below.

Score Explanation

49-75: Mild alienation. You behavior should not be damaging to your children. You may be considered a naïve alienator.

76-100: Moderate alienation. Your behavior will at times harm your children and their relationship with their other parent. You may be an active alienator. Try to apply what you learn from this book.

101-above: Significant alienation. You are probably damaging the relationship between your children and their other parent. You may be considered an obsessed alienator. Practice what you have learned from this book, and if the tension does not improve, seek professional help.

Now that you have completed the Parental Alienation Scale, take a moment and think about what the results mean. Don't get too upset if you are dissatisfied with your score. Your score gives you some idea of how much work lies ahead. In the following chapters, you will learn more about specific symptoms and strategies for changing how you cope with your own alienating behavior as well as that of your ex-spouse.

How Parental Alienation Affects Children

"Has anyone asked you where you want to live?" inquires the evaluator. Jodi, a dimpled six-year-old, nods emphatically. "Oh yes! All the time," she replies. "When mom asks, I say with her, and when dad asks, I say with him. I guess I have them pretty confused." But not nearly as confused as she often feels herself.

"How does parental alienation affect children?" may seem like a simple question with a simple answer. Anyone who understands alienation agrees that parental alienation hurts children, probably for many years. But this answer is not as simple as it appears because divorce itself, even without the complications of alienation, hurts children in the best of circumstances. A simple example is how Jodi may have felt when her parents were asking her to choose between them. Imagine for a moment if Jodi made an open pronouncement in front of both parents that she intended to live with her father. What would have been the emotional aftermath to Jodi and her parents, in particular her mother? What would this do to the relationship between her parents? When parents are tempted to use the children as pawns to hurt, control, or exclude the other parent, as is generally the case with PAS, youngsters find it difficult to heal.

Before answering the question "How does parental alienation affect children?", you must understand that changes you see in your child's behavior, even disruptive changes, are not always caused by parental alienation, the divorce, or your ex-spouse's behavior. Children's attitudes, behaviors, and feelings change with age and maturation. Some behavior changes are healthy and normal, even if they are disruptive or irritating for parents and other family members. But divorce is different from the typical problems your children have at school or with friends. Divorce forces your children to completely change the way they think about family, their future, and ways to relate to others, particularly their parents. They have no experience to know how to cope with these changes. All they know is from television or what they see with their friends. Your children may know other children from broken homes, but that doesn't prepare them for what is coming. Often, your children will adjust to the divorce in the same way they have adjusted to other major changes or disappointments in their life. Their personalities will probably have more to do with how they adjust than anything else. This is not to say you can't help them, because you can.

So how do you sort out all this confusion? How do you discriminate between disruptive behavior that is normal and behavior that is a symptom of alienation? When do you need to consider getting your son or daughter professional help? To help you better understand these distinctions, I have divided this chapter into three sections: how children typically cope with stress (in both healthy and unhealthy ways), symptoms of alienation, and when to get professional help if you believe your child's behavior is getting out of hand.

How Children Cope with Stress

Change is inevitable. Even if your children never have to face the prospect of a broken home, they will have to cope with many painful and even devastating changes in their lives. The death of a loved family member, moving from friends and familiar surroundings because of a job change, the family's loss of income, betrayal by a friend, and the death of a favorite pet are but a few examples of the traumas that your children may face. As hard as you try, you cannot shelter them from the hurt caused by these losses. But you can be there for them, reminding them of your love and your desire to protect them. Somehow, even with your support and love, they will have to come up with their own emotional resources to cope with the pain and heal from it. You must be patient. There is only so much you can do to ease their suffering.

Some children tolerate change better than others, and children's reactions to stress are as unique as their personalities. You know whether your child's recovery is usually fast after a disappointment or whether the hurt tends to linger. One child may brood for days or weeks, while another just keeps going on as if nothing happened. This is confusing to parents, who may worry that a child who avoids discussing a traumatic experience will suffer serious emotional problems later on. Most of the time, these fears are unfounded. Because of differences in temperament, what is traumatic for one child may be less so for another. Some children do well with a divorce, even if they refuse to talk about it. In fact, if you and your spouse have a history of fighting or violence, they may even welcome the divorce.

How children react to stressful events depends a great deal on their age. Younger children will react faster and are usually more expressive of their feelings. They may act out with temper tantrums, have nightmares, act younger than their years, revert to baby talk, or become clingy. Boys are more likely to act out their feelings, while girls become more withdrawn and depressed. Older children and teenagers may defy your authority, become more aggressive by hitting or punching their siblings, withdraw from the family, fight with their friends, escape to their room for hours at a time, show less interest in pleasurable activities, neglect their school-work, or become overly sensitive and critical.

Most parents can attest to feeling frustrated because their teenagers refuse to talk. Teenagers typically deny feeling anything. They frequently respond to your questions by saying "Nothing" or "I don't know," leaving parents to infer how their teenagers are feeling by observing their behavior. If teens continue to maintain their grades, appear reasonably happy, remain active with their friends, and behave themselves, the parents can usually assume they're doing fine.

Criticizing your child's behavior will close the door on any opportunity to understanding and helping your child. There is an important distinc-tion between correcting the child's behavior and criticizing the child. (How to set up a positive mentoring relationship is discussed in chapter 8.) When you make up your mind to talk with your child, you must think about what you say and do. This may be difficult if you are also going through a rough time, but remember, putting your needs aside is what parenting is all about.

Healthy Coping Behaviors

The list below describes specific behaviors that will help you better under-stand what you can expect to see when your son or daughter is making an adequate adjustment to the divorce or, for that matter, any major stress in life. It may be helpful to you while reading the list to think back and remember how your child handled past disappointments. Remember how long it took for your child to bounce back. What did you do to help the healing?

1. During the bad times, your child will still sometimes talk sponta-neously about his or her feelings.
2. Usually within a couple of weeks, your child should be back to his or her old self.
3. Your child should continue with fun activities and friends. Any withdrawal from them should not last more than a couple of weeks.
4. Your child should continue to act interested in being a member of the family.
5. If your child misbehaves or acts out, when things have calmed down, he or she should be able to express remorse about that behavior.
6. After regaining composure, your child should be able to have some insight about his or her inappropriate behavior.
7. During this period of adjustment, your child should continue to show a need for emotional closeness and support from the family. Preteens and some teenagers may not want physical closeness, like a hug, but you should not interpret this as not wanting to be close. Your past experience with your child will tell you how to interpret the avoidance of physical contact.
8. Your child still needs—and should still respond to—praise and encouragement.

Maladjusted Behavior Caused by Divorce

It may be difficult for you to tell how your children perceive the divorce and how well they understand what is going on. As discussed earlier, many children avoid talking about their thoughts and feelings. The most effec-tive way to learn how your children are adjusting is by watching their behavior. If their behavior is appropriate and consistent with past behavior, their adjustment is probably adequate. If there are unsettling changes in your children's behavior, you may need to talk with them and offer help.

There has been considerable research on how divorce affects children and what factors influence a child's adjustment. The results from these studies will give you some insight about what you can do to help your chil-dren make the transition to a single-parent home. You will learn that some changes don't have to be devastating to your children, providing you and your ex-spouse don't get caught up in alienation. Letting alienation get out of control is the one thing that will completely destroy any attempts you make to ensure your children's future. (Remember, as discussed in chapter 1, some degree of naïve alienation goes on in virtually all divorces, but it is active and obsessed alienators who risk damaging their children the most.)

When researchers study how children are affected by divorce, they usually look at the children's academic performance, school attendance, symptoms of depression or anger, behavioral problems, and social skills as indicators of adjustment. They reason that children who are making an adequate adjustment will bounce back from the stress, maintain their grades, continue to socialize, and behave themselves. Children making a poor adjustment will withdrawal, appear depressed or angry, act up, and lose their motivation and interest in school. The results from many of the studies are limited because they do not answer the question "What are the variables influencing a child's adjustment to the divorce?" This question is important because knowing children from divorced families do worse in school than children from intact families is not helpful to parents who are trying to help their children adjust to divorce. It is more important to know why some children from divorced families adjust well while other children from divorced families adjust poorly.

Many studies on divorce adjustment can be criticized because of small sample size, inconsistent results, and the complexity of the circumstances that can influence adjustment. Age, sex of the child, sex of the custodial parent, step-parents, intelligence, and other variables can all influence a child's adjustment. These are the reasons that you need to be cautious about interpreting research results.

Wallerstein and Kelly have done the most extensive research to learn how children of different age groups react and adjust to divorce. They found that young preschoolers, ages 2 ½ to 3, often become more aggressive. Middle preschoolers, ages 3 ¾ to 4, are more irritable, aggressive, self-blaming, and bewildered about the divorce, while older preschoolers, ages five and six, are more anxious and aggressive. When the children reach ages seven or eight, they may appear more depressed or fearful. They begin to experience the grief from their loss. They may have thoughts about the divorce being their fault, which would help explain their divided loyalties and anger toward both parents. As they get older and are able to think more independently, nine and ten year olds may feel betrayed, rejected, and powerless to mend the family. They hate the idea of having to choose between parents. They feel a divided loyalty with fantasies that their parents will somehow reconcile. It continues to surprise me how many children still hope their parents will reconcile, even after their parents have remarried.

Adolescents, eleven years and older, react to a divorce in a variety of ways. They may feel sad and resentful about having their life turned upside down. There is now a lot of uncertainty about where they are going to live, whether they will have to leave their friends, how will the loss of money will affect their lifestyle, and what their friends will think.

Wallerstein and Kelly did a follow-up study and found that 52 percent of the latency age children (ages nine to eleven) living in a stable home environment made an adequate adjustment after the first year from the divorce. They appeared to others as relatively content with their family and friends. Although their adjustment appeared complete, the children continued to have intrusive memories of the divorce that stirred their anger and hostility. The children saw neither mothers nor fathers as being predominately at fault for the divorce. Both were equally targeted by their children for blame.

The study showed that many of the children continued to have problems adjusting to their parents' divorce after one year. They showed signs of depression and lowered self-esteem. A sizable number (24 percent) of children actually showed more serious symptoms of maladjustment. They were more seriously depressed and had more behavioral problems compared to a year earlier.

To help you better understand the problems you may encounter with your children; I have outlined a concise summary of studies identifying variables associated with your children's adjustment to divorce. When reading the summaries, be careful not to overgeneralize the results or assume that the results have to specifically apply to your family. Doing so will cause you unnecessary worry. Keep in mind that the summaries identify variables that affect many children, but not all children, adjusting to a divorce.

RESEARCH ON CHILDREN'S ADJUSTMENT TO DIVORCE

- Children appeared better adjusted to a divorce after two years than they did after one year.

- Children having emotional problems before the divorce will have greater problems adjusting after the divorce. These children will likely need counseling.

- Divorce does not have to interfere with a child's normal psychological growth. This is comforting because the study implies that children are necessarily harmed by the divorce.

- Younger children have more problems adjusting to divorce than older children.

- Children from divorced families are more aggressive, demanding, unaffectionate, disobedient, and angry.

- A child's understanding of the divorce did not aid in their adjustment. In other words, telling children all the reasons for the divorce does not help them handle it any better. Some things are better left unsaid.

- Boys have greater difficulty adjusting to a divorce than girls. Also, the negative effects of divorce last longer for boys than girls.

- The less conflict between parents after the divorce, the better the children adjust.

- Boys from divorced families score lower on intelligence tests as well as math and reading achievement tests and are more likely to be placed in special educational programs or held back in school than boys from intact families. This was not true with girls.

- The children having a positive relationship with their noncustodial parent had better academic and social adjustment.

- Children adjust better to divorce when they attend school in a small district. They had less absenteeism and retentions and better grades.

- Boys who maintain contact with their father adjust better to the divorce than boys who do not maintain contact.

- A parent's consistency and regularity with visits is more important to a child's adjustment than frequency of visits.

- Frequent visits are only beneficial if the noncustodial parent is not overly emotionally.

- If there are hostilities between the parents, frequent visits are not beneficial to the children's adjustment.

This is but a small selection from many studies that have researched the effects of divorce on a child's adjustment. Although the studies provide some important insights, many of them do not completely answer the question, "How can I raise my children to minimize any damage to them because of the divorce?" The interpretation of the studies' results is limited because the researchers usually contrast the adjustment of children from divorced families with that of children from intact homes. The results have consistently shown that children from intact homes are better adjusted than children from divorced homes—in other words, divorce is not good for children. This conclusion should surprise no one.

So what have we learned from these studies that will help you? Unfortunately, knowing that divorce is not good for children does not deter the increase in divorce rates. Children will continue to go through this ordeal, while parents sincerely try to do what they believe is best for their children. They will do whatever they feel is necessary to prevent the children from being victimized by the divorce process. The most important thing you can learn from these studies is knowing there are things you can do to help your children adjust to reduce their suffering, such as minimizing conflict between divorced parents (or at least children's exposure to it), and maintaining children's positive relationship and regular visits with the noncustodial parent.

Symptoms of Parental Alienation

Parental alienation is one possible result of divorce—especially if the divorce goes badly between the two ex-spouses. To help you better understand parental alienation and parental alienation syndrome; I have listed its more obvious symptoms, with one or two examples of each. Some of these behaviors will look familiar to you, but others may come as a surprise because you hadn't really thought of them as something that would hurt children.

- Your son or daughter refuses to give reasons for not wanting to visit.
  "I don't want my dad to see me play soccer. He doesn't deserve to watch me play."

- The child is unable to express reasons for hating you or your family.
  "I hate you! You're mean. I don't want to see you again."

- You allow your children to choose whether or not to visit, knowing that the court has not empowered you or your children to make that choice.

"Billy is old enough to decide for himself. If he wants to visit, he'll tell me. Until then, I'm not going to force him."

• Telling your children everything about why the marriage failed and giving them the details about the divorce settlement.

"Billy, come here and look at these papers. See why we don't have the money for you to take Lindsey to the prom. If you want to go, ask your father for the money."

• Refusing the other parent access to medical and school records or schedules of extracurricular activities.

"If your father wants to see your soccer schedule, let him go to the coach and get it himself."

• Blaming your ex-spouse in your child's presence for not having enough money, changes in your lifestyle, or other problems.

"If your father wasn't driving around in a new car and taking his girlfriend to fancy restaurants, we would have money to go out once in a while."

• Not acknowledging that your children have personal property. Children should have some control over where they want to take personal possessions.

"Sweetheart, you can't take your new doll home to mom's. I bought you the doll and it should stay here."

• Becoming rigid about the parenting time (or visitation) schedule for no good reason other than getting back at your ex-spouse.

"I don't care if you are fifteen minutes late. The court order says you are to be here at 6:00. That doesn't mean fifteen minutes after 6:00. If you are early, you can wait in your car until 6:00."

"I'm not going to swap weekends! You wouldn't trade weekends with me when my brother came to town. Forget it!"

• Assuming that your ex-spouse is dangerous because he or she has threatened you in the past during an argument.

"I'm not going to let that bastard take Jenny out of my house. How do I know that he won't hurt her like he said he was going to hurt me? I'll never forget when he threatened to smash my face in."

• Making false allegations against the other parent of sexual abuse, using drugs or abusing alcohol, or other illegal activities.

"I know he's touching her. I can tell by her look when I ask her."

• Asking your children to choose you over the other parent.

"Hon, just wait until you live with me. We'll be able to have fun like this every day. Wouldn't that be great?"

• Reminding your children that they have reason to feel angry toward their other parent.

"Billy, it's okay to let me know how you feel. It's understandable why you are angry with your mother after she left me for her boyfriend. You know how hard I tried to keep the family together."

• Suggesting an adoption or change in name should you remarry.

"Billy, after Jim and I get married, wouldn't it be great if he adopted you and became your real father?"

"I didn't tell Billy to use Jim's last name. That's his choice."

• Giving children reasons for feeling angry toward the other parent, even when they have no memory of the incident that would provoke the feeling. It is safe to suspect that someone is keeping the children's anger alive when they cannot personally remember the incident.

"I know you're too young to remember when your dad used to beat me, but I can never forget it. He still scares me. Now you go off and have a fun visit with your father, but don't get him angry."

• Having special signals, secrets, words with unique meanings, or a private rendezvous suggests to your children that there is something wrong with the other parent. To avoid being caught with the secrets, you are encouraging your children to lie.

"Lindsey, you know how much I love you and miss you. I'll tell you what. Why don't I meet you at recess by the playground so we can see each other. But you mustn't tell your mother, because you know how angry she will get. This will be our little secret. Okay?"

"I know you can't talk freely on the phone because your mother is listening. I'll tell you what. If you say 'I want to get a new CD,' that will be my signal to meet you at McDonalds. How does that sound?"

• Using your children as a witness against their other parent.

"Lindsey, I need you to tell the judge about how mom lets her boyfriend spend the night. Okay?"

• Asking your children to spy or covertly gather information to be used later against the other parent.

"Billy, you need to tell me if your dad lets one of his girlfriends spend the night."

"Lindsey, this is really important. I need your help. Could you go into the top desk drawer and look into mom's checkbook and find out the

balance. I need to know if she's paying the bills. Don't let her see you. You know how crazy she can get."

- Setting up temptations that interfere with parenting time.

  "I know you want to go to Cedar Point next weekend with Jim and his kids and me, but you can't. You're suppose to visit your dad that weekend. Why don't you talk with him, but you know what he'll say."

- Giving your children the impression that it will hurt your feelings if they have a good time on a visit.

  "Billy, how was your visit?" "Great, Mom. The Rock and Roll Hall of Fame was cool." Dejected, mom says, "That's nice."

- Asking your children about your ex-spouse's personal life.

  "Lindsey, has your mother started dating yet? Where did your mom get the money for the new TV?"

- Rescuing your children from the other parent when there is no danger.

  "If your father gets angry or if you get bored, just call me and I'll come and get you."

These are a few of the symptoms of alienation. One common characteristic of all the symptoms is that the alienator's behavior causes the child tremendous anxiety and conflict. More detailed examples with various strategies on how to combat alienation are described in later chapters.

Severely alienated children are the victims of the obsessed alienator's relentless campaign to destroy their relationship with the targeted parent. These children may appear to others like normal, healthy children until the topic of their targeted parent comes up. Immediately, their demeanor changes. Their friendly, pleasant expression turns to anger and contempt. This is the child that Gardner is describing with his definition of parental alienation syndrome.

WHAT DOES A SEVERELY ALIENATED CHILD LOOK LIKE?

- He has a relentless hatred toward the targeted parent.
- He parrots the obsessed alienator.
- The child does not want to visit or spend any time with the targeted parent.
- Many of the child's beliefs are enmeshed with the alienator.

- The beliefs are delusional and frequently irrational.
- The court does not intimidate him.
- Frequently, his reasons are not based on personal experiences with the targeted parent, but reflect what he is told by the obsessed alienator.
- The child is not neutral in his feelings; he only feels hatred and is unable to see the good.
- He has no capacity to feel guilty about how he behaves toward the targeted parent or to forgive any past indiscretions.
- He shares the obsessed alienator's cause. They work together to denigrate the hated parent.
- The child's obsessional hatred extends to the targeted parent's extended family without guilt or remorse.

The parental alienation syndrome child needs special help. If he maintains his stance of hatred, he will lose out on a potentially loving and supportive relationship with his targeted parent. The loss can last years, if not a lifetime. Frequently, a relationship with the targeted parent's family or the grandparents is also lost to the severely alienated child. For these reasons, courts, mental health professionals, and even legislators have been trying to find valid treatment protocols for deprogramming these children. Courts and frustrated targeted parents have been looking to force the obsessed parent's cooperation with sanctions such as: forcing the child to spend time or even live with the targeted parent, jailing the alienator, hospitalizing the child, using visitation centers, placing the child with neutral family members, or fining the obsessed parent. Though there are anecdotal examples (Rand, 1997) of these sanctions working, there are still no studies with adequate sample sizes showing that these techniques do in fact promote greater cooperation with the obsessed parent, reduce alienation, and alter the child's attitudes toward the targeted parent.

The long-term effects of these interventions on the child must also be considered. Whatever strategies prove most effective must not only strengthen the relationship between the alienated child and the targeted parent, but the relationship with the obsessed alienator and the child must also be preserved. After all, the child needs both parents, not just one parent at the expense of the other. This is why parental alienation syndrome should not be a political issue of one parent against the other. Both parents and the child must be winners.

The severely alienated child is not a psychologically healthy child. An important aspect of a child's development as he grows older is a differentiation between the child's beliefs and those of his parents. In psychological terms, the child develops an ego or an identity that is unique and separate from his parents. This begins with the terrible twos and continues through adulthood. The obsessed alienator fights this important developmental process, at least where the targeted parent is concerned. In effect, the obsessed alienator doesn't want the child to have his own beliefs and feelings toward the targeted parent. He will do whatever is necessary to enmesh the child's perceptions, beliefs, and feelings with his own. I have not talked to a parental alienation syndrome child who appeared well rounded and happy. Every one was defensive, angry, depressed, and had an "us versus them" mentality. Anyone who didn't share in his and the obsessed parent's beliefs about the targeted parent was the enemy.

When Is Professional Help Needed?

Not all children cope well with a divorce. Even fewer survive parental alienation without emotional scars. On the other hand, every time your child is upset about something or gets belligerent, you don't have to run to the therapist. The issue is "How do I know if my children are not coping and need professional help?" There are no hard-and-fast rules about when to get children help. You will have to use your own judgment and trust your instincts when things are not right. You know the hurt is not healing if, in a reasonable time, your children don't return to their old selves.

The question "How do I know if my child is not coping with the divorce and needs professional support?" may also reflect your insecurity about your parenting instincts. Feeling insecure is not uncommon for parents going through a divorce. Unfortunately, my profession is partially to blame for why many parents feel this way. Some psychologists and family therapists have done an injustice to parents by reinforcing insecurity with their obsessive critique of what parents are doing wrong with their children. Some parents, hopefully not you, no longer trust their own instincts and judgment about how best to raise their children. Instead, the parent will seek reassurance and affirmation from others who are sometimes less informed than themselves. They innocently search for guidance and reassurance from mental health professionals, books, talk shows, or newspaper columnists. Even this book may shake your confidence, though I hope not.

Seeking professional help can be frightening for both you and your child. Getting help is not an admission of your failure. Both you and your children have gone through a unique experience without the benefit of having been taught how to handle a divorce. When all else fails, getting help is an admission of your competency and good judgment. Competent parents know when they need professional guidance. An incompetent parent will place his or her personal need to save face above the children's need for help. Listed below are guidelines describing what you can look for that when your child needs professional help. It is never clear cut, but this should make the decision easier for you.

WHEN TO GET YOUR CHILD PROFESSIONAL HELP

- Your child's disturbing behavior persists beyond a month or two.
- After a stressful event, your child does not bounce back to his or her old self.
- Your child's grades on the most recent progress report have significantly dropped.
- Your child tells you about sexual or physical abuse.
- Efforts to get your child to change his behavior have repeatedly failed.
- You suspect your child is drinking or abusing drugs.
- You begin to see changes in your child's behaviors that are common with kids who are abusing alcohol or drugs. A lack of interest in the family, a change in friends, a drop in school grades, a defensive attitude when asked about her behavior and how she spends her time, dramatic changes in dress, a loss of interest in social activities, a depressed or agitated mood, and old friends no longer coming by the house are all signs of possible abuse.
- Your child is no longer interested in doing what he or she once considered fun. He or she no longer wants to play sports, date, or hang out with old friends.

This list of reasons for seeking professional help is not exhaustive. You may notice other behaviors that raise concern about your children's adjustment. Deciding to seek professional help will depend a lot on how much control you believe you have over what is happening to your children. If you have a game plan for helping your children and feel confident about your parenting skills, professional help may not be necessary. If instead, you are confused about what to do, you should speak with a therapist.

Asking for help is sometimes hard because you feel embarrassed about telling a stranger your problems. It may seem like an admission of failure or you may be afraid that you will be told, "This is all your fault." Either way, trusting someone to help and not knowing what our children will say can be scary. That is why it is important to find someone who is qualified and makes you feel comfortable.

While deciding on counseling for your son or daughter, the first thing you will probably do is to ask the children if they want to talk to someone. This sounds reasonable, but most of the time they will say no. After all, children are masters of avoidance and the prospect of talking to a stranger makes them nervous. They may complain about not knowing what to say or worry about what the counselor will say to their mom or dad. Now you feel bewildered. You may not know whether to respect you children's wishes or force them to see a counselor. The answer to that question depends on how badly your children are behaving. If you believe your children are not coping and their behavior is getting worse, they should have no choice but to see a counselor. It is up to the counselor to work with your children's resistance and develop a rapport.

Sherry and Jim

Sherry didn't know what to do. She knew that her son needed help because his fits of anger were getting worse. One day, he kicked his foot through his bedroom door, complaining that he just wanted to be left alone. Sherry pleaded with her ex-husband, "Jim, you have got to stop and listen to me. We've got to get Jerry help. For months, he's been tearing the house apart and sneaking out late at night. You don't even know who his friends are anymore. Remember Larry? He doesn't even come around anymore. And there's no talking to him without a fight. You have got to do something. All he does is go into his room and listen to that rap music. For all we know, he's on drugs."

Feeling attacked by Sherry's accusations, Jim snapped back, "If you would stop nagging and leave him alone, you wouldn't have these problems. Jerry doesn't act like that around me. It's your fault. If you let him come and live with me, there wouldn't all these problems. He's great when we're together. He behaves himself and is not a problem. He doesn't need to see a counselor. What he needs is for you to just back off and give him some breathing room. Let him decide where he wants to live. He'll be all right."

Therapy During a Custody Battle

Sometimes parents, like Sherry, are involved in a custody battle and worry about what the court will think if they seek professional help for themselves or the children. The fear is that the court will hold it against them when it comes time to make a custody decision. In general, the opposite is true. Rarely will the court have a problem with you or the children getting professional help. This is not an issue the court will consider when making a custody decision. In Jim and Sherry's case, Jim would have greater difficulty justifying his behavior, especially if Jerry was found to not be treated for a drug problem. The court's concern will have more to do with the parents conduct and why the children need counseling. The court will be concerned if it finds that the child should have been getting professional help and one of the parents actively interfered—for example, by not giving the other parent the insurance card. Some courts would even consider this child neglect, which is potentially punishable, or grounds for not awarding custody.

Finding a Therapist

Finding a qualified mental health professional doesn't have to be difficult, especially in larger metropolitan areas. It's important to find someone who understands families, children, and divorce, parental alienation, and knows the workings of your domestic courts. Usually, the therapist is a licensed psychologist, social worker, family therapist, or a mental health counselor. It is unusual to find a psychiatrist who counsels children and families. Typically, they work with other therapists and limit their practice to administrating and monitoring medication.

A therapist or counselor may make a recommendation that is against an existing court order. For example, a therapist may tell you to stop visits until a particular issue is resolved in therapy. Perhaps your child is angry at his father and doesn't want to go, his tantrums suggest unconscious conflicts such as possible child abuse, he's too young to be away from his mother that long, etc. Even if the therapist is well meaning, in most states a therapist cannot tell you to do anything that would violate an existing court order. If the counselor makes such a request, ask whether he or she has the authority to do so. If you feel strongly enough about his recommendation, you should consult your attorney for advice before taking any action. Otherwise, you may be in contempt of a court order.

For information about working with a counselor and deciding whether to consult one for yourself, see chapter 13.

Giving Your Children What They Need

"You want to raise a child to be patient, compassionate, forgiving, loving, and honest. Well, children learn those things from parents who are patient, compassionate, loving, and who tell the truth. The qualities you want passed onto your children can only be passed along by those of you who show you have them yourself."

Referee Alex Savakis
Trumbull County Family Court, Ohio

Betsy and Robert

"Excuse me. Excuse me!" The school psychologist practically had to shout to get Robert and Betsy's attention. They had been bickering and sniping at each other since they walked into his office, arguing viciously for the past ten minutes. After tossing off another barbed comment or two, the couple, who had divorced eight months ago after a nine-year marriage, finally turned their attention to the psychologist.

"I asked you here to talk about Tommy," he said. He had already explained that their eight-year-old son's teachers were concerned about changes in his behavior and frequent requests to go to the nurse's office.

Both Robert, a thirty-four-year-old small business owner, and Betsy, a thirty-seven-year-old office manager, looked confused. "I thought that was what we were doing," Betsy commented.

"Well, then, maybe I missed something," the psychologist quietly proposed. "I heard you two mention child support, each other's spending habits, and who's responsible for Melanie's coat that turned up missing. Hardly a word was mentioned about what Tommy feels or needs or is going through right now."

"Are you sure?" Robert asked.

But of course, he was. The school psychologist was also quite certain about what he experienced while they were arguing in his presence. "I felt frustrated and powerless," the school psychologist reported. "I was afraid that you would get violent right here in the office. I was feeling somehow responsible for bringing you together and causing this fight. Most of all, I wanted to stop you, but I felt helpless to. And I'm an adult," he pointed out. "So I must ask you if you two fight like this in front of your kids?"

Betsy wanted to deny it, but the truth was that they did. They fought when Robert picked up the kids for visits and when he dropped them off. They fought over the telephone with the children near enough to overhear. And, Betsy admitted, just last week she had allowed Tommy to stay up past his bedtime because Robert was stopping by with some tax papers. She thought she and her ex-husband would be more likely to control their tempers with their son in the next room. They argued anyway.

Fights with Robert often reduced her to tears, Betsy told the psychologist, and Tommy would try to comfort her. "It's okay, Mommy. I love you," he'd say. On more than one occasion, she had replied, "I know *you* do, honey. It's your father who's going to be the death of me." According to the psychologist, Tommy seemed to have taken that statement literally.

"Children don't always realize when you're exaggerating or using cliches," he said. "I know Tommy worries about you. And I have a feeling that he sometimes pretends to be sick and goes to the school nurse hoping she'll send him home where he can keep an eye on you."

Betsy was beginning to feel sick herself. As she thought about the other signs of stress Tommy had been showing—falling grades, difficulty concentrating, going off by himself during recess, occasional bedwetting—the destructiveness of her incessant arguing with Robert finally hit home.

"I'm always telling Tommy that I love him and won't let anything bad happen to him," Betsy remarked, her voice quivering. "But something bad happens every time his father and I speak to each other. It has to stop."

This realization hit her like a bucket of ice water, dousing her anger and forcing her to take action, positive action this time. Betsy began to monitor her behavior, to be more aware of the nuances in what she said, and to recognize when her words or actions were adversely effecting her child and her child's relationship with his dad.

Regaining Perspective to Focus on Your Children's Needs

The prevention of parental alienation syndrome becomes possible when you begin to recognize the impact your words and behavior have on your children and make a conscious effort to address the unique needs and feelings they have developed because of your divorce. This requires sensitivity and a more charitable attitude toward your former mate than you've had in some time. To understand this attitude, try to remember the frame of mind you were in when you were first dating the man or woman who is now your ex-spouse. Way back then, you paid attention to almost everything your new love said or did. You noticed his reaction to your comments. He, in turn, kept a mental record of the things that seemed to please you. And you both chose not to behave in a way that might adversely effect or completely derail your budding relationship. Although you no longer *feel* the way you did then, for your children's sake, you can behave with the same sensitivity.

You are no longer lovers or even sparring spouses. You are divorced parents with a mutual interest in your children's welfare. Although you may have had some trouble adapting to those roles up until now, by remaining attuned to each other's feelings and negotiating when behavior changes seem to be called for, you and your ex can make your new co-parenting relationship work.

Of course, you may not feel ready or willing to do that. You may still be too angry or hurt. The memories of infidelity, verbal abuse, or violence may be too fresh in your mind. Perhaps you're thinking, "That louse doesn't deserve to be treated sensitively," or "I'm not the one who should be monitoring and changing my behavior. She walked out of our marriage. Let her change," or "He's a nut case. We'd all be better off having no contact with him ever again." And you may be right.

If your ex-spouse is truly dangerous—incapacitated by a mental illness or addiction or for some other reason completely incapable of caring for your children—the recommendations found in this chapter won't always apply. But in all other cases, you owe it to your children to at least try to heal, forgive, and parent cooperatively.

Parents usually have good instincts about what their children need to grow into healthy adults. Unfortunately for all, divorce often distracts parents just when their children's needs are the most intense and heartfelt. As Robert and Betsy discovered, it's easy to lose sight of what is happening to your children—even when you know they are probably going through the biggest adjustment of their young lives.

Children of divorced parents have essentially the same emotional needs as children from intact families. However, when children of divorce turn to their parents for nurturing, attention, or reassurance, they are often turning to two people who are overwhelmed by their own problems and no longer available to each other for mutual support.

If parents have to adjust to new roles, time may be a precious commodity. Their struggles to make ends meet financially or pull themselves together emotionally may leave them too drained to deal with their youngster's demands. Yet, even in the midst of all this chaos, it is possible to refocus and, if it seems necessary, to revamp what you're doing to help your children through a difficult time of transition.

Below I have described some children's needs that frequently get neglected during a divorce. After each description, you will be asked to evaluate your recent efforts to meet that specific need—not to make yourself feel guilty or like a failure but rather to reawaken your sensitivity and rethink your behavior.

EXERCISE: HOW WELL ARE YOU MEETING YOUR CHILDREN'S NEEDS?

Your children need a number of things from you in order to feel secure and thrive. How well do you feel you've done in each of the following areas since your separation or divorce? Rate yourself on a 1-10 scale, with 10 meaning "completely satisfied" with the way you've addressed this need and 1 meaning "completely dissatisfied."

1. Your children need you to be there for them. They want to know that you're emotionally available, willing to answer their questions, and able to show affection without going overboard. Devoting every waking moment to them is more than they'd ask for. However, knowing that they can get your attention when they need comfort or help with a problem is essential for them to feel safe and secure. Your rating _____

2. Your children need your approval and encouragement. They look for clues that you cherish and feel proud of them. It reassures them to see that you carry pictures of them in your wallet or to hear you brag to friends and family about their

accomplishments. Receiving compliments and congratulations from you directly has an even greater impact. Your rating _____

3. Your children need you to recognize that they are unique individuals with their own personalities, perceptions, and preferences, and to treat them accordingly. They need you to remain sensitive to their adjustment to the divorce and listen to their feelings even if they are different than your own. They experience more success in general and find it easier to adapt to the divorce when your expectations are realistic. So be aware of where they are developmentally and try not to ask more (or less) from them than you would expect from any other child at their developmental level. Your rating _____

4. Your children need you to encourage them to have a positive relationship with their other parent, or at least not stand in their way. Yes, you might be happier if you had less contact with your ex-spouse. Like many custodial parents, you may see your ex's presence as an intrusion, a privilege he forfeited when he divorced you, or a potential hassle that you'd rather avoid. It would be more comfortable and convenient for you if your former mate stayed away from your children's activities. But what feels good for you is not always what's best for your children. Research has repeatedly shown that children who are actively involved with both parents without conflict make the best initial and long-term adjustment to divorce.

   Your children want to feel free to have fun during a visit or to invite their other parent to see them in school plays or championship games. They don't want to feel as if they're betraying one parent by having a good time with another or as if they're the prize in a tug-of-war between the two of you. You need to assure your children that they don't have to choose sides, that it's possible to love both of their parents, and that they are causing you no harm by doing so. Your rating_____

5. Your children need you to show them how to respond to stressful situations in emotionally healthy ways. They need to know that you won't fall apart under pressure. They count on you to cope without using drugs or alcohol and without becoming violent or verbally abusive. Your children need to see you express anger without losing control. This ensures that they won't be afraid of you when you're angry.

   They also need you to demonstrate that the hurt and anger linked to the demise of your marriage can heal. Your children will feel safer and more secure once you've gotten beyond the initial pain and confusion of your divorce. In the meantime, they need you to be honest about your feelings (while exercising a reasonable amount of self-control) and to let them know that it's okay to feel sad or angry. By watching you manage your emotions, they can learn to manage theirs. Your rating____

6. Your children need you to maintain as many family or community ties as possible. Although you might like to pack up, move away, and start a new life far away from everyone you now know, making such a major change so soon after your divorce isn't always advisable. Your kids have already "lost" one full-time parent and family life as they knew it. They need the comfort of familiar surroundings and ongoing contact with their network of grandparents, cousins, friends, neighbors, scout leaders, doctors, and teachers. Encourage them to accept support from these people, and accept some yourself, especially if you are a working parent. Your rating____

7. Your children need you and your ex-spouse to make every effort to peacefully resolve any differences of opinion on how to raise them after the divorce. They need examples of flexibility and two people working together rather than rigidity, back stabbing, and one-upmanship.

Cooperation and communication between divorced parents is crucial for children's present and future well-being. If your children observe a reasonable degree of cooperation between their parents, they will be more relaxed and less fearful in the aftermath of your divorce. They won't learn to dread the times when you and your ex are together the way youngsters who've come to expect arguments between their parents do. For these children, the moments immediately before and after a visit when they are "passed" from one parent to another are among the worst. They lose their spontaneity and ability to enjoy the time they spend with their family. Insecurity plagues them everywhere they go.

Watching their parents argue over visits reminds children of the other fights they've witnessed over the years. If they have previously been drawn into their parents' battles, they'll silently shrink back or slink away, hoping that neither parent will notice their presence and ask their opinion. They learn to dread any question concerning parenting time.

Other children react to fights between their parents by

blaming themselves. They think, "If it weren't for me, there would be no visitation and nothing to fight about." And they look for ways to prevent future arguments. Many will keep the peace by keeping their mouths shut when they'd like to ask for a change in the parenting time. Knowing that there will be an argument if they're late getting home, they don't dare ask to stay at Mom's until the end of a Star Trek episode. And they won't risk starting a fight between their parents by letting on that their best friend's sleepover party falls on a parenting time weekend. Instead, they just don't attend. They sacrifice their desires to make life easier for their parents instead of the other way around.

If sacrifices must be made to bring about some semblance of family harmony following a divorce, parents ought to be the ones making them. Swallowing some pride, passing up opportunities to argue, and uttering a kind word now and then doesn't hurt anyone. It can do wonders for your kids. Your rating_____

Note: If your ratings in one or more areas weren't as high as you'd like, try not to be too hard on yourself. You probably weren't being malicious when you lost sight of your children's needs. You may have been detoured (or stopped dead in your tracks) by various obstacles. Some blinded you to your own behavior and its impact. Others may have kept you too worked up to do what was best for your youngsters.

Obstacles to Effective Parenting

Let's take a look at some of the emotional obstacles that may be preventing you from recognizing your children's needs or may be interfering with your ability to parent cooperatively. As your awareness in this area increases, so will your ideas about what to do differently in the future.

Stuart and Mary Beth

"It's the same argument over and over again," Stuart complains. "I call to ask for a change in visitation and she goes nuts." To prove his point, the forty-three-year-old investment counselor produces a tape recording of a recent telephone conversation. It begins with his ex-wife, Mary Beth, reacting to his request to take the kids for the upcoming weekend instead of the one after it.

"You'll never change," Mary Beth says with disdain. "You're the same selfish, self-centered bastard you were when we were married."

"And you're still a controlling bitch." Stuart retorts blandly. He's been down this road before. "Can I see my children this weekend or not?"

"You don't care about your kids. If you really loved them, you'd stop disappointing them. Don't you think they're sick of you not showing up when you're supposed to? Why should they change their plans whenever it suits you?"

"What kind of plans?" Stuart attempts to ask. But Mary Beth goes on as if she has not heard him.

"I thought you'd be different once you stopped drinking, but you're just as inconsiderate and unreliable as ever," the thirty-seven-year-old registered nurse says.

Stuart cuts in angrily, "This isn't about my drinking. There's a convention in Vegas next weekend."

"Right. And it will be something else the weekend after that," Mary Beth snaps. She lists the out-of-town meetings, camping trips, business dinners, and once-in-a-lifetime Super Bowl tickets that have interfered with parenting time over the past few months. "You've got some life Stu, running all over creation having a good time while I'm here working double shifts, taking care of your kids, and trying to explain why Daddy can't fit them into his busy schedule again."

Although the conversation would continue and escalate into a loud exchange of insults and accusations, Mary Beth hit the crux of the matter here. After enduring more than a decade of Stuart's alcoholic binges, week-long disappearances, and inability to hold onto a job, she had finally divorced him. But she was still struggling. He had gotten sober, landed a high-paying job with lots of perks, and adopted an exciting, carefree lifestyle that Mary Beth alternately envied and resented.

"It isn't fair," she thinks. "Not after all he put me through." She feels he owes her something—some courtesy, some consideration, or at the very least, some predictability so that she can manage her time. Instead, he repeatedly asks to change the parenting time schedule.

At first, Mary Beth had tried to accommodate Stuart. But his excessive requests disrupted her routine, interfered with her plans, and left the kids uncertain about when they would next see their dad. Over time, she became more and more resentful about his requests, his carefree way of life, the years she "wasted" on him, and more.

"I'll show him," Mary Beth decided, and began to refuse Stuart's requests regardless of the circumstances, igniting his anger and leading to bitter confrontations. Now, each sees the other's actions as spiteful and malicious. From their entrenched positions, they get into what Stuart originally referred to as "the same old argument again and again."

When this occurs, Stuart and Mary Beth appear to be arguing about parenting time schedules. But visitation is actually the battleground for a war that began before Mary Beth and Stuart were divorced. They are struggling for power, control, retribution, or the resolution of some old, personal business between them. And once these ex-spousal issues get mixed up with the parental issues they set out to discuss, their children's interests or desires are completely lost.

Obstacle 1: Ex-Spousal Issues

Fighting about why he left you, who gets the tax refund, or her mother's meddling has nothing to do with what's best for your children.

The confusion between ex-spousal and parental issues is the first and most common obstacle to doing what's best for your children following your divorce. Pain, anger, sadness, and feelings of inadequacy or failure that began while you were married don't just go away when your divorce is final. These feelings can fester and influence how you relate to your former spouse for years. When bitterness from the marital relationship bleeds through to interactions about the children, as it often does, you get interactions like Mary Beth's and Stuart's. The inability to separate ex-spousal issues from parental ones is a major contributor to ongoing dissent between formerly married couples with children.

Ex-spousal issues are emotionally-charged topics that have nothing to do with your children or how to raise them. They stem from your relationship with each other and probably caused the break-up of your marriage. These sources of continuing conflict, confusion, outrage, or hurt feelings might include the following:

- A lingering sense of betrayal that dates back to the day you found out your spouse was having an affair.
- Anger about having to lower your standard of living (because you must pay child support or no longer can depend on your spouse's income).
- Feeling old and inadequate compared to your ex's new mate.

- Memories of being controlled, belittled, abused, or lied to by your spouse during your marriage (and anticipating that you will be again).

As they did for Mary Beth and Stuart, these ex-spousal issues and others like them tend to come up again and again, making almost any interaction between ex-spouses a potential battleground.

Parental issues are focused on your children's needs and problems: their health, safety, progress in school, adjustment to the divorce, visitation, developmental milestones, and so on. Why is Julie failing math? When will Megan be old enough to date? How will we pay for Sam's braces? Should Pete be involved in two after-school sports, computer classes, and trumpet lessons? Although answering questions like these can still push some buttons and lead to disagreements, parents are generally able to discuss them objectively and in a relatively calm, rational manner—unless ex-spousal issues creep into the conversation, creating so much emotional interference that communication virtually grinds to a halt.

When ex-spousal issues bleed through to discussions of parenting concerns, they distort your perceptions, cloud your judgment, and impair your ability to decide what's best for your children. Nothing gets accomplished. In fact, the feelings aroused by your unfinished relationship business may be so intense (or the ensuing argument so brutal) that you'll never get around to talking about parenting issues much less resolving them. To avoid this outcome, you must make a continual, conscious effort to separate ex-spousal issues from parental ones. The following exercise can help.

EXERCISE: IDENTIFYING EX-SPOUSAL AND PARENTAL ISSUES

The purpose of this exercise is to help you differentiate between ex-spousal and parental issues.

First, think of any topic that triggers feelings of anger, jealousy, grief, frustration, bitterness, resentment, or other strong emotions and tends to start arguments between you and your ex-spouse. List these topics on a sheet of paper.

Next, when you're satisfied that your list is fairly complete (you can add more issues at any time), go back over it and write the letter "P" beside the items that pertain solely to the needs, problems, and upbringing of your children.

Then go through the list a second time and write the letter "E" next to

DIVORCE CASUALTIES

items that involve only you and your ex-spouse, not your children. All items should be marked with either an E or a P.

Ex-spousal ("E") issues should not have any bearing on your decision to seek changes in custody or parenting time and should never be discussed in your children's presence. These issues are none of your children's business.

But what about "P" issues? Can't they trigger arguments and cause tension that's bad for children too? Certainly they can. Almost any parent will become defensive when the other parent makes unsolicited comments about their parenting skills. Inflammatory statements such as "I know more about raising kids than you'll ever know," or "I have to tell you what to do, for the children's sake. You don't know the first thing about parenting," ignite arguments. Tense discussions become full-fledged confrontations.

Go back over the "P" issues on the list. Check those that seem especially explosive. Think about what might make these parenting matters so upsetting or difficult to resolve. Could there be an ex-spousal issue hidden below the surface? How about a fear (of losing your children's love, for instance) or a desire (to protect your children from unpleasantness of any kind) or a conviction (that kids need to go to church every Sunday)?

Simply knowing that these underlying currents exist can help you manage your emotions more effectively and work out parental issues more reasonably than you have in the past. If ex-spousal issues are not resolved and continue to interfere with your calmly dealing with parental issues, you may consider getting counseling.

Resolving Volatile Issues

Always calm down and regain self-control before asking your ex-spouse to explain his behavior with the children or confronting her about an emotionally charged matter. When you start to argue and voices get loud, take a time out. Announce your intention to cool off, then walk away, or allow the other person to withdraw. Try again when you both have your anger under control.

When someone's speech becomes loud and pressured, your chances of getting through to that person or resolving a problem are nil. You can't "win" or even get your message across because the other person is not listening to what you have to say. Instead of pursuing this futile endeavor, acknowledge that the discussion has obviously stirred up some strong feelings and suggest that you both back off for a while. Agree to discuss the

49

issue at another time, and for the time being, do nothing about the matter that led to the argument.

Before following up on a concern voiced by your children, ask yourself whether the matter is really worth discussing with your ex. Is it important enough to risk starting an argument or could you simply reassure your youngsters and move on?

When children tell you something that is inconsistent with what your ex-spouse has said, do not automatically conclude that your kids are correct and your ex-spouse is lying. You may have a biased desire to believe your children rather than your ex-spouse (especially if honesty wasn't his strong suit previously), but there could be other explanations for the discrepancy—a misunderstanding on your part or your children's, for instance, or an attempt by your children to manipulate something out of you. In addition, calling your ex a liar is alienating and provokes tension between your children and the other parent.

Obstacle Two: Theorizing

Human beings are naturally inquisitive. They want to know what makes people tick and why they do what they do. If they don't understand why someone is behaving in a particular way and no one offers them a reasonable explanation, they will come up with one of their own. Then they will emotionally react to their theory as if it were fact.

If you've had a stormy marriage or gone through a hostile divorce, you may be predisposed to see your ex-spouse's behavior in a negative light. Your negative interpretation arouses negative feelings that intensify animosity toward your former partner. You may be quick to judge and prone to misunderstand because you're looking at your ex's actions through a lens clouded by pain, anger, bitterness, and memories of past experiences that turned out poorly. Or your misinterpretations may stem from a desire to protect your children from harm—although the threat to their health and happiness is mostly in your head.

Ron and Susan

Divorced parents in their mid-thirties, Ron and Susan had initially managed to keep conflicts over parenting to a minimum. A little over a year after their break-up, Susan, the custodial parent, was shopping with nine-year-old Brett and seven-year-old Mary in a local mall and ran into Ron. She glanced at Brett and Mary to see how they were reacting. Instead of rushing over to Ron and affectionately greeting him as she'd expected, they both wore blank expressions and stood listlessly several feet away from her. From Susan's perspective, they seemed scared to approach Ron.

"What has he done to make them afraid of him?" she wondered. "If he's hurt them in any way, I'll kill him." She could barely resist the urge to grab their hands and rush away.

Ron also noticed how emotionally withdrawn his children seemed, but he interpreted their demeanor differently. "They're clearly unhappy with their mother," he concluded. "She must be making their lives miserable." He was angry and wanted to wrench his children away from Susan on the spot. Although neither Ron nor Susan acted on their impulses, the damage was done.

Reacting to their respective theories, each felt protective and became increasingly suspicious of the other. They grilled their kids about what went on when they were with the other parent and were constantly on the look out for signs of abuse. At one point, Ron even considered seeking custody. Susan thought about cutting off visitation—all because of what turned out to be a totally invalid theory.

Brett and Mary didn't feel afraid or unhappy but rather awkward and unsure about how to handle a situation they'd never encountered before (running into Dad while they were with Mom). If they rushed over to greet their father, they might hurt their mother's feelings. But if they stayed right next to their mother, their father might feel rejected. They resolved their dilemma as many children would, by removing themselves from it.

Brett and Mary withdrew physically by taking several steps away from their mother and emotionally by avoiding eye contact and taking on the most non-committal look they could muster—a blank, almost trancelike expression. They didn't need rescuing or protection but reassurance and direction. If either parent had realized this, or if Susan had reserved judgment and simply mentioned to her kids that they were welcome to go over and say "hi" to their dad, months of wrangling would have been avoided.

The only way any of us can ever really know the meaning of another person's actions is for that person to explain his or her behavior to us. People rarely volunteer that information, though, and we rarely ask. Instead, we formulate theories. We interpret other people's actions based on our previous experiences with them, recent events, how we would behave under similar circumstances, and so on.

Although they sometimes do prove to be accurate, we tend to believe that our interpretations are correct even when we have no evidence to support our theory. This is a trap. As Ron and Susan discovered, we stir up all sorts of turmoil by emotionally reacting to our theories as if they were facts. Particularly where children are concerned, they often are not.

Children Avoid What Makes Them Uncomfortable

"Leaving the scene" the way Brett and Mary did is a fairly typical childhood reaction to confusion, discomfort, and awkwardness. Youngsters will use it when they get caught sneaking cookies from the pantry or have to endure Aunt Jane's cheek pinching at a family gathering or are torn between pleasing their teacher by telling her who hid the chalkboard erasers and being loyal to a friend by not telling. It's a mainstay escape mechanism among children whose divorced parents have trouble getting along.

As I've said, arguments and icy silences between their parents upset children. Tense situations that come with the territory of divorce confuse them. Just saying goodbye after a visit can pose a dilemma for them, especially if they know you are watching from the doorway (or suspect that you're looking from a window). How affectionate can their parting from their other parent be without hurting you? And how enthusiastically can they greet you without hurting their other parent?

It's just too complicated for their five- or eight- or ten-year old psyches to handle. So they tune out their surroundings, turn off their feelings, and get that familiar blank expression on their faces. Because they don't know how to explain their feelings in words they withdraw instead, or deny being bothered, or without being conscious of their motives, let out their feelings in some other venue (by getting into fights on the playground, for instance, or having stomach pains that require special attention from the school nurse). Unfortunately, parents don't always realize that a simple desire to avoid unpleasantness or escape discomfort is behind the blank looks on their children's faces and the almost depressed quality to their appearances.

The Temptation to Blame

When you don't like what's happening and don't know why it's happening, your first inclination may be to blame somebody for it. According to this theory, when little Billy does something troubling or that you don't expect after visiting his other parent, it easy to assume that what Billy did was the other parent's fault.

When you notice that your children have become distant, deflated, or unable to speak above a whisper or look you in the eye, your parental instincts kick into gear. You want to protect, to help, to make everything all better and prevent this bad thing from ever happening again. Unfortunately, you don't really know what that bad thing is.

Not knowing can make you feel helpless. Coming up with a plausible theory to explain your children's upset temporarily relieves that helpless feeling. And one of the easiest theories to come up with is that the problem is all your ex-spouse's fault.

If you're still angry or disgusted with your ex for his past behavior, you're primed to believe your theories. It is consistent with what you already believe about the man or woman to whom you were once married. Blaming or targeting the other parent also keeps you from feeling guilty or responsible for the situation. Unfortunately, taking yourself off the hook in this manner will ultimately intensify your anger and add to your sense of powerlessness. After all, if your ex is totally to blame for your children's unhappiness only he—and not you—can stop your children's pain.

Naturally, things can go wrong during visits, and children sometimes do go into their "zombie" imitations in response to an ex-spouse's inappropriate behavior. You may even have good cause—based on past experience—for being suspicious, but you are still theorizing and reacting to a premise that could be anywhere from slightly off the mark to completely untrue.

To reduce misunderstandings and needless conflict, try to examine your reactions before you act on them. Take a moment to ask yourself, "Have I drawn a conclusion based on something I actually saw or heard or know to be true and not merely something I think happened or believe could be true? Did I consider and eliminate other explanations before coming up with this theory of my own?"

Tips on Avoiding the Blaming Trap

1. Before automatically blaming or rushing to any other conclusions, do these things:

- Learn to recognize when you start theorizing.
- Remind yourself that your "explanation" is really an interpretation that could be wrong. Before you spring into action, check out your theory.
- Ask for clarification from the person whose behavior you're trying to explain. The mere act of asking reduces your chances of overreacting. It gets you to slow down, listen, and hopefully make a thoughtful, conscious decision about what you'll do next. This is a vast improvement over blindly following the trail of convoluted reasoning winding through your mind.
- When seeking clarification from children, you won't always get clear, concise answers. They rarely come right out and say, "I feel sad about Dad not living with us anymore," or "I was afraid that I'd hurt your feelings if I hugged and kissed Mom in front of you." Instead, they might tell you they felt "weird" or "icky" or simply not interested in kissing. Sometimes they will tell you what they think you want to hear rather than taking the risk of upsetting you by being honest.

2. Although its not nearly as bad as the catastrophes you're apt to conjure up in your imagination, when children can't express affection toward their other parent in your presence, there is still a problem.

- Stop and ask yourself "Why would my children feel nervous about kissing or hugging my ex when I'm around?"
- If you don't know for sure, ask your children. If they can't answer immediately, gently offer some options.
- Let your kids know that they won't get in trouble for answering your questions. But don't press. Help them feel safe, and they will, sooner or later, let you know what's going on with them.
- If they tell you that they didn't kiss Daddy good-bye because they didn't want to hurt you or cause trouble between you and your ex, assure them that it's okay to openly express affection to their other parent.
- Repeat that message frequently. More often than not, reassurance is what your children want and need. What they can do without is the feeling that they are doing something

wrong by maintaining a relationship with their other parent or seeing their other parent getting blamed for something he didn't do.

3. Occasionally, there will be incidents involving your kids and your ex-spouse that do require your attention. Here's what to do when this occurs:

    *   Listen to what your children have to say without getting upset, making judgments, or assigning blame. Otherwise, you will alarm your children, causing them to temper their story, or you'll get yourself so worked up that you'll distort what you're being told and later feel like a fool for not getting your facts straight.
    *   Consider the possibility that your children may have misunderstood what occurred or are unable to describe the incident accurately.
    *   After calmly listening to your children's story, take some time to think through what you've heard and decide whether or not you need to discuss the matter with your ex-spouse.

Obstacle Three: New, Blurred Boundaries between You and Your Ex-Spouse

If your dad, who's retired and living on a fixed income, drove up in a brand new, high priced sports car, you might have no qualms about saying, "Nice wheels, Dad. But can you afford them?" Yet you'd never think of pulling up next to the same car driven by a stranger and asking the driver, "How much money do you make to afford a car like that?" You wouldn't want to offend the other person.

Likewise, you would hesitate to use vulgarity in front of a nun or reveal your sexual history to someone you'd just met—even if no one ever came right out and told you not to. That's because human behavior is continually shaped by a set of unwritten rules of conduct. These rules will change over time or with a change of circumstances like a divorce. The trick is to keep up with them.

Rules are relatively succinct for most young children who come from intact families free of conflict. Expectations are few and consequences clear cut. Whether you obtained your knowledge through first-hand experience or by observing the experiences of others, you quickly grasped that misbehavior led to disapproval, criticism, punishment, or some other unwanted outcome. Then you learned to anticipate those negative outcomes if you misbehaved.

Rules became more complex as you grew older. You learned more layers and nuances, particularly during your teen age years when the desire to fit in with your peers by adopting behavior they found acceptable was a powerful motivator. You had to make your way through a maze of social dos and don'ts, knowing all too well that if you veered too far from the path, your peers would get you back on track with their criticism.

Finding yourself in a situation where you don't know the rules can be extremely uncomfortable. For example, on your first day at a new job you may feel as if you're tiptoeing through a minefield trying not to offend anyone. You may cautiously watch people for clues about the company's unwritten code of conduct or signs (in the form of stern or pitying looks) that you have inadvertently crossed the invisible line between appropriate and inappropriate behavior, which I refer to as a boundary.

A boundary is a mental stop sign that gets us to stop a behavior before we violate a code of conduct. Usually when we're about to cross a boundary, we'll feel uneasy or concerned about how other people will judge us. This anxiety is similar to guilt, only we experience the feeling before doing something we think is wrong. (Guilt is the feeling you get after you have crossed a boundary.)

Most of us have different boundaries for different situations. For example, because codes of conduct are generally stricter at work than at home or in social situations, more behaviors are out of bounds there. We also have different boundaries for different relationships. Less personal information is shared with colleagues than with friends and less with friends than with our mates, who are often privy to the most intimate details of our lives. So what happens when we're no longer married to our mates? Our boundaries move.

Once you and your spouse separate, many of the behaviors that used to be acceptable are not acceptable anymore. Previously, either of you could enter the house without calling ahead or knocking on the door or giving any thought whatsoever to what might be going on inside. When you were hungry, you could go to the refrigerator, see what there was to eat, and take whatever you wanted. It didn't matter who brought in and opened the mail delivered to your family's address. Now it does. In fact, every one of these actions could be considered offensive and an invasion of privacy once you and your spouse are no longer living under the same roof.

Never underestimate the impact of acting as if a separation or divorce hasn't changed the rules. Even a nonchalant "So what did you do this weekend?" can evoke a strong negative reaction from your ex-spouse. Defending your remark by saying you were making small talk or trying to show interest in her activities may not wash. You gave up your right to know her whereabouts when you got divorced. By asking her about her activities now, you will violate a boundary and offend her. Of course, people are different. Even after a divorce, what is offensive for one person is not necessarily offensive for another. It is going to take patience and sensitivity to figure out just where your new boundaries are.

You may unintentionally violate many boundaries while you are going through your divorce. Grief, uncertainty about your future, lack of experience with the legal system, fear of losing custody of your children, and other intense emotions associated with your divorce can impair your judgment about rules and boundaries. As a result, you might do any of the following:

- Call your attorney or a judge at home
- Rummage through your ex-wife's purse or examine your ex-husband's checkbook
- Put children or friends in the uncomfortable position of gathering information about the person your ex is dating
- Secretly record telephone calls between your children and their other parent
- Intercept and read your children's mail from their other parent or pick up an extension and eavesdrop on their phone conversations
- Not give children gifts sent to them by their other parent

Generally speaking, you should know that these behaviors violate other people's right to privacy or possession. Before engaging in them, you ought to have a sense that you're about to do something that most people consider inappropriate. Due to your lack of experience in this situation and the intensity of your feelings, you run a high risk of missing the usual emotional cues. To compensate, you must mentally identify inappropriate behavior and consciously commit yourself to respect those boundaries.

After a separation, some awkwardness is to be expected. Because neither you nor your ex are sure of the new rules, occasionally one of you will inadvertently cross a boundary and get an earful from the other. Your best bet is not to take any rights for granted. Assume that all of your old permissions have been withdrawn. Don't touch intimately, show up unannounced, open drawers or cupboards, or ask "Who was that blond you were biking with in the park on Sunday?" unless you're ready to argue.

When children are involved, determining the rules and abiding by them becomes an even more complicated task. The fine line between looking out for your children's welfare and checking up on your ex-spouse is easy to cross. Once again, actions that might have been accepted while you were married can cause arguments or lead to alienation after your divorce, making it all the more important to redefine and respect the boundaries between yourself and your former wife or husband.

EXERCISE: IDENTIFYING NEW BOUNDARIES

The purpose of this exercise is to help you recognize and respect the new boundaries in your relationship with a former spouse.

First, on a sheet of paper, list all the ways you used to behave that now seem to offend your ex-spouse, as well as things your ex used to do that now seem immodest, improper, or an invasion of your privacy.

Next, think ahead six months or so and list any boundary violations that might occur in the future. In other words, what might you or your ex-spouse do to inadvertently or unintentionally offend one another?

Finally, write new rules by answering the following question for each item on your list that relates to your behavior: "How can I change my behavior or way of thinking to comfortably fit this new boundary?" (Please notice that I have not asked you to determine how the other person could change. Their behavior is beyond your control, and trying to convince them that their boundaries are unreasonable will only cause another argument.)

Questions Frequently Asked by Divorced Parents

We have just looked at several major obstacles that sometimes prevent divorced parents from focusing on their children's needs. I'd like to close this chapter by answering some common questions asked by divorced parents who are doing the best they can for their children but aren't always sure how to go about it.

How Can I Tell Whether My Child Is Adjusting to the Divorce?

Parents are usually good about knowing how their children are adjusting to trauma. Though children may not talk about their feelings, their behavior will give you some idea about how they are coping. Your experience with your child tells you if their behavior is out of the ordinary. A sudden drop in school grades, frequent fights with friends, or retreats for hours at a time are hints that something is wrong. You will want answers now so you can come up with a game plan to help your child.

Rather than just reacting to how your child is behaving, approach your child by trying to understand the reasons for his hurt or changes in his behavior. Begin by closely watching your child's behavior and think about what has happened during the past few weeks that may help explain the changes. Then plan to make a conscious effort to take time to talk and listen to what your child has to say.

The game plan to help your son or daughter must begin with effective communication. The ability to help your child—and to improve the quality of your relationship with your friends, colleagues, and even your ex-spouse—depends on sound communication skills.

How Can I Improve Communication with My Child?

The first step in developing skilled communication is effective listening. Relating to others is impossible without "fully hearing" what they have to say. This means that sometimes we should be listening to what is said rather than talking and trying to justify our point. One way of knowing that you are not listening is when you think more about what you are going to say next than what the other person says. Frequent interruptions are a clue that someone is not listening.

Listening for how your child is feeling rather than debating the merits of their feeling will bring the two of you closer. Children, like anyone else, don't want their feelings to be judged as wrong, stupid, and silly. Instead, they want someone to recognize what their feeling and why they feel the way they do. Once they know that their feelings are understood, you may be able to clarify a misperceptions, or offer comfort to your child. But don't do this too fast, or your child will feel cut off.

For children to talk freely, they must feel physically and psychologically safe. Give yourself and your child ample time. You don't want to be in a rush or stop in the middle of your conversation because you have to be somewhere. Turn off the television so there are no distractions. Find a comfortable and safe setting to talk, then encourage your child to talk about how she feels.

Learn from listening to what your child has to say. Let your child know that you understand why he or she feels the way they do. This is done by repeating back to the child or paraphrasing what you just heard. Resist any temptation to defend yourself when it is not necessary to do so. Instead, be patient and listen. Your child's spontaneity will give you an idea about how you are doing as a listener. When your child pauses and appears to be watching his or her words, your child is not yet comfortable or, for whatever reason, you lost him. You must be patient and let him set the pace of the conversation. You do not have to finish the conversation in one sitting.

When your child starts to get restless or distracted, this is the time to stop talking. You can come back later to talk. End the conversation by telling your child how good you felt talking with him. Do what you can to reinforce that talking together was a positive experience. Also, be warned, that how the conversation ends is what the child will remember next time. If the conversation ended badly, he will be hesitant to open up and talk to you later.

What Should I Do If My Children Don't Want to Talk about Their Feelings?

Don't push them. Most children will adjust fine to the divorce even if they don't want to talk about it. Usually you will know what they think by various comments they make. Remember, the problem with most kids, particularly male teenagers, is that they try to avoid talking about anything uncomfortable. When you raise the question about, "How are you feeling about…?", they go blank or say, "I don't know." This response can be confusing. The only choice you have is to take your child at face value and believe everything is all right. Be patient, open the door by giving them permission to talk, and then back off and let them take the initiative.

Should I Ask My Children Where They Want to Live?

No. Don't ask your children to make decisions about custody or visits when they obviously don't want to. In fact, the decisions is usually not up to them anyway. It is the court's decision. Be patient with your children. If they have something to say, let them spontaneous tell you when and if they are ready. Usually, when a parent prods the children for an answer, they are doing so to reduce their own anxiety rather than having concern for their child's welfare. If your children have strong feelings about custody and wants you to know, they will tell you in time. Many children want to be left alone and have the adults make the decision for them. In this way, your child does not have to be responsible for hurting someone they love.

Children would rather be able to rationalize that the decision was the court's rather than their own. In this way, the children are not rejecting anyone. To children, rejecting one parent over the other can be equated to "not loving" a parent. This belief might be used by an alienating parent to influence their children's feelings.

How Long Will It Take My Children to Adjust to the Divorce?

There is no simple answer because children are different. Like adults, some children recover quickly while others can take years. You must be patient. Adjustment is a process that takes time. The issue isn't whether or not your children are adjusting, but whether their behavior tells you they are getting better at excepting the divorce and getting on with their lives. Children should be doing better after a year from the divorce and even better after two years. This is also true for parents.

How Important Is It for the Children to Have an Active Relationship with Their Father?

Extremely important. Children need their fathers, particularly boys. It appears from the research that boys have more problems adjusting to divorce than girls. I wonder if this isn't due to the fact that most boys end up living with their mothers and have less contact with their fathers. Growing up in an all-female household without a male's influence can be hard on some boys because they don't get an affirmation of their own masculine behavior. Many boys feel insecure about growing up to be what society thinks of as a man.

Sadly, a lot of fathers have psychologically abandoned their sons and, for various reasons, have little or no contact with their children. This can be devastating to children, particularly boys, who need a role model and a mentor to teach them how males get along in this world. They need the assurance that their dad isn't rejecting them and is available show him how to play sports, hunt, or do those other "male" things. It's true that sometimes dad is not the healthiest influence for your son. In this situation, mom needs to encourage her son to get involved in activities that will give him the positive affirmation he needs to build his self-esteem.

Girls also need their fathers. Dads give their daughters appropriate male role models who teach them how to understand and relate to the male culture. He is the one who tells them how pretty they are, raves about their successes, and later gives them insight about what guys think and feel. Dad helps to affirm their femininity.

My Children Are Always Moody. What Can I Do?

There is a lot you can do. Begin by accepting the fact that children, and particular teens, get moody. Kids get cranky, complaining that they are bored. When asked to pick up their socks, hang up their jackets, or turn the music down, you may be confronted with a smart comment or a whiny, "I'll do it later." They will talk back, acting as if you know nothing or you're nuts: "FINE, I'll do it, I don't care"; "It's a free county and I don't have to." You may think to yourself during these times that your child is "going through a phase" or "it's the hormones kicking in." This becomes even more complicated with children of divorced parents because the parent may not know who to blame for the children's problems. Resist the temptation to blame your ex-spouse or the stressful parenting time schedule. Parenting never stops. Once you think you have one problem worked out with your child, another problem surfaces. If you are lucky, you will get a rest between problems.

I Know My Children Hear Our Fights. Will This Hurt Them Later?

It sure can. Exposing your children to your hostilities will do more to hurt them than almost anything else you can do.

To help your children make the best of the divorce, your goal should be to keep your hostilities toward your spouse under control and away from the children. You must control your feelings. This is the most important point we have learned from multiple studies on divorce.

When children see their parents yelling, cussing, and threatening each other, they are terrified. While they are sitting on the floor watching television, they may act as if they don't hear you, but don't you believe it. Remember when you were a child, how you would lie in bed and strain your ears to hear what your parents were saying if you heard one of them mention your name? Kids, like adults, are nosy and will eavesdrop. Refer to chapter 4 for guidelines on how to sidestep power struggles; these suggestions, and others throughout this book, will help you control fighting with your ex-spouse.

How Can I Help My Children Adjust to the Divorce?

There are number of things you can do to help your children. Begin by resolving the conflict and anger between you and your ex-spouse. If you and your ex-spouse need counseling to do this, then please get counseling. Next, continue your parenting role and responsibilities. Your children need you to maintain the structure and routine in your home, which includes appropriate limits and expectations about how they behave. When your children violate those limits, administer appropriate discipline. This is also true during visits. Visits are not the place to throw out the rule book. Once the rules are gone, it is difficult to get them back without a major revolution.

Children respond well when you make a conscious effort to keep the communication between you and your children open. Take time to be with your children, without distractions. Don't forget that your children are fun to be with. Find mutual interests and enjoy them together. A mutually satisfying relationship between you and your children will do wonders for their emotional well-being.

Children need family and family traditions. Let your children know the importance of loving relationships with all members of the family. Encourage them to participate in family traditions with both sides of the family. Let family and friends be a source of support for both you and the kids.

Children need to feel prized by their parents, both for who they are and for what they achieve. Make it clear to your children that you enjoy spending time with them. Brag to your children and others about their accomplishments. They need to hear excitement in your voice when you tell them they've done something well. Reassure them that they are loved and that you will do what you can to keep their lives stable. Children become anxious about change they don't understand or can't predict.

How Can I Prevent My Children from Feeling That They Must Choose Between Loving My Ex-Spouse and Me?

Occasionally children have the mistaken belief that if they love one parent, love for the other parent or a step-parent will diminish. They feel torn between wanting to express their love for one parent while not wanting to hurt the other parent. One adolescent said it well: "I hate to hurt people's feelings and disappoint them, but when you are in the middle, trapped, you got to go to someone's side." This child does not understand his capacity or his parent's capacity to love. His mistaken belief is forcing him to choose between his parents. Children need to be continually reassured that they can love both parents and step-parents.

Is It Important to Display Physical Affection toward My Children?

Yes, but there are exceptions. You must be sensitive to how your children feel about physical affection. Many older children are uncomfortable and will pull away if you try to hug or kiss them. Don't take this personally. Respect their boundaries and find other ways to show your love. As for the children, they may be uncomfortable initiating affection to your other the other parent. Explain to them that there are other ways to express their feelings like writing a letter, sending a card, buying a special gift, making unexpected phone calls, continuing a family tradition, or acknowledging birthdays and holidays. Older children may rationalize their hesitation by saying, "I don't need to do that. Dad knows I love him." Even though your children are teens, they need continual encouragement and guidance in helping them express their positive feelings.

How Can I Protect My Children from Being Hurt?

Often you can't. Divorce has tremendous potential for hurting children, and often the hurt cannot be avoided. You may remember the hurt on the children's faces the first time their father did not show up for a visit or when their mother didn't come to a recital. You understandably felt angry and protective. Perhaps you tried to make excuses for the other parent to lessen the hurt. The fact is that you cannot keep making excuses for the parent's behavior. In time, the children will form their own opinions about both parents, based not on excuses but on their own personal experiences. Dad's relationship with the children will depend more on how he behaves toward them rather than what you or he tells them. In time, the children will no longer believe his excuses. After your children have learned to draw their own conclusions, they usually will not be honest and say anything about how they really feel to that parent. They may act as if everything is fine when it is not. Their behavior toward the parent will give you some clue about how they actually feel.

Brianna Listening to *60 Minutes*

Brianna, my oldest daughter, was about three at the time when she was sitting on the floor playing with her doll while my wife and I were watching a story on *60 Minutes* about a rape. I don't remember exactly what the story was about or the words the commentator was using other than he mentioned sodomy. To our surprise, our daughter blurted out, "That would hurt." We were amazed for many reasons. To begin with, we didn't think Brianna would be listening to a television show like *60 Minutes*. Secondly, she obviously understood what was being said because her response was accurate. We didn't understand how she would have made the association between sodomy and pain. To this day, I couldn't explain her reaction. But we did learn some valuable lessons from this experience. First, we can't always protect children from what they will hear on television. Second, children listen when you least expect it. And last, they understand more than we think.

Just Roll Up Your Sleeves and Do the Best You Can

If you want to bring stability and tranquility back into your children's lives following a divorce, you'll need to focus on their needs more than your own. That won't be easy to do. The most effective parents are able to consciously put their personal needs aside in deference to their children's needs. They find a balance between the time they need for themselves and the time they give to their children, and they do not feel bitter about the sacrifices involved in parenthood. Less effective parents are frequently resentful when their children's needs come before their own.

Looking at how you've behaved since your marriage ended and at what your divorce may have done to your children is both enlightening and discouraging. After a while you may feel you can do nothing right. You may lose all hope of being a "perfect" parent. But no one can make that claim. All you can do is aspire to be better.

Why Parents Alienate

"It's only a matter of time before your father will hit you like he hit me."

Alienating parents act under the assumption—conscious or unconscious—that all their problems with their ex-spouse will go away if they can convince the children to hate that targeted ex-spouse. But I have never met an alienating parent who was happy about what he or she was doing, and the reason is simple: for these purposes alienation does not work.

There are many different reasons why a parent would try to alienate the children from the other parent, though they are not usually conscious of their motives. Some reasons are irrational while others seem justified. Trying to resolve guilt for abandoning the family, an inability to control rage after feeling betrayed, and getting defensive at the thought of losing a parental identity are all possible motives. Whatever the reasons, the result for the children, and usually both parents, is hurt and bitterness that can last for years, if not forever.

Alienation to Avoid Guilt

"Your father wouldn't have left you if he really cared."

Guilt is a terrible feeling that everyone tries to avoid because it is painful and can linger for years. In fact, that is the purpose of guilt. Guilt, or the fear of guilt, is intended to keep you from misbehaving. The problem is that you may not know what causes the feeling, and if you know, you may not know how to get rid of the guilt. Guilt implies that you did something wrong. Some parents think that they should be punished for their sins.

One mother's assertion "I know I'm getting what I deserve. How else can I explain why I feel so miserable?" is a typical statement from a parent who is struggling with guilt. If you are a newcomer to divorce, you know how easy it is to find reasons for feeling guilty. All you have to do is think about what you did wrong—even vague generalities like "I know I could have tried harder in my marriage."

Parents who feel hurt and betrayed are often driven to absolve their guilt and regain their self-esteem in the most irrational ways. Some parents believe that they will be exonerated from their guilt if they reinforce, in their mind, the belief that they care more for the children than their ex-spouse does. Guilt-ridden parents look for opportunities to prove their point to themselves, their children, and their ex-spouse. They do this by cutting down the other parent, reminding the children of the other parent's faults, or leaning on the children for comfort and reassurance of their self-worth.

There are many ways parents deal with their guilt. Parents can either blame others for their problems, overcompensate by being the "super-parent," make excuses, or just feel depressed or angry and do nothing. Most of these tactics don't work. True, time sometimes helps the pangs of guilt fade, but usually the feeling is just pushed aside or is masked by stronger emotions such as resentment or self-contempt. Learning to understand and resolve guilt is absolutely necessary if you are going to adjust to your divorce, go on with your life, and be a more effective parent.

Playing "supermom" or "superdad" is a fairly good tactic because you look good to others. After all, how can a superparent think any bad thoughts that would hurt the children? The problem with many alienating superparents is that they try to look good to others while aggressively degrading the other parent's competency. They are usually critical and, often unconsciously, look for every little fault in the other parent. The guilt-ridden superparent seems to believe that the worse the other parent looks, particularly in the children's eyes, the more likely they will appear as the loving and competent parent. If they can somehow carry this off, their hope is that their guilt will go away. Unfortunately, their tactic is doomed for failure because the hurt will continue to fester as long as they continue to alienate.

EXERCISE: WHAT DO I FEEL GUILTY ABOUT?

To help you better understand how guilt could motivate you, complete this exercise. Try to be honest by resisting the temptation to blame your ex-spouse. Remember, no one will read what you write, so don't hold back.

Think back over the past year or two and remember the things you did that caused you to feel guilty. Write these things down on a sheet of paper. You can be brief. After completing your list, look at each item and imagine for a moment what you could have done differently at the time (not what someone else could have done). Finally, try to focus on how you might have felt if you had behaved differently.

Jill

Jill, a rather timid and unassertive mother, decided not to seek custody of her two children because she could not withstand her husband's nagging and harassment. Jill knew that she had to get out of the marriage to stop his degrading verbal abuse, and she believed that her children loved their doting father. Already regretting her decision, Jill agreed to give their father custody. Visits went well though Jill continued to feel plagued with guilt. Summers were particularly hard on Jill because her children's friends would come over to the house wanting to play. Feeling embarrassed, she would tell the little friends that her children were not home. The friends persisted in wanting to know when Jill's children would return home. Though Jill had no reason to feel embarrassed or guilty, she continued to dread the friends' inquiries. In Jill's mind, the friends' questions were a reminder of her inadequacy and failure.

Sexist Attitudes Contribute to Guilt

Our society continues to adhere to many sexist beliefs. One example is a mother feeling stigmatized for not choosing to seek custody or, for whatever reason, losing custody. She knows that she has more to lose than the father. She expects to be harshly judged by both men and women for her apparent abandonment of the children or her loss of her maternal responsibilities. If a mother loses custody, she is looked at with suspicion. People will raise such questions as "What's the matter with her?" or ask the dreaded question "Where are your children?" The questions remind her of the stigma of not having custody of her children. This threatens her self-esteem and sense of competency as a mother.

When the father seeks custody and loses, he is disappointed but admired by others as a loving parent for his effort. Fathers rarely struggle with feeling stigmatized if they do not get custody. In fact, he can use society's sexist attitudes as a rationalization to protect his ego and self-esteem. He is able to rationalize losing custody by arguing that the mother always wins.

Many fathers believe they have done nothing wrong to deserve having their children taken from their lives. In recent years, these fathers have developed a conviction for their right to have an active relationship with their children. Being a part-time, weekend father is not enough to satisfy them. They are willing to fight their wives and the court to assure their active relationship with their children. Many fathers have joined support or political groups to vent their frustration with the legal system. They are fighting for both legal and social changes that support their position that they have the same rights as the children's mother to be the custodial parent.

Mothers, too, often feel betrayed and angry when they learn of their husband's desire for a divorce. Mothers often feel frightened and vulnerable at the prospect of losing custody of their children. Their hurt is held in while their anger grows in intensity. They may express their feelings of betrayal and ownership of the children by stating "That's my baby. He has no right to have her." Though they are conscious that more fathers are being given custody, most mothers try to deny the possibility of their not being the custodial parent. Ironically, no-fault divorce has inadvertently heightened animosity between the parents. One parent may feel betrayed while the court does nothing to protect his or her rights. Betrayed parents seeking retribution from the court are often disappointed and angry when they learn that the court will not champion their cause. This can contribute to ex-spousal issues dragging on for years to come. (To distinguish between ex-spousal and parental issues, refer back to chapter 3.)

Social attitudes and prejudices are slow to change. Frequently, the state's legislative body and the courts are slow to respond to society's demands for change. Nonetheless, change is occurring. Courts are responding to fathers' demands for more active involvement with their children. The cry from mothers about the inequities of child support are starting to be heard. Both men and women are becoming more conscious of the unfairness to mothers for stigmatizing them for not having physical custody of their children. Unfortunately, it is still easy to feel impatient and frustrated because change is slow. Either way, sexism plays a role in alienation because traditional attitudes influence how you feel about yourself and how you think others will judge you. We take these attitudes into the court with us and back home with our children.

Terri and Robert

Terri divorced Robert because she just couldn't take his verbal abuse and putdowns any longer. They seemed to not have a day without yelling and screaming "over the stupidest things." Survival was all that Terri was able to think about. During one of those rare moments when she wasn't paying any attention to the children, Terri let Robert have it with both barrels. She lost all control, pounding Robert's chest with her fist, yelling for him to "Get the f_ _ _ out of this house!" Reflecting years later, Terri still felt guilty about the terrible scene she had caused in front of the children. She never said anything to either Robert or the children because she had hoped that the feeling would just fade away. Anytime the topic of the divorce came up in conversation, Terri would immediately get embarrassed and fear that someone would say something about what she had done. Gently, she would steer the conversation in another direction.

Take Constructive Action to Absolve Guilt

Terri's guilt may not be earth shaking. In fact, hitting Robert in front of the kids may be just one of many things that have occurred over Terri's life that caused her to feel guilty. What's important is that Terri's guilt is still not going away. Instead, it's influencing how she behaves and feels around her children. If Terri is going to get rid of the guilt, she must change her behavior and do something different. She must take action. Terri could begin by honestly talking with her children by sharing her regret and guilt about what she did to their father. She could assure them that it is understandable if they were hurt and disappointed by what she had done. If Terri asked, the children might even forgive her. This way, her action will help the guilt to fade away.

If you suspect that you are feeling guilty because you have been alienating your children from their other parent, you must begin by owning up to the truth, changing your behavior toward your children and your ex-spouse if you want any hope of ridding yourself of the guilt. To do this, identify the specific behavior that is causing your guilt. Look back at chapter 1 and your results of the parental alienation scale. The items that you rated 4 or 5 will give you some ideas about what you are doing that may explain your guilt. These inventory items should give you some direction about what you can do to feel better.

Take, for example, item 23. Suppose you rated the statement a 5, acknowledging that you feel you always have good reasons to be critical of your ex-spouse. Though you may believe in your heart that this is true, your attitude can be what's causing your guilt. Let's try an experiment to see whether you can reduce your guilt. Let's start with the notion of being less critical and recognize that the other parent has his or her own competencies, perhaps different from your own. As abhorrent as it may sound, giving the other parent credit for what he or she does well and stopping the critical comments to the children will help absolve your guilt. I know this is hard to believe, but if you can keep from getting sick to your stomach, try it. You may be surprised. Forgiving and saying kind words, especially to your ex-spouse, can take you a long way toward feeling better.

Often superparents criticize targeted parents about parental issues even though their bitterness has more to do with ex-spousal issues. This is confusing for the targeted parent, who asks "What's the big deal?" Of course the big deal for the superparent is "How can you let the children outdoors without a coat?" or "Shouldn't they be in bed by 9:00 P.M.?" or "How can you let Johnny use his roller blades in the street?" The tip-off that the superparent is probably still dealing with unresolved ex-spousal issues is the intensity of the accusing parent's voice. The rage is usually out of proportion to the offense. These parents cannot talk about what is troubling them; they have to yell, demean, or scream. The intensity of their rage can be a carry-over from feeling betrayed by their ex-spouse, bitterness caused by the drop in standard of living, and so on.

Before the superparent can find peace and stop being so critical, she needs to understand the ex-spousal issues that continue to cause hurt or guilt. Then, maybe with the help of therapy, she can find a way to heal. This is usually done by finding new ways to thinking about the past. For example, instead of saying to yourself, "That bastard can't be trusted with my children," change your self-talk to something like, "I need to get him to understand the importance of not bringing the children home late on school nights." Your self-talk is probably different from my example, but you get the point. Changing your self-talk and behaving differently will help lessen your guilt and add some much-needed peace to your life. Be patient and give yourself some time to change. Saying something nice to your ex-spouse once is not enough to absolve years of guilt. Keep trying.

Admit Your Mistakes

Worrying that others will discover your mistakes will cause you to feel guilty and fearful. Rather than fearing that your mistakes will be discovered, openly admit them when you are wrong. You will be surprised how much better you will feel.

Sometimes parents find themselves defending against an allegation that is true. They get defensive and start arguing for no rational reason and hold on to the belief that they cannot let the other person see that they did something wrong. Admitting mistakes is an easy and effective way of avoiding these meaningless arguments. This also does wonders for reducing guilt.

For example, let's say you are accused of not caring for the children because you are always late picking them up after a visit. Hearing the accusation, you feel defensive and want to attack. The fact is, you usually are late. What is not true is that you do not care for the children. Now you have to make a choice. You can either counterattack with your own accusations or admit that you are usually late. Admitting that your usually late will defuse the attack. After all, how can you be hurt by what you admit is true and you don't defend? Defending your actions in this example will only incite more fighting. Instead, you and your ex-spouse can begin discussing how to solve the problem of your tardiness.

Stay out of the Blaming Trap

Blaming is another common tactic for trying to avoid guilt. Successful blaming, meaning that you believe your accusations, is a way for blamers to maintain their sense of self-worth. The purpose of saying "It's your fault" is to absolve the alienating parent from taking any responsibility for what is wrong. Unfortunately, it is easier to find fault with others than to admit our own shortcomings. But blaming only makes matters worse because the blaming parent will get more angry while waiting for the other parent to fix the problem or change the annoying behavior.

Now the tensions build and the accusations fly. The blaming parent will rally around the parental role and accuse her ex-spouse of causing all her troubles. The allegations against the ex-spouse are intended to protect the ego and strengthen the blaming parent's self-worth. Degrading the targeted parent, particularly in the eyes of the children, helps assure the blaming spouse of her value as a parent. But like the alienating super-parent, the blaming parent is using a tactic that never works.

The irony with this tactic is that you actually empower the other parent at the expense of your own power. When your ex-spouse fails to respond to your satisfaction by fixing the problem, you will feel victimized, even though your ex-spouse usually doesn't understand what is happening. Believe it or not, it is common for the blaming parent to become depressed. After all, depression is akin to helplessness, a victim's unwelcome companion.

Don't Spoil Your Children to Make Up for the Past

Some divorced parents try to align themselves with the children by giving them extra attention, taking time to play games, frequently taking them to the mall, and so on. This can be a strategy to diminish guilt and make up for past neglect. The parent finds solace from "buying the children" while the ex-spouse is passively excluded from the activity. Though the exclusion is usually unconscious, the activity with the children is a subtle form of alienation. It sends the children the message, "I bet your mother isn't this nice."

Of course, give your children the attention they need. But overindulging will only spoil them. It will not resolve your guilt.

Alienation Because of Feelings of Entitlement

"I'm his mother. You aren't the one who gave birth."

Being a parent is a special status that should be worn proudly. I still get more of a thrill being called "Daddy" than being called "Dr. Darnall." I'm sure this is also true for mothers. Motherhood and fatherhood are both very special.

Some parents are motivated to alienate because they hold the mistaken belief that they are entitled to their role as a custodial parent because they gave birth, because they paid the bills, or because their personal identity and sense of self-worth is dependent upon their parental role. Unfortunately the courts inadvertently reinforce this belief because custodial parents usually do have more rights and privileges.

Feeling entitled is different from believing you are the better parent to raise your children. The difference is knowing that your children are truly better served by what you can give them rather than what the children give you. Your children's interest must come before your self-interest, even if you are hurt by the realization.

Your Children Are Not Your Possessions

You may think you are entitled to your child's custody much as you are to any other prized possession. Losing custody is tantamount to losing your identity. "After all, if I am not a mom, what am I?" The prospect of not having the primary responsibility of raising your children is personally threatening. You may complain about your ex-spouse being less deserving and "only seeking custody to hurt me." Perhaps your assertion is correct. But usually such a statement is shortsighted because it reflects a belief that your ex-spouse has fewer rights than you or is a less competent parent. Neither of these beliefs may be true. Instead, the beliefs may be a reflection of your insecurities or arrogance.

Neither you nor your ex-spouse owns your children. They are in your temporary care. The children are no more your possession than your ex-spouse's. If your ex-spouse makes statements suggesting ownership of the children, ignore them. Such statements are meaningless and are only intended to incite an argument.

Sometimes a parent, usually the mother, fears that the ex-spouse will challenge the children's custody, so she vehemently defends her position while attacking the ex-spouse's claim to the children. Both parents consciously or unconsciously strive to align their children to their side, thus reinforcing the belief that they are winning the custody war. The children struggle with being pulled in opposite directions by their parents. Wanting to avoid the conflict and tension, the children feel they have no choice but to emotionally withdraw from both parents. When a parent raises the question of preference, the children look away, avoiding eye contact and speaking softly. What they say to the inquisitive parent should not to be trusted. The children are likely to tell the inquisitive parent what he or she wants to hear. In this way, the children avoid feeling disloyal or fearful of the parent's rejection.

Believing that you are entitled to the physical possession of your children sets the stage for alienating and, in time, a possible custody battle. While you give your ex-spouse occasional reminders about who is in charge of the children and who is responsible for their care, your ex-spouse will feel the chasm you are creating between him and his children. This leads to resentment and eventually hate and a fight that no one wins, especially the children.

Conquer Entitlement by Revising Your Self-Talk

If the expression "They are my children" is more comfortable than the expression "They are our children," perhaps you need to rethink your reasons for seeking custody. If your motivation for seeking custody is entitlement, you are probably already fueling alienation. The reason this occurs is because "entitled" parents usually sound angry when discussing the idea of the ex-spouse having custody and are typically overly protective and defensive when questioned about their parenting. Frequently, the children will witness the parent's defensiveness, causing them to feel confused.

Overcoming entitlement must begin with the recognition that you are holding on to beliefs that are both false and damaging to your children. These beliefs can be heard in your self-talk. They are important because you will emotionally react to them as if they are true. If you expect your feelings to change, you must begin by identifying the beliefs or self-talk that provokes the feelings. Take the belief that women are always better parents. If you believe this is true, you can't help but feel threatened or offended by the idea of the father having custody. Another example is the belief that "I'm the parent and I always know what's best." Any suggestion otherwise will anger the entitled parent. Your anger and desire for retribution will, in time, hurt your children. To eliminate these feelings, the parent must begin by recognizing that the irrational belief is damaging to the children, and the parent needs to change his or her self-talk to a more rational belief. The belief "I'm the parent and I always know what's best" could be restated as "I'm one of my child's parents and I would like to think that sometimes I know what's best." Believe it or not, consciously changing the self-talk will change the feelings. If this is awkward, fake it for the time being. It takes practice and requires your patience.

Alienation Because of Protective Feelings

"He's abused me. I know it's only a matter of time before he abuses our children."

It is natural for you to want to protect your children when you believe their physical or psychological safety is threatened. You will do whatever is necessary to safeguard your children from any perceived threat, even if the threat comes from your ex-spouse. But this is where you have to be cautious. There is a difference between what you think is a threat and what you know is a threat. You need to know rather than just react to what you think; otherwise, you're heading for big problems. If you react to your beliefs by getting angry and threatening the other parent to withhold visits or return to court, he will naturally prepare to retaliate.

To avoid this dilemma, first realize that you do not know the reasons for the other person's behavior. Instead, you are making an interpretation that may be wrong. Secondly, you must ask your children to clarify what they are feeling and why rather than guessing. The act of asking for clarification will help prevent your emotional reaction to your interpretation because you now have to listen rather than think.

In this crazy world of ours, every day we hear about the abuse, neglect, and even death of children. Hearing these horror stories is enough to scare any parent. It is easy to become overly sensitive to anything that we think can pose a risk to our children's safety. "Anything can happen when he's drinking and getting stoned," you may think. Having suspicions or even hearing subtle suggestions from your child is not reason enough to panic and take immediate action. Before jumping to conclusions and stopping visits or calling the local prosecutor, take a deep breath and think about how to calmly proceed. Though your feelings may be understandable, it doesn't help you or your child if you are hysterical. Take some time to think about what action you are going to take rather than just impulsively acting in a way you may later regret.

For more on allegations of sexual abuse, see chapter 11.

Physical Abuse and Neglect

If you suspect physical or sexual abuse, immediately report the incident to the appropriate child welfare agency. If you see physical evidence of the abuse, take the child to a hospital's emergency room for examination. By law, the hospital must report the suspected abuse to the authorities. If you see physical evidence of suspected abuse on your child's body, taking pictures may be helpful. However, be warned that most photographs of bruises do not show up well. Photographs tend to wash out the contrasting colors of the bruises unless you have additional lighting. For this reason, it is best to take your child to the hospital or the authorities to document the bruises.

Courts are suspicious when an allegation of abuse is raised for the first time during divorce litigation. The courts question why the allegations weren't raised sooner, particularly if there was a risk to the child's safety. Though suspicious of a false allegation, the court will usually take the allegation seriously rather than exposing the child to further abuse.

Parents knowing that their former spouse was a victim of childhood physical abuse causes some parents to worry about whether the former spouse could, in time, abuse their own children. The fear comes from the popular notion that all abusers were also victims of abuse. While it is true that most abusers were also victims, this is not the same as saying that all former victims will abuse their own children. Kaufman and Zigler (1986) conducted a thorough critique of studies assessing the risk of a victimized parent abusing their children. They found that the best estimate of intergenerational abuse appears to be about 30 percent ± 5 percent . This is six times the estimated rate of 5 percent for the general population. From their estimates, they concluded that the majority of parents who were abused did not abuse their children.

You should always take your children's accusations seriously but proceed cautiously. Your first concern must be your child's immediate health and safety. If your child requires medical attention, go to your physician or an emergency room. Otherwise, call your local child welfare agency. Keep in mind that your idea of physical or mental abuse may not be the local definition. Bad parenting isn't always abuse. For example, there continues to be a debate, even among mental health professionals, about the advisability of spanking. One school of thought is that spanking teaches children to resolve conflicts with violence. Others argue that controlled spanking teaches valuable lessons, particularly when children run out in the street or do something else that threatens their safety. Whatever you choose, spanking should always be controlled, never cause bruises or abrasions, and never use an object like a cord, paddle, or belt. These are weapons of abuse and can cause serious harm. I personally believe that children can be taught without physical punishment.

Alcohol and Drug Abuse

Parents enter the divorce arena knowing each other's history and habits. Information once trusted with your spouse may now be used against you in a contested custody case or when your ex-spouse tries to restrict parenting time. You could have a serious problem in court if you used illegal drugs during your marriage. An angry parent will sometimes bring this up in court to use against you in a custody dispute. (What I find interesting is that the parent who makes the accusation usually admits that they also used drugs with the ex-spouse.) To play it safe, you must assume that courts will never tolerate using illegal drugs in your children's presence. This includes marijuana. Whatever your beliefs are about marijuana, domestic court is not the place to take a political stand.

Regardless of whether you are accused of abusing drugs or whether you are concerned about your ex-spouse's use of drugs, you must understand what an abuser is before you decide to take the issue to court. Drinking, by itself, is not illegal unless your drinking causes you to behave in an illegal manner or you jeopardize others' safety. The most obvious example is drinking while driving with your children in the car. This behavior is inexcusable and illegal in all states. Your excuses mean nothing if you are caught.

Alienation is not uncommon when a parent is abusing alcohol or drugs. When one of the parents is abusing, there are usually allegations going back and forth: One parent making the allegations and the other defending or blaming others for why they drink. What you now have is a power struggle where one parent is angry because the other parent is telling them how to behave. At the core of many of these arguments is whether or not the person is actually abusing alcohol or drugs.

To help clear up any confusion you may have about alcohol and drug abuse, it may be helpful for you to know something about what constitutes alcohol and drug abuse. The generally accepted definition of abuse involves these factors:

- Significant life problems because of using alcohol or drugs, such as failure to fulfill major role responsibilities at work, home, or school.
- Legal problems such as domestic violence, disorderly conduct, and driving under the influence.
- Recurrent use in physically hazardous situations like driving or operating machinery.
- Continued use despite ongoing interpersonal or social problems like arguments with family members or physical fights.

This definition assumes that the abuser does not have control over their alcohol or drug use; the substance is causing them serious problems, but they still continue to use it.

To learn more about alcohol and drug abuse, contact your local help hot line or an appropriate agency listed in the Yellow Pages.

The criteria for alcohol and drug abuse were not given with the idea that you make a diagnosis for yourself or your ex-spouse but to make you more aware of your use, or your ex-spouse's use, of alcohol or drugs. You need to recognize if you, or your ex-spouse, are heading for trouble. Drinking in front of your children is not illegal. On the other hand, if your drinking is causing your children distress or you are risking their safety (such as drinking and driving), the court can order you to have a drug and alcohol evaluation and order you to not drink in your children's presence. If you violate the court order and risk your children's safety, the court can change custody or stop visits.

A history of alcohol or chemical dependency does not have to hurt you in court, providing you can show that you are recovering and managing your life successfully. Steady attendance at Alcoholics or Narcotics Anonymous will help tremendously. Many recovering parents win custody and do well raising their children. Problems arise if you currently abuse alcohol or drugs, the symptoms are apparent to everyone, particularly your children, and you do nothing about it. This is a serious problem because the court's first commitment is to protect the children, even if that means keeping them from you until you get treatment. For example, would you want your children driving around with a parent who is drinking and doesn't see that he has a problem? Yes, parents have problems, but there is little excuse for not getting help. At least that is the way the court will see it.

Mental Illness

A parent who is mentally ill may have a tainted perception of what is happening during and after the divorce. A dependent father will become more frightened at the prospect of being alone. A paranoid mother will become more suspicious, believing that others are plotting to deliberately hurt her; she may easily become an obsessed alienator. Even the added strain of the litigation itself will magnify the severity of the symptoms. These parents become vulnerable, struggling to cope with the stress from the divorce and having to rebuild their lives.

A parent's mental illness may have contributed to the breakup of the marriage and may continue to be a problem during the separation or after the divorce. There is little doubt that some of the symptoms of mental illness can contribute to alienation. If you suspect that this is true of your ex-spouse, you may want to talk with your attorney about getting a professional psychological evaluation of both of you. The evaluation should be unbiased and not be an attempt on your part to have a "hired gun" come to court and blast away at your ex-spouse. Instead, the evaluation could help assess the seriousness of the mental disorder and make recommendations to the court about the need for treatment, custody arrangements, and parenting time schedules. A good evaluator will always consider what is best for the children in making the recommendations.

If you have a history of a mental disorder, you may need additional counseling or medication to get through a divorce. Prior symptoms can return at a stressful time. It is important that you let your therapist know what is going on; otherwise, he or she can't help you.

Nearly all of us have moments when we question our sanity. To cope with these difficult moments, remind yourself of your capacity to heal. Spend time relaxing with friends or in surroundings you enjoy whenever you can. Make a conscious effort to do things that are fun and refresh you. If you feel truly overwhelmed by problems, you may want to consider seeking qualified help. Therapy can help you understand yourself better and teach you how best to cope under stressful circumstances. Perhaps you will feel reassured knowing that many of your feelings are normal and you are coping fairly well. See chapter 13 for information on how to find a good therapist.

As with recovering alcoholics and drug abusers, parents with a history of mental illness can win custody and do a good job of raising their children. However, the same logic applies: they must show that they are getting treatment for their problems, responding well, and managing their lives successfully. The court will look skeptically at a parent who is too depressed to get out of bed in the morning and see the children off to school and who doesn't actively participate in their lives.

Alienation Due to Hurt and Anger

"Your mother's a tramp. She doesn't deserve to see you."

A betrayed parent feeling hurt because of a sudden pronouncement of divorce often has no place to vent feelings. Trying to keep composed, the parent suppresses the hurt. In time the suppressed hurt turns into anger. Since the parent feels victimized by the ex-spouse, he or she directs the anger towards the ex-spouse using the only issue they have left in common, the children, feeling justified because of some rationalization or distorted perception.

Anger and hurt are powerful motivations for a parent's alienation. Often there are good reasons for having these feelings. Many parents have no interest in resolving the anger but, instead, are driven to show the world how they have been wronged. They focus their blame more on ex-spousal issues rather than addressing what is best for the children.

During an interview with a parent, I may suspect alienation when I cannot get direct answers to my questions. I may ask a mother, "How would you encourage your children's relationship with their father?" Instead of talking about the children, the mother responds by going into a diatribe about her ex-husband. She vengefully attacks him for his infidelity or his lack of concern for the children. She cannot stop talking about her betrayal and anger toward her ex-husband, forgetting the original question.

Anger, hate, and hurt are powerful feelings that can be hard to overcome. For some people, especially the obsessed alienator, these feelings rarely heal. For others, like the naïve and active alienators, time helps the healing.

Learn to share your hurt rather than your anger. You will get further.

Tony and His Parents

Tony's parents have been divorced for about two years. He is eight years old and has been living with his mother. His father has standard visitation that reportedly has been going well. His mother has adjusted well to the divorce and has been dating the same person for about eighteen months. Then Tony's father suspected that the boyfriend had been spending the night and felt resentful. Though Tony described the boyfriend as "nice," his father was critical of the boyfriend's behavior. Father explained to Tony that mom's boyfriend was a "drunk, who shoots animals and eats them." The father's interpretation of the boyfriend's behavior implied there was something wrong with him.

Upon further inquiry, Tony's father disclosed having no information to support his belief that the boyfriend was a drunk. He came to this conclusion from gossip. The gossip supported the father's own self-interest, so he used it to influence his son's attitude towards the boyfriend. He tried to strengthen his argument by suggesting something was wrong with his mother's boyfriend using the negative connotation that he "shoots animals and eats them." In all likelihood, the mother's boyfriend is a hunter and probably does what most hunters do: shoots and eats animals. The false perceptions were intended to alienate Tony from his mother.

The father's allegation had a second implication that reinforced the alienation between Tony and his mother. There was the suggestion that something was wrong with his mother for having a relationship with a person who would do such terrible deeds. Though the implication is subtle, over a period of time such suggestions have a damaging influence on the relationship between Tony and his mother. Tony may feel hesitant toward his mother and her friend because of his father's subtle criticism. A child's hesitancy or a lack of spontaneity may be symptomatic of alienation.

Alienation to Save Face

"I don't care what he says. I'm a good mother. My kids think so, and all the neighbors do too."

Like it or not, we do worry about what other people think about us. And what we think they think influences our behavior and how we feel about ourselves. All of us have this ideal of how we want others to see us, especially about us as parents. This is even more an issue for most women because our society places more emphasis on their role as parents. For example, when you see a mother and father at the store and their child has a tantrum, which parent is expected to get the child under control? Usually the mother is the first to intervene. The father may be waiting and hoping that his wife will get things under control, or he may even be oblivious to the problem. Meanwhile, the mother may feel embarrassed and desperate. Perhaps the father eventually intervenes with his stern authority to subdue the child. His intervention may not be any more effective than hers. Nonetheless, in most marriages, the responsibility for initially subduing the crisis still rests with the mother.

Which parent's competency is most harshly judged when children have behavioral problems? There are variations in attitude from one part of the country to another, but in general, our society is usually a harsher critic of mothers than of fathers. So when there are problems with the children, which parent has the most self-esteem to lose? The mother.

Self-esteem develops from a history of successful accomplishments. The accomplishments have to have been challenging and had a personal value to be meaningful. Initially, the success from painting a room may have enhanced your self-esteem, but as you completed more projects around the house, the value to your self-esteem lessens. If you do not place a personal value on painting a room, then the accomplishment may be nothing more than just getting another thing done. The greater the challenge of the task, the greater the potential for building self-esteem. This involves taking risks. For example, writing this book will do more for my self-esteem than staining the patio deck. I may feel good about accomplishing both, but my esteem will be enhanced more by the book because of the greater challenge.

Children as a Reflection of the Parent's Competency

Many parents' self-esteem is dependent upon their personal perception of their competency as parents. This is particularly true for women because they are looked upon as the primary caretakers in our society. Fathers are typically less dependent than mothers on their parental role for their self-esteem. In our society, fathers usually have a number of other resources for building their self-esteem, such as their paid work, recreational activities, hobbies, and the friends they meet through these activities. Mothers who stay home with young children have fewer resources outside the family.

Parents are typically unaware of their strengths and weaknesses. Even incompetent parents who lack sensitivity and effective parenting skills will believe, contrary to the evidence, that they are competent and caring parents. They will defend and rationalize their incompetent behavior, often blaming the children or others for their personal shortcomings. Parents want to believe they have more strengths than shortcomings. Any challenge from their ex-spouse as to their competency in fulfilling their parental role is seen as a threat to their self-esteem. These parents will react to the threat with anger and vengeance to protect their favorable self-perception. This is why custody litigation is so painful. The court proceedings afford the opportunity to publicly attack your competency while you have to sit back and listen. You have to depend on your attorney to defend your character.

Parents with good ego strength and self-confidence are not easily threatened; parenting is only one of many resources for building their self-esteem. Those who are dependent on the parental role as the exclusive source of self-esteem are more quickly threatened by any suggestion that someone else could effectively assume their parental responsibilities. If you find yourself with parenting as your only source of self-esteem, you need to start doing other things. Many divorced parents find it difficult to schedule a lot of hobbies and activities just for themselves, but pick one that really appeals to you and fit it in somewhere. Remember, in some ways you have an advantage: every other weekend, you don't have the kids! Your married counterparts are not so lucky.

EXERCISE: WHO AM I?

Being an active parent is one of the most important, and hopefully satisfying, things you can do with your life. But being a parent is not all of who you are. You represent other valuable things to other people. You may be a teacher, a good friend, a skilled craftsman, or many other things. These other roles are also who you are.

Take a moment and write down on a sheet of paper as many of your roles, skills, and attributes as you can that other people see and value. If you have trouble making the list, consider enriching your life by getting involved in new interests, making new friends, or finding new ways of having fun that don't involve parenting. I hope you find making the list easy.

Do Fathers Merely Babysit, While Mothers Parent?

Have you ever heard of a mother who has an appointment and asks the father to "babysit"? Why would the father taking care of his children be considered babysitting rather than parenting? No one thinks of mothers as babysitters. The different sexist messages our society communicates to parents influences their self-esteem. Mothers may feel less entitled to a life outside their role of a parent while fathers are relegated to the subservient role of babysitter.

Today's parents are less accepting of traditional sex roles handed to them by society. In the 1990s, mothers are becoming more involved with full-time jobs, and assuming household tasks that were traditionally considered "man's work." Fathers, too, are changing their interests by becoming more involved in their children's activities. Fathers are seen more frequently at school conferences, ball games, dance recitals, and open houses. The demise of rigid sex roles is a healthy trend that allows both sexes more choices and opportunities to involve themselves with their children. Neither parent should be excluded from any of their children's activities because of their gender.

Parents want to believe that other people see them as loving and competent. Even the opinion of their ex-spouse is important. Parents need their ex-spouses' support and reassurance that they are doing a good job parenting. Even the comments made by grandparents are important because the parent's confidence is usually weakened by divorce. Parents are sensitive to even the perception of a criticism. During this time of readjustment, they are likely to be overly defensive and easily angered when their competency is challenged. Parents do not want to hear about what they are doing wrong or have their motivations questioned. Instead, they want to be reassured that they are doing a good job.

If you suspect that your ex-spouse has poor self-esteem and this is a cause for his or her defensiveness, consider what you can do to help. Remember, people get defensive if they don't feel safe in the relationship. If you are critical or demanding, your ex-spouse will either wither to your demands or retaliate. Either way, you and the children lose. Instead, help build your ex-spouse's confidence. Give praise when it is due. Remind your ex-spouse that you are there to help, and then be of help without criticism or wisecracks. As soon as I suggested giving your ex-spouse praise, you may have thought that there was nothing to say because your ex "can't do anything right." It is important to see that you are wrong. Complete the exercise in this section and then take the opportunity to share these comments to your ex-spouse. You will be amazed by your ex-spouse's reaction. If you keep giving sincere compliments, in time your ex-spouse will feel safer and less defensive.

EXERCISE: WHAT DOES MY EX-SPOUSE DO RIGHT?

Write down five specific examples of when your ex-spouse displayed good parenting skills. It makes little difference how significant these skills are. If you find it difficult to come up with examples, be patient and take time to think.

_____
_____
_____
_____
_____

The next time you notice your ex-spouse displaying these skills, sincerely complement him or her without any critical innuendoes. In time, the results may surprise you.

Mary and Jim

Mary, a loving and devoted mother, had long hated her ex-husband, Jim. Though Jim had custody of the children, he always cooperated with parenting time and encouraged the children to spend time with their mother. Jim reasoned that if he were going out for an evening, he would give Mary first choice to babysit. She wanted to babysit but could not reconcile in her mind the idea of helping her ex-husband. Mary felt that she would be "giving in" if she accepted Jim's offer. Mary stated during an interview that she refused to babysit because she resented Jim telling her what to do. She misunderstood Jim's intentions. Jim was not demanding that Mary babysit. Regardless, Mary refused Jim's request believing that she won the power struggle. Mary inferred too much from Jim's request. She had the mistaken belief that saying "no" was punishing Jim and reminding him of her bitterness.

Alienation for the Sake of Winning

"I'll show her that she can't tell me what to do."

Some parents can't tolerate the idea of losing anything, particularly losing a battle to a person that has in the past hurt or betrayed them. Losing is humiliating because, in your mind, it implies to all around you that you are wrong and the other person is right. Of course, this is not true. The mere thought of losing control and having to obsequiously bow to the other parent's demands ignites a rage that is felt in every muscle of the body. They do all they can to keep from exploding.

Mary's rationalization was flawed because her stubbornness and need to win caused her to lose valuable time with her children. Other than the inconvenience and the children missing time with their mother, Jim was not hurt by Mary's rejection. His hurt was nothing more than Mary's fantasy. She and the children would have been winners if she had put her resentment aside and accepted Jim's invitation.

Children Always Lose in the Parents' Power Struggle

Some parents get so wrapped up in their own anger and power struggles that they can't see what they are doing to their children. They can't see how they are hurting the children by their actions because they believe "No one is going to tell me how to raise my kids." Some parents fight for longer visits or seek custody with no reason other than to prove that they are in control. These parents are not concerned for the children. Instead, they are compelled to push on for what they want because they have the irrational belief that winning is the only hope of ridding themselves from their awful feelings. What these parents don't realize is that winning does not heal the wounds.

Little things can incite a power struggle. Forgetting to return a jacket, returning Johnny from a visit ten minutes late, or Sue outside playing and not wanting to take your phone call can trigger a fight because the behavior, whether it is the child's or parent's, is seen as an act of defiance. Even when the child's behavior is causing the problem, the angry parent will challenge the other parent, saying, "Why can't you control Sue? You know she should be waiting by the phone for my call." Such a statement reflects the parent's belief that his needs or desires are more important than his daughter's. However, once Sue finally comes to the phone, her father will sound loving and gentle.

A power struggle between two parents happens when one parent wants to control the other parent's behavior and the targeted parent refuses to be controlled. It is not always easy to recognize a power struggle. The most obvious sign of an impending power struggle is when someone gets angry at any suggestion or demand of being told what to do. Any suggestion, whether or not it is a good suggestion, triggers the anger. It doesn't usually make much difference if the suggestion or demand comes from the court or the other parent. Either way, the parent is angry and wants retaliation.

When parents believe their motivations are challenged or a critic is closely watching their behavior, they will get defensive, fight back, or withdraw into secrecy. Withdrawing becomes a matter of self-protection. Letting someone know how they feel is thought of as too risky and an open invitation for an attack.

Sometimes what parents say will tell you that you are heading for a power struggle. "I know what's best for my children. What do you know about raising kids?" are common attacks that imply to the receiver that they know nothing about child rearing and should just do what the attacking parent says. You can see examples of items on the parental alienation scales that reflect the liklihood of a power struggle.

Typical Rationalizations for Alienating Behavior

- "I am the one who makes sacrifices for our children. You don't do a thing to help out."

- "You're a bad influence on the kids. I know that boyfriend of yours stays overnight. What are they supposed to learn from that?"

- "You have no experience in raising children. You didn't even change diapers. How can you take care of the children?"

- "I know what's best for the kids, so do it my way and they'll be fine."

- "It's absolutely ridiculous how much I have to pay for child support. I'm paying an arm and a leg. You get the house and everything, and I get the bills."

- "I can't ask you anything. All we do is fight every time I try to talk to you."

If these rationalizations sound familiar and are heard from an angry voice, you can be assured that you have been in a power struggle.

Some parents will fight for their belief that their way of parenting is best. The quarreling about whose approach is better causes power struggles that should be avoided. Sometimes parents will rationalize their insistence that their way is better by proclaiming that "children need consistency." Of course, consistency means that their standards, and not the other parent's, are to be followed. The insistent parent wants total control and domination as to how the children are to be raised.

Guidelines for Sidestepping Power Struggles

- Stay calm and try not to make demands. Instead, make suggestions and negotiate. If you can't keep down the tension, agree to come back to the issue later.

- Be specific in stating what you want. You should be able to describe it in a way that the other person can literally visualize in their mind. If they can't get a mental picture of what you are talking about, they won't understand you. If you are unable to find the words to give a visual picture, then you are asking the other person to understand something that you can't explain. That is not fair.

- Try to avoid telling your ex-spouse that they are wrong. People don't like to be judged. Instead, tell your ex-spouse that you have a different idea about how to handle a particular problem.

- Realize that you don't always have to agree. If parents can "agree to disagree," it is much better for the children than if their parents continue to fight in front of them.

- Take a moment and ask yourself, "On a scale of 1 to 10, with 10 being the most important thing you have to handle (new job, buying a house, planning your estate) and 1 being of no importance, how important is this issue?" If it rates 4 or less, maybe it isn't worth the trouble. In other words, put the issue in perspective before making a big deal about it.

- With every power struggle, there is an implied demand. People are sensitive to the notion of fairness. "Why should I bend to your desires if I get nothing in return?" they think. If the other person feels that you are unfair with your demands, they will either fight you or passively back down to your will and get back at you later. If you are making a demand, think ahead of time about what you are willing to give in order to get what you want in return. (You could give time, give emotional support on other issues, transport the children to the doctor, help with a household repair, etc.)

- When you negotiate, remember that you will not always get everything you want. Instead, both of you should get some of what you want.

Power is defined by some as the ability to influence another person's behavior. This is obvious with children. As long as our children do what we tell them, we will feel in control. When children refuse our demands, we become frustrated and angry. The battle line is drawn for the power struggle. Now the issue is whose will is going to prevail. The issues for the children and parents are different. Parents cannot allow their children to win without feeling degraded and incompetent. Children are fighting to avoid feeling uncomfortable for having to do what they are told.

A source of frustration is an unconscious awareness that your child saying "no" is more powerful than your demands. Hearing "no!" or listening to nagging is enraging. A fight will surely ensue unless your child backs off or you give in. Giving up does nothing more than allow you momentary relief from your frustration. Of course, your child learns that nagging is good and more nagging is even better. This is probably not the lesson you want your child to learn. To break the cycle, you must realize that your persistence will cause your child's behavior to get worse before it gets better.

Don't Let Yourself Be Manipulated

We all know that grinding sensation in the stomach that comes when we feel we are being manipulated. When you have the sensation, the best thing to do is nothing. Tell the demanding person about your discomfort and state clearly that, "I can't give you an answer now. I have to think about what you are asking." Be firm but polite in stating your position. Don't let the other person talk you into doing something you will later regret. If it is easier, give the person some excuse so you can excuse yourself and leave. Once you are alone, take some time and think about what you want to do. Without the pressure to make a decision, your thinking will be clearer because you have sidestepped a potential power struggle. You can avoid feeling guilty if you do not let people manipulate you into doing something that is contrary to your values and beliefs. It is you, and not others, who are accountable for your behavior.

Overcoming power struggles is difficult, especially for two parents who already have a history of not being able to resolve differences. Mediation can be helpful, though I have see this fail when a power struggle is at the heart of the parents' conflicts. Usually, the parent who feels they are losing the power struggle will regain their status by quitting the mediation. After all, the one who says "no" wins. Now, the targeted parent and the mediator are lost. What does one do when one parent asserts their power by doing nothing? Typically, the only thing left to do is to get the alienating parent into therapy. This is not easy to do unless it is court ordered and someone gets the parent to see how he or she is hurting the children. There is hope if the parent is either a naïve or active alienator. If the parent is an obsessed alienator, the outlook for making things better is poor. That is why it is important to recognize these problems early and act quickly, before the alienator becomes entrenched in a hostile position.

Alienation Backfires in the Long Run

"Why did you lie to me all those years? I went to see Dad last week, and now that I'm older, I can see that he's not half as bad as you always said."

It is important for alienating parents to understand that, when children get older, many have an inquisitive desire to make some kind of contact with the targeted parent. They are curious to know more about this person they have been told to hate. Once the children are older, perhaps adults, some things will have changed. They will make their own judgment about the targeted parent based on their personal experience rather than on what the alienating parent has said. In addition, the targeted parent is usually a little wiser and more mature. He or she won't be the same person who had been described years before as some ogre. This now causes a discrepancy in the adult children's minds.

When they come to believe that the alienating parent has filled their heads with lies, the children can feel betrayed and become angry and bitter. They feel victimized all over again, but this time by the alienating parent. They may resent the years they lost with the other parent and his or her family, so that the final results of alienation are to taint the children's adulthood as well as their childhood.

No matter what your reasons are for wanting to alienate your children from their other parent, you owe it to them to think long and hard about what you are doing.

5

How Parents Alienate

"We were going to live happily ever after. I would be the perfect hus-band and father. She would be the perfect wife and mother. And we were pulling it off—until Claire told me she was in love with some-body else and wanted a divorce. I couldn't believe it and I'll never forgive her for it. I get furious every time I think about her and Stanley living out my dream in my house with my kids. I can hardly stand picking up my kids because I have to act happy and pleasant when I would rather kick Stanley's butt."

Charles, divorced father

Parents alienate in many ways. Some are obvious and even offensive to an observer. Others are more subtle. In fact, you may have not even thought of what you are doing as alienating until it's pointed out to you. An off-handed criticism of your ex-spouse, a look of disgust, or a slip of the tongue can all have alienating effect on your children. None of these things that most parents do at one time or another will have a devastating affect on your children. In fact, most children just brush off the comment as meaningless or they think, "mom's just in a lousy mood." However, over time, such comments (usually made by a naïve or active alienator) can have a cumulative affect on how your children feel toward their other parent. Obsessed alienators are typically more blatant in their comments and actions against the targeted parent. Either way, an important step in preventing alienation is being able to recognize alienating behavior, whether the behaviors are subtle or blatant.

Whatever motivates the alienator, the results are almost always the same. The alienating parent strives to strengthen the children's psychological dependency on himself while sacrificing the children's relationship with the other parent. This dependency is an interesting phenomenon. The children are taught to not trust their own perceptions and feelings about the other parent and, instead, are told to trust and believe in what the alienating parent says about the targeted parent. Whatever the children thinks about the other parent, the alienating parent will somehow subvert the beliefs and replace them with their own. Over time, the alienating parent succeeds in having their children become their parrots. They no longer have their own opinions or beliefs. When this happens, the obsessed alienator is ecstatic and triumphant. You can imagine what this does to the children's self-esteem and sense of individuality.

Alienating parents don't one day just say to themselves, "I'm going to ruin my children's relationship with their father." They have reasons that they believe justify their behavior. Their excuses are endless. Most often the alienator believes that they or the children were victimized by the targeted parent, and in some cases this is true. The problem is that alienated parents often do not know what they are doing, or if they do know, they have no idea of the consequences in store for them and their children.

A Common Cycle of Alienation

The alienating cycle begins when one parent triggers an emotional response in the other parent. This cycle typically goes through four phases.

Phase 1: Parent A Triggers an Emotional Response in Parent B

When couples marry, they bring into the relationship a history of experiences, a way of seeing and interpreting their world, and beliefs about that world that influence how they behave in the future. This composite of experience, perceptions, and beliefs is what is their personality. It tells us something about how the individual is predisposed to react in their environment.

A trigger is any stimulus or activity that sets off an intense emotional reaction in someone. A trigger may or may not have anything to do with the divorce. It may be nothing more than an innocent comment that sets off an emotional tirade. In fact, sometimes one parent triggers the other parent without even realizing it. Or if they see an intense emotional response, they are confused about what happened. Triggers usually have symbolic significance, so the reaction is out of proportion when compared to how most people would have reacted (see chapter 7).

Any action or comment from your ex-spouse can trigger an emotional reaction that sets off a maelstrom of hate and contempt and possibly alienation. Requesting a change in—or denying—a visit, buying your daughter a new bike, being late with your support check, returning your children thirty minutes late, and a change in your child's mood can all trigger the alienator into action.

Claire's ex-husband, Charles, whose quote prefaced this chapter, is a good example. Seeing Stanley when he picks up his son triggers an intense emotional reaction. The reaction may have nothing personally to do with Stanley. Stanley, in fact, may empathize with Charles. The issue is that Stanley has become a symbol of betrayal and loss. This is what he triggers in Charles. Now the issue for Charles is how he is going to respond. Up to this point, he feels victimized. How he reacts will determine whether he becomes an alienator. Will he retaliate and begin a trail of alienation, or will he find another way of dealing with his hurt without involving the children and his ex-spouse?

EXERCISE: WHAT ARE MY TRIGGERS?

This exercise will help you become more aware of comments or actions of others that can trigger the alienating cycle. This exercise is divided into two parts.

First, think about ways that your ex-spouse behaves that trigger your anger or hurt. Think of the things that just irritate you to death.

1. _____
2. _____
3. _____
4. _____
5. _____

Now, try to remember comments your ex-spouse has made that upset you. Write these down.

1. _____
2. _____
3. _____
4. _____
5. _____

Phase 2: Parent B's Defenses Are Raised

When you are triggered, your immediate reaction is to defend your behavior or retaliate. (Often common sense dictates that you resist that impulse.) Alienators and even targeted parents are quick to defend their behavior because it is hard to admit that you may be wrong, especially to your ex-spouse who is ready to pounce on you. Parents in the heat of a divorce are sensitive and vulnerable to attack or anything they construe as criticism.

Like everyone else, you have an idea of how you want others to view you. If you are like most people, you want others to think of you as a good and loving parent, compassionate, honest, or all those things that you think you should be. This idealized image is like a facade around our true soul, how we really are but often don't want to admit. This wall is our armor, an insulator from the outside world. When someone speaks about "not letting anyone in" or "putting up a front," they are talking about this protective wall. If, either intentionally or by accident someone threatens to penetrate this wall, the person's defenses immediately go up to strengthen the wall and prevent the person from being hurt.

The risk of getting close to someone is that they will learn your vulnerabilities and how to get through your defenses to hurt you. This is the reason trust in a relationship is so important. You need to be able to trust the person you love and who learns of your vulnerabilities and know that they will not use them against you. Who better than your ex-spouse knows these vulnerabilities? The very person you loved, went to bed with, and grieved with is now the very person you fear will say things that hurt you. You will try to defend yourself, but your defenses will not always work.

Phase 3: Parent B Responds to the Perceived Attack

The third phase of the alienating cycle is how you respond to your triggers. There are many ways you may react when you are triggered. Blaming, rationalizing, and denying are just a few. You may react without thinking but make excuses for how you behaved. You may retaliate with your anger, deny there is a problem, blame others, or force yourself to walk away from the conflict. Some of these are more effective than others.

Whatever you do, this is a good point to stop the alienating cycle. It is one thing to get angry or tell your ex-spouse about your hurt, but it is quite another if you include your children in your response or react in a way that harms the relationship between your ex-spouse and the children. The first scenario is two adults who have something to work out between themselves; the latter is alienation. So what is the difference? Alienators focus on hurting the other parent's relationship with the children instead of preserving that relationship. Parents who are trying to preserve the relationship will consciously try to recognize the symptoms of alienation and behave in a way that prevents it. As mentioned in chapter 1, this isn't difficult for naïve and aggressive alienators but is nearly impossible for obsessed alienators.

Many times parents react quickly and later regret their how they handled a situation. You are better able to prevent alienation if you make a commitment to yourself to stay calm or regain your composure anytime you feel triggered. You will be amazed how much this helps prevent alienation and preserve your own sense of integrity.

What is important during this stage of the alienating cycle is that you have choices about how you will react after you have been triggered and are feeling defensive. If you think you can't control your behavior, you should consider getting therapy. Otherwise, you must assume responsibility for what you do. How you react to alienation is not always a simple matter of doing what you think is correct. It can involve a change in attitude and a realization that you have to put your personal needs aside in deference to your children's. Remember what I said in chapter 4: If you want to change how you feel, you must begin by changing your way of thinking and your behavior.

Phase 4: Parent A Uses that Response Against Parent B

When a parent uses an alienating tactic, the targeted parent may react with anger and retribution. The counteroffensive, ideally, is to get the alienated parent to back off and stop what they are doing. This rarely happens. Instead, the alienating parent will use the targeted parent's furious reaction against him, affirming to the children that their criticism against the targeted parent is true. This reinforces the alienating parent's belief that they were right all along and their behavior was justified; for example, "I told you your father would have a fit if you asked him to stay home and go with us to the beach."

How you break up the cycle will depend on whether you are doing the alienating or are the targeted parent. In reality, you probably do some of both, even if you started out as the target. You can stop the alienating cycle by intervening anywhere at any point and by not doing anything that seems to reinforce the other parent's alienating tactics. The best way not to reinforce the alienation is not to react to the alienating behavior until you have time to think about what you want to do and develop a strategy. You may need to talk to a counselor or a mediator to help you develop this strategy. What you don't want to do is wait for the alienation to get worse. Remember, there is a point at which alienation is near impossible to cure.

Common Alienating Tactics

The specific tactics listed below are among the weapons in the alienator's arsenal. They can serve as triggers in the alienation cycle described above. They can also be deliberate retaliation methods.

Making Derogatory Comparisons

"You're just like your mother."

When children hear such comments, they know that Dad is not paying them a compliment. These statements hurt children. Though the reasons you are hurt may be understandable, this isn't an excuse to hurt your children by making such reckless comments. You must learn to avoid making derogatory comparisons between your ex-spouse and the children. If you cannot control what you say, consider getting professional help. Not being able to stop the comparisons is probably caused by your inability to heal your hurt or anger. If you keep tearing down your child's self-esteem, in time, even your apologies will not be of any comfort.

Name Calling

"You can have a beer. Your mother won't know any difference cause she's stupid."

Children feel uncomfortable when they hear one parent calling the other parent names. Children may not know how to react to what they hear. Should they agree with the name caller, ignore what is said, or defend the victimized parent? Name callers would be shocked to hear their children openly agree with what was said. Imagine your child saying "Mom, I think you're right. Dad is a bastard. Someone should kick him in the ass for not paying child support." Most parents would be offended hearing their children make such a comment.

Children usually learn to snub their parent's belittling comments. They keep the blank expression on their faces and go on with what they are doing without so much as a flinch. Though they appear disinterested, your children will listen to what you say. They will keep to themselves any reactions to such comments. Typically, you will not know what your children think or feel about either you or the victimized parent. For this reason, you must be alert to your children's reactions.

Parental alienation syndrome is thought of as one parent trying to alienate the children against the other parent. But this is not always true. Alienation can occur in the reverse. A parent may unintentionally alienated themselves from the children because of derogatory comments said about the other parent. Children who hear their father is a "jerk" or their mother a "bitch" are put in an awkward position. The derogatory comments may weaken the children's relationship with the accusing parent while strengthening the bond with the victimized parent. Usually the name caller is unaware this is happening.

Children of different ages will have different reactions to name calling. Younger children are quicker to believe the disparaging comments while older children are more skeptical about what they hear. As children grow older, they are less likely to be fooled by their parents' comments. Rather than taking these comments at face value, they learn to use their own experience to form an opinion about the other parent. This is why name calling can backfire.

Name calling is more serious for children already alienated from the other parent. These children are more inclined to believe the alienating parent's disparaging remarks. The comments strengthen the children's erroneous perceptions of the targeted parent. Their alienation becomes more deeply entrenched. For this reason, these children and the accusing parent need to get therapy because serious damage has already occurred to the relationship between the child and the victimized parent. Unfortunately, most parents will not agree to get therapy because they do not see that they have a problem. Instead, they quickly blame the ex-spouse for the children's alienation.

Name calling or making derogatory comments about your ex-spouse must stop. You must learn to control what you say in your children's presence. Otherwise, you are taking the risk of hurting your children and alienating them from either you or your ex-spouse. Many times, you will not know whether it is you or the other parent that is being hurt by your comments. Do not expect your children to tell you.

You need to find a healthier avenue for venting your anger. Maybe a friend or a counselor can help. When times are bad, everyone needs a confidant, whether it be a professional or a friend. Consider getting professional help if your ex-spouse continues to be a source of pain and you cannot control what you say in front of your children. Otherwise, your children will continue to be torn by your animosity. After all, it is their mother or father you are degrading.

Revealing Inappropriate Information to the Children

"I have no secrets with my children."

Is honesty the best policy? Your desire to be honest with your children may be commendable—providing you are sensitive about the nature of the information you share. Some information about the divorce or your private life is none of your children's business. Children may not always understand the significance of what they hear. Though you believe your children are bright and mature, they still do not have the same capacity to understand as an adult. They want to know what is happening with their parents because of their love for them and fear of the future. To reduce their insecurity, children will listen for any clue about what their future holds. They will eavesdrop and listen to their parent's conversations through the walls. Parents need to respond to their children's fears while being discrete with what they say. They need to be reassuring without causing the children excessive alarm by projecting their own fears onto the children.

Parents may wrongfully assume children will ask questions when they do not understand something. This is not always true. If your children believe a falsehood, they will have no reason to ask for clarification. After all, why should they? Children, like most adults, have difficulty giving up their misperceptions and assumptions. When asked if they understand what they are being told, they may nod in agreement. Only later will you learn they did not. To reduce misunderstandings, ask the children to repeat back to you what they think you have said. If what they say is wrong, you can then correct the misunderstanding. Just keep in mind that children are more likely to remember inaccurate information than to ask a parent for clarification. Any school teacher can give examples of how children will not understand something and yet not ask questions.

Telling your children everything about the divorce is not in their best interest. Many of the reasons for your divorce are private. Children, as well as teenagers, do not need to know the details of their parents' sex lives, who is having an affair with whom, or the details of the family finances. Children want to feel secure believing that you and your ex-spouse will always be there for them and financially provide for the family. Usually when a parent wants "to be completely honest," he or she is sharing information with the children to strengthen their own position and, at the same time, alienating the children from the other parent. A common example is a parent showing the children the divorce papers. The alienating parent typically focuses on the financial aspects of the settlement so they can blame the other parent for the family's financial sacrifices. This tactic may backfire because the children could feel guilty or protective toward the victimized parent.

Divorce can cause a financial hardship and a drop in the family's standard of living. There is only so much money to go around. It is usually the custodial mother that suffers the greatest financial hardship because her capacity to earn money is frequently less than the father's. The discrepancy between the parents' income may be a sore point, particularly for the parent who has suffered the greater loss.

A parent who shows the children the divorce papers is usually stirred by their anger and desire to get back at their ex-spouse. Feeling hurt, many parents show the financial settlement hoping to be vindicated for not being able to give the children all they want and saying to the children, "See! It's your father's fault that you can't have the Air Jordan™ shoes." Showing the divorce papers serves no other purpose other than to alienate the children from their father. You may personally believe their father deserves such treatment, but this is not fair to your children. Your children must understand that the family will have to make some sacrifices that will, at times, be difficult. Even after the divorce, both parents must work together to ensure that the children's basic needs are met. On occasion, both parents will have to say "no" to the children when, in the past, they could have said yes. You should avoid blaming the other parent for not having as much money as you once did.

Parents need to be selective about the type of information they share with their children. They must decide beforehand if the information they want to share is in the children's best interest or, instead, serves their own purposes. Do not share information with your children that is likely to be distressing or harmful to their relationship with the other parent.

It is good to be cautious and suspicious of a parent's motives when he or she makes a public pronouncement about being honest about sharing information with the children. Parents will propagandize their children by selectively giving them information that would further their cause to alienate. They can share the reasons for the divorce, reveal past physical abuse, or declare, "your father left us to be with his girlfriend." The intent is to suggest to the children that they and the disclosing parent were victimized by the other parent's abuse or neglect. Even if the information told is true, the children do not necessarily need to know it.

There are times when parents share information with each other that will stir strong feelings or serve as a trigger. Discussing medical bills, changes in parenting time schedules, or deciding on how to pay for braces can cause either parent to feel nervous talking to the other parent. Sometimes a parent will use the children's presence during the discussion to control the tension they feel with the other parent. When children are used in this manner, they usually feel trapped. They cope with the tension by trying to isolate themselves with play or involving themselves with some other activity. They act as if they are not listening. Though they appear engrossed in play, they are probably listening to the conversation. You must remain sensitive to how the children would feel if they overheard your conversation. To prevent them from any unnecessary discomfort, pay attention to what you say in their presence.

EXERCISE: A LESSON IN ALIENATION

The aim of this exercise is to help you improve your ability to recognize alienation techniques. Below is an actual letter (including misspellings) that a father mailed to his two children, Josey, age thirteen, and Ray, age eleven. Read the letter and underline the statements that are examples of alienation. (Better yet, copy them onto a separate sheet of paper, and write why you think each phrase or sentence you have chosen shows alienation.) When reading each sentence, think about who is being hurt by the statement. Imagine being a child hearing your father making the statement.

Dear Josey and Ray,

Josey you are well aware of the situation that we are living with as far as money goes, and you both know that I have been honest with you both and Terry [children's stepmother] has been honest with you both also. If I could have had you guys during the summer. By that I mean the times that I didn't pick you up because of no money. The reason for that was that during the summer when I have you on days off it always before pay day and I never had any money. Plus we were in negotiation for a contract that still has not been settled.

Now that the adoption has gone through and we have a son we have to pay for him, and just because there is another baby in the family that doesn't mean that Terry and I love you kids any less. I don't know what your mother is telling you and to be perfectly honest I don't really care, because you will learn soon enough who is telling the truth to you kids and who isn't. I am thinking about talking to a lawyer about having the support payments stopped because ever since Jimmy has come into our lives there has been one excuse after another as to why you can't come over, I want very much for you kids to see and get to know your step brother. Terry and I are not blaming you kids for not coming over, because I and Terry know deep down that it is not your guys fault. The only people being hurt by this are you guys. If I stop the support payments I want you kids to know that it has nothing to do with you guys. And I also don't know if you were allowed to read the letter that Terry sent to your mom or not, but Terry had every right to send that letter after the remarks that were made over the phone. I will not go into detail about it because I don't think you kids should be brought into it. If you kids have any questions at all please call us or write a letter and you will be given the facts. We haven't lied to you kids yet and there is no reason to start now. Well that is it for now, I hope you understand this and remember that we both love you both and have no intention of hurting you kids.

Love, Dad & Terry

Now that you have completed the exercise, you may want to compare your answers with mine. I give a reason why I believe each statement is an example of alienation. Your reasons may be different than mine, and that is fine. The point is to make you more sensitive and aware of alienating behavior in your own relationship with your ex-spouse and children.

> "Josey you are well aware of the situation that we are living with as far as money goes,"

This statement implies that the children know too much about their father's finances. This could be fine if the children are not made to feel responsible for the tight budget. Their father may cause the children to feel guilty or responsible for the money problems which is unfair to the children and may cause them to feel alienated from their father.

> "you both know that I have been honest with you and Terry [children's stepmother] has been honest with you both also."

Father's statement has the subtle implication that he is virtuous and honest while mother is not. This statement would alienate the children from their mother.

"If I could have had you guys during the summer. By that I mean the times that I didn't pick you up because of no money."

Children will not buy the argument that father did not see them because he had no gas money. Even if this is true, children will continue to have the illusion that father has more money than he is willing to admit. If you do not have the money, the children will always think you can get it if you want. Children feel a sense of security embracing this belief, even if the belief is clearly false.

"The reason for that was that during the summer when I have you on days off it always before pay day and I never had any money."

Children are not stupid. They will not believe their father's argument that he will have no money for a weekend visit. Instead, the children will usually think, "I'm not important enough for my dad to see me." The children will feel rejected.

"Plus we were in negotiation for a contract that still has not been settled."

Father assumes his children will be understanding because he cannot see them because of a contract negotiation. The children probably do not know what a contract negotiation is. Again, the statement suggests that the children are gullible.

"Now that the adoption has gone through and we have a son we have to pay for him, and just because there is another baby in the family that doesn't mean that Terry and I love you kids any less."

Father is saying that they are less important than the new baby. The children would question, "Why would you adopt a baby if you cannot afford to visit us?" What is preposterous about father's statement is the suggestion that he loves his children. The children would not accept father's reasoning. They would feel hurt and rejected, even if father's reasoning was sound, which it is not.

"I don't know what your mother is telling you and to be perfectly honest I don't care"

Father is suggesting that their mother's statements are not important. He is planting the suggestion in his children's minds that he, and not their mother, is the truthful figure in their lives.

"because you will learn soon enough who is telling the truth to you kids and who isn't."

Father is continuing to suggest that he is honest and their mother lies.

"I am thinking about talking to a lawyer about having the support payments stopped"

This statement is the bomb ready to go off. Father is saying, "I have a new baby that I value more than you. To pay for our new baby, I will stop supporting you."

"because ever since Jimmy has come into our lives there has been one excuse after another as to why you can't come over"

Father's statement implies that he has been too busy to see his children. The children would feel alienated and rejected by their father.

"Terry and I are not blaming you kids for not coming over, because I and Terry know deep down that it is not your guys fault."

The implication is that it is their mother's fault for the children not visiting. Father is attempting to alienate children from mother.

"The only people being hurt by this are you guys."

Father is suggesting to the children that they are victims because of their mother's efforts to keep the children from father when, in fact, he is alienating them from their mother.

"If I stop the support payments I want you kids to know that it has nothing to do with you guys."

If the children are old enough or have any reasoning ability, they would not believe this argument. This is an example of a parent causing his or her own alienation from the children.

"And I also don't know if you were allowed to read the letter that Terry sent to your mom or not,"

The suggestion is made that Mother is withholding information while Dad is being honest and virtuous. Another attempt to alienate the children from their mother.

"but Terry had every right to send that letter after the remarks that were made over the phone,"

The comment suggests, without being specific, that the children's mother made derogatory remarks about Terry. Father was attempting to make the children feel alienated from their mother by suggesting that their mother said something wrong. She may have, but what is the point of Father's statement?

> *"I will not go into detail about it because I don't think you kids should be brought into."*

This statement will tease the children by suggesting that the children are not entitled to know what is going on.

> *"you will be given the facts."*

In other words, "I am the good guy, I'll give you the facts." Father's emphatic use of the word "facts" suggests that someone, probably Mother, would not give them the facts. The intent, again, is for Father to look good at Mother's expense.

> *"We haven't lied to you kids yet and there is no reason to start now."*

Father is implying that someone may be lying to the children, and that he is virtuous because he would not lie. He is raising the question in his children's mind, "Is Mom lying?"

> *"have no intention of hurting you kids."*

Father is suggesting that his children may be hurt by his statements in the letter. The question he should ask himself is "Could the painful statements have been avoided?" I think so. His letter did little, but cause his children to feel alienated and rejected.

This letter was a rich source of examples for illustrating alienation. You can see that some statements would cause the children to feel alienated from their mother while other statements would backfire, causing the children to feel alienated from their father. It is understandable why the children would be hurt and confused after reading this letter.

Making Excessive Demands on the Children

> *"I expect to be able to call my kids anytime I want. They are my children and no one is going to tell me when I can talk to them. They know I love them."*

Demanding parents believe they have rights beyond what is ordered by the court. They are quick to anger whenever anyone refutes or hinders their wants. They often speak with a sense of entitlement with little or no regard for how others feel.

In the portion of a taped conversation below, you can hear this attitude in Megan's father's voice as he demands that she stay on the phone rather than ride her pony. Six-year-old Megan's tears don't even deter him from his desires. In fact, her father counters Megan's protest by blaming Megan's mother for the fact that she could not ride her pony earlier.

Father: Megan, talk to Daddy.

Megan: I want to ride my pony. I just came back from school.

Father: I know, you've been home for an hour.

Megan: I want to ride it before it gets dark.

Father: Well, you can ride it in the barn.

Megan: No, I can't. My mom's gonna take the new stalls out. She puts horses out to close the stalls.

Father: Oh, I see.

Megan: The stalls are not that big.

Father: Megan, Megan, you're not going to talk to Daddy?

Megan: I'll call you back!

Father: Well, Daddy'll be in bed by then. I'll be sleeping.

Megan: I'll call you back when I'm done riding. This ain't a good time to be talking.

Father: Well, this isn't a good time for you to be riding your pony.

Megan: Why?

Father: This is going to be the time that I call you from now on.

Megan: Huh?

Father: I'm going to start calling you at 5:00.

Megan: Mummy, is it 5:00?

Father: It's after 5:00. This is when I'm going to start calling you.

Megan: Daddy's going to call me at 5:00 every day.

Father: Megan

Megan: What?

Father: Now why are you getting upset?

Megan: I want to ride my pony.

Father: Well, Megan, you know how bad you want to ride your pony? You know how bad that is? That's how bad I want to talk to you.

Megan: I want to give you to Grandma.

Father: No, you talk to me.

Megan: Daddy, I want to hang up!

Father: Megan, listen to Daddy.

Megan: What?

Father: Megan, are you crying?

Megan: Yes.

Father: Well, do you think that's fair to Daddy when I call you, you want to go and do something?

Megan: 'Cause I didn't ride my pony last night!

Father: Well, is that Daddy's fault? That's your Mummy's fault. Because

	she should have let you ride it and she didn't, so that's her fault.
Megan:	Nuh-huh!
Father:	That's not Daddy's fault, okay? So don't blame Daddy for this, okay? You understand this?
Megan:	Okay.
Father:	It's still daylight out. You'll still get to ride your pony.
Megan:	No, I won't. It gets dark sooner.
Father:	No it don't. I'm calling now for you to talk to me, okay? And I want you to talk to me, okay? I don't want you to cry; I want you to talk to me. Okay? You understand? Do you understand, Megan? Huh?
Megan:	Yes.
Father:	Now, what did you do in school today?
Megan:	Nothing.
Father:	Don't be upset. Don't you be upset with Daddy, okay? Because remember I told you me, and you are gonna get to go team pen soon. I'm going to come out, and me and you, and we're going to take two horsies and we're gonna go team penning.
Megan:	Hello?
Father:	Hello?
Megan:	Daddy, I'm getting dressed. Hang on for a second.

As you read the script, how do you feel about Megan's father? Was he interested in his needs or those of his daughter? Was he trying to alienate Megan from her mother? I think you know the answers to these questions. What Megan's father fails to see is how he is hurting himself. He is causing his own alienation because he is trying to blame his ex-wife for the problems that he's creating with Megan. Do you think Megan will see this? She probably couldn't verbalize what is happening but she knows how and why she feels the way she does.

Cheryl and Larry

Cheryl was protective and concerned about her son's welfare. Jason, age thirteen, had a good relationship with his father, Larry. Larry was often overpowering and demanding. He insisted on making phone calls to his son anytime he wanted. He told Jason, "You are old enough to make your own decisions, and you don't have to listen to your mother. If you want to talk to me, you don't have to ask her." Cheryl was angry at Larry for encouraging Jason to snub her authority. She felt frustrated and harassed by Larry's insistence to talk with Jason whenever he wanted. Because the phone calls were upsetting Jason, Cheryl insisted that Larry call before 9:00 P.M. She reasoned that limiting the phone calls would allow Jason time to calm down before bedtime. When his father called later in the evening, Jason would toss and turn trying to fall asleep.

Larry interpreted Cheryl's edict as an attempt to interfere with his relationship with Jason. Jason, like most children, wanted to avoid the entire situation. He would not tell his father anything about how he felt. Larry believed that Cheryl was trying to alienate him from his son when, in fact, Larry was causing his own problems. He did not take the time to empathize with his son's feelings.

Making Idle Threats

"If you go and live with your mother, I am not going to see you anymore."

All parents have said things to their children they later regretted. Sometimes angry parents make hurtful statements that are absolutely meaningless. An example is threatening your children with never seeing them again or saying you will find a new family. These statements will serve no purpose other than scaring your children and satisfying a selfish need to vent your anger.

Imagine for a moment how life would be if you were accountable for everything you have ever said. When you are angry at a person who cut you off with an automobile, you may want to ram your car up their tail pipe. Should the person driving the other car take your threat seriously? When you say to your child, "I could kick your butt," should they bend over and wait? Though the threat to your children is inappropriate, should they take what you said literally? Of course not. Interpreting the statements literally is irrational and serves no purpose other than creating more chaos.

Going through a divorce does strange things to our reasoning abilities. All of a sudden, you may start to take threats literally. Your ex-spouse is now accountable for everything that is said. In fact, some of the statements said may even be brought up in court. Now more than ever, you should learn how to express your anger and frustration in a way that does not hurt your children or the relationship with your ex-spouse. I continue to be amazed how a spouse will threaten their spouse with some kind of terrible legal action as if they are some kind of expert. Statements like, "You will never see the kids again" or "I'll take you for all you are worth" are absurd. If you are concerned about a threat by your ex-spouse, talk to your attorney.

You cannot reason with someone who has loud and pressured speech. You will lose the argument because the other person will not listen to what you have to say. Instead, focus on regaining control of your feelings by suggesting that both of you back off and discuss the issue at another time. For the time being, ignore the topic of the argument. If you find that nothing works in helping you regain self-control, seriously consider getting therapy.

Threatening Violence

"I'm going to kick your ass if I find out you lied to me."

There is a disturbing increase in family violence with today's divorces. Husbands and wives seem to have less control over their behavior. This is especially true while the marriage is failing. They act impulsively with little thought to how their behavior harms themselves or the children. The violence may surprise everyone, including the offender. There are many occasions when the offender has had no previous history of domestic violence.

After the divorce, the victimized parent cannot assume that the offender will offend again. A single violent act is reason to be cautious but does not mean that future violence is inevitable. Although, the common view today is to believe that once you offend you will always be an offender, this is not supported by research.

The violence is likely to recur if the person assumes no responsibility for his or her behavior but blames others; this gives the perpetrator reason to justify future violence while offering no incentive to change. A professional rather than an ex-spouse should assess a parent's potential for violence. In all fairness, even professionals do poorly in predicting violence. The individual's history of previous violence and their abuse of alcohol or drugs are the best predictors. Psychologists can only assess a person's personality and give some insight into potential violence.

A victimized spouse sometimes uses his or her experience with the ex-spouse to foster arguments that prevent parenting time (or visitation). Professionals and the courts must be cautious before taking away a parent's right to visit because of a past violent incident, however. The argument "He abused me, so he will abuse my son" does not always hold water.

Fearing violence because of your ex-spouse's past treatment of you does not always justify stopping parenting time without a court order or a recommendation from your attorney. (For an exercise that may help you assess whether your ex-spouse is really a threat to your children's safety, see chapter 9.)

In recent years, women have become more violent. Many have been known to attack their husbands and cause serious injury. Weapons can be a tremendous equalizer when a woman assaults a man. Even when the woman is clearly the aggressor, it is still the man who frequently gets charged with domestic violence. This is true for a couple of reasons. First, men still feel embarrassed that their wives have assaulted them. They may think it's degrading to report the assault to the police. Second, the person who gets charged with the assault is usually the second person who gets to the police. Men take too long thinking about what to do while their wife is on the phone.

After years of living with your spouse, you learn the vulnerable spots in each other's armor. You know what to say that will drive your spouse crazy. When the marriage was good, spouses trusted that their partner would not push those buttons. When the marriage falls apart and there is a loss of power, a spouse may react by pushing buttons to equalize their advantage. One spouse may accuse the other of being fat, being a lousy sex partner, never having time for the family, etc. Whatever the accusation, it sets off a fury of hurt and rage and perhaps a threat of violence. If violence does erupt, everyone may feel guilty and scared afterward.

EXERCISE: KEEP YOUR FINGERS OFF THOSE HOT BUTTONS!

After having been separated or divorced for a time, it is easy to forget those little digs or criticisms that drove your ex-spouse crazy. This exercise will help remind you of those criticisms that trigger your ex-spouse's hurt and rage.

Take a few moments and remember back to the arguments you had. Think about what would trigger an argument. If you are having trouble remembering, think back to the topics or comments you would avoid saying to prevent a fight. Make a list of those comments below.

1. _____
2. _____
3. _____
4. _____
5. _____

It is likely that any of the things you have just listed can still trigger a fight between you and your ex-spouse. If you want peace and cooperation, do not make any comments about these topics. If you push any of these hot buttons, you can be assured you are going to be the loser. Remember, you have your own hot buttons that can be pushed.

Harassment

"He calls me in the middle of the night and just laughs and then hangs up."

Some parents complain about being frequently harassed by their ex-spouse. Harassment is sometimes subtle and other times explicit. Either way, the behavior is damaging and will always cause alienation. Here are some examples of subtle harassment:

- Unannounced visits.
- Demanding frequent phone calls at unreasonable hours.
- Having the other parent wait to the exact minute before you allow them to leave your house with the children.
- Listening on another telephone to your children's conversation with the other parent.
- Nagging and criticizing the other parent in the children's presence. Usually the nagging parent will obsess on one subject such as drinking, cleanliness, or money.
- Frequent changes in parenting times.
- Insisting on making frequent phone calls to your children when they are with the other parent. The children may feel they are the ones being harassed. The harasser, of course, denies the allegation. They believe they are just showing their love toward the children.

If any of the examples above describe your behavior, think about what you are doing to your children. If you continue such behavior, you are just hurting yourself and your relationship with your children. Do not fool yourself by believing your own excuses for what you are doing. Your excuses are not justified. You are deluding yourself by thinking that your actions will heal your hurt and anger. This will not happen.

The harassing parent typically denies any wrongdoing. They either make excuses for their behavior, blame the other parent, or complain that the ex-spouse is getting what he or she deserves. They do not see themselves as doing anything malicious. Instead, they see themselves as a virtuous and loving parent who only wants a relationship with their children. They are blinded by an obsession that the other parent is trying to interfere in the relationship with the children. Unfortunately, they cannot see how their behavior is hurting the children.

Harassment is a vicious form of a power struggle between two people. Children, family members, and ex-spouses are all potential targets for the harasser. The harasser is an angry parent who believes he or she has been wronged by the ex-spouse's power to keep him or her from being involved with the children. To gain vindication, the harassing parent has an obsessive desire to destroy the other parent's power. Ironically, the harassing parent believes he or she, and not the ex-spouse, is the victim. The harassing parent will threaten and intimidate the targeted parent until he or she feels beaten down and succumb to the harasser's demands. The harassing parent intimidates to win the power struggle. Sadly, the tactic often works. After feeling beaten down, the targeted parent may surrender to the harasser's demands and complain, "It just isn't worth fighting anymore."

Harassment is more complex than just one parent repeatedly annoying or attacking the other parent. Both parents believe they have been victimized by the other. Each feels frustrated by their belief that they have no power to stop or influence the other parent's behavior. The hostilities between the parents intensifies while the children helplessly watch. The children are torn by not knowing where to place their loyalty.

Most harassing parents assume that the children will sympathize with their position and pull away from the other parent. This is not always true; it depends on the children's perception and interpretation of both parents' behavior. The targeted parent usually tries to explain the harassing parent's behavior to the children. She does this to gain the children's sympathy and understanding. But sometimes the targeted parent will actually cause her own alienation from the children if they sympathize more with the harasser because of the targeted parent's degrading comments or retaliation. Both parents are risking alienation because it is difficult to predict which parent will gain the children's sympathy.

Harassment can escalate to an intensity that is frightening and even dangerous. Harassers have been know to stalk their victims, peep into windows, and break into houses. They make excuses for their behavior, believing it is virtuous. An example is a harasser who broke into his ex-spouse's home, arguing that he wanted to see if she left the children alone while she went out for the evening. He made the excuse that he was looking out for his children's interests. Instead, his ex-wife and his son were home. The two of them were scared to death when they heard someone coming through the bedroom window. The father was lucky he didn't get his head blown off.

Harassers, like abusers, can threaten to hurt you or retaliate against you if you tell anyone about what they are doing. They depend on you to say nothing. If you give into the harasser's demands, you are perpetuating the harassment. Your best protection and hope in stopping the harassment is to make your ex-spouse's behavior public. Talk to your attorney, file a complaint with your local police, or speak to your therapist. Will your ex-spouse get angry? You can count on it. He knows that his ability to intimidate you depends on your silence.

You should never tolerate harassment in any form. Although harassers, like abusers, may threaten to hurt you if you tell anyone about their behavior, the harasser rarely follows through with the threats. This is not to suggest that harassers cannot be dangerous. Some harassers are dangerous if they have a history of violence and drug and alcohol abuse. Your best protection against the harasser's threats is to report them to the authorities. If you file charges, don't drop them unless you are advised to do so by your attorney or the prosecutor. After the harasser sees that you are serious, they will beg for forgiveness, cajole, and make all kinds of promises. Though they sound, and perhaps are, sincere, don't take their word for it. In addition, if they drink or use drugs, the risks are even greater that they could hurt you. This is all the more reason to report the behavior. The problem with harassers and abusers is their lack of control over how they behave. They will have more control if they know that they are being watched by either the police, a probation officer, a therapist, or someone who they perceive as having authority. Of course, this is not guaranteed, but it helps.

6

More Alienation Tactics:
Secrecy and Spying

"Paul, honey, does Dad ever smoke pot when you're visiting? I'm just curious."

Secrecy and spying are among the most blatant and damaging forms of alienation. Parents who ask their children to keep secrets from the other parent or to serve as spies to gather information about them are placing their children in a painful conflict where they must choose between their parents. The children also learn to be deceitful and to betray someone they love. Obviously, this is very damaging to children.

The Difference Between Casual Questions and Spying

It is natural for a parent to ask their children upon their return home, "How was your visit?" or "Did you have a good time?" Such questions are harmless, and you should not become paranoid about asking your children innocent questions about visits. There is a difference between these casual questions and asking for specific information. The latter is spying.

You need to be aware of how your children feel about your casual questions about the other parent's home. If they spontaneously answer, there is little reason to be concerned. If your children appear uncomfortable, you should probably back off from asking any more questions.

Expecting Your Children to Keep Quiet

One of the less malicious forms of secrecy is wishing that your children would not tell your ex-spouse what goes on in your home. Sometimes you may wonder how you can keep you child quiet and have any privacy. After all, there are some things that are none of your ex-spouse's business. They shouldn't judge what you do in *your* home, right?

Hypothetically you may be correct, but your beliefs can be unrealistic and lead to alienation. Let's face it: Children will talk, especially if they are unhappy about something going on in your home. Expecting them to keep secrets is unfair and teaches them to lie with your approval. Telling your child, "Don't tell your mom (or dad)," places them right in the middle of both parents. They have to choose their loyalties, which is exactly what they don't want to do. Instead, you and your children will be better off if you live your life with the belief that you have no secrets and whatever goes on in your home is open to public scrutiny, and that includes your ex-spouse.

If you think about it, how much really goes on in your home that anyone cares about? Your children should be free to say whatever they want, without being afraid that they will offend you or violate your trust. They should not have to censor what they say to anyone. If you expect your children to keep their mouths shut, you are taking the risk that you are causing your own alienation because they may be more uncomfortable with you than with your ex-spouse.

Both your ex-spouse and the court will pass judgment on misbehavior if it is brought to their attention. Feeling this scrutiny is uncomfortable, especially if your behavior is questionable. The solution to feeling uncomfortable is simply to behave yourself. Don't live a life that depends on secrets. There should be nothing that you do in your children's presence that anyone would care about. It may not always be easy, but you will be amazed how much better you will feel.

EXERCISE: MUST MY PRIVATE LIFE BE SO PRIVATE?

Often parents believe that their lives are not only private, but they have to keep certain secrets from their ex-spouse. To help you better understand what actually needs to be a secret, complete this exercise. Below, write down five secrets that your children know about but you don't want your ex-spouse to know.

1. _____
2. _____

3. _____
4. _____
5. _____

Now review your secrets and answer the question, who cares? Do these things really have to be a secret or are you making an issue about something that has little significance to anyone. If you conclude that the issue is important and must be a secret, maybe you need to rethink about how you're behaving, whether your children should be exposed to this behavior. You could be putting your children in a very awkward position. Do you think you are causing some alienation?

Having Secrets and Codes with the Children

Having secrets, special signals, a private rendezvous, or words with special meaning are damaging to your children's relationship with their other parent. It is one of the most blatant forms of alienation. Telling your children, "Don't tell your mother," "This will be our little secret," or "When I say "whimsy," call me tomorrow," creates an exclusive relationship that psychologically excludes the other parent. The secrecy implies there is something wrong with the other parent that justifies such behavior. The victimized parent is portrayed as not understanding or someone who "doesn't want us to have fun." Regardless of the excuses, the results are the same: The children are alienated from the victimized parent while the other parent is characterized as a special person who understands.

Sara and Bobbie

In the middle of the night, Sara went downstairs to get a drink. Looking out from the kitchen window while drinking her juice, she saw a car parked across the street blinking its headlights. Sara recognized the car and the silhouette of the driver: It was her ex-husband, Bob. Sara was stunned by what she saw. She couldn't believe her eyes, although her daughter, Bobbie, had been acting strange lately. Sara always prided herself about bring a rational person, able to stay calm and not get caught up in petty bickering with Bobbie's father. Now she began to understand why Bobbie has been acting the way she has. For no apparent reason, Bobbie has been withdrawn and "kinda secretive. We use to be able to talk about anything together." Lately, Bobbie would just pull away and appear indifferent when Sara would try to talk. None of this made sense other than perhaps Bobbie going through one of her moods. Now Sara realizes that Bobbie and her father were up to something. Sara felt excluded, pushed away by Bobbie. Jealous because Bobbie and her father seem to have something special. Sara ran upstairs, fuming.

Sara didn't expect to learn that Bobbie and her father had secret rendezvous. She was overcome by jealousy—the idea that she was excluded from part of Bobbie's life. I suspect that any parent can understand Sara's hurt. Sometimes the actions or comments are less obvious than what Sara experienced. They may be more symbolic (as explained in Chapter 7).

There are many reasons a parent would have secrets or private rendezvous with their children. The most frequent excuse is that the ex-spouse "will not allow me more time with my children." "She would have a fit if she knew the truth about the times I see my children." Sometimes, the alienating parent feels powerful for having a special relationship with the children. It is almost like "getting one over" on their ex-spouses. The children become unwitting vehicles for the parent's hostility.

Do not blame your children when you learn they have secrets with your ex-spouse. Without being punitive, ask your children about the secrets. Try to understand how they feel about your finding out about the lies. Explain to your children that they did nothing wrong but that you need to discuss the secrets with their mother or father.

When you are alone with your ex-spouse, tell him or her that you have learned about the secrets. Without attacking or degrading your ex-spouse, explain your concern about how they place the children in the uncomfortable position of having to lie and deceive. Try to understand why your ex-spouse was asking the children to lie. Usually, an ex-spouse will ask the children to keep secrets when they expect that you will get angry about something or try to restrict the ex-spouse's activities with the children. Rather than asking the children to keep secrets, see if you and your ex-spouse can come to some agreement about the issue. If you can't reach an agreement, consider taking the children to a counselor or have your attorney discuss the issue with your ex-spouse's attorney. or mediator

Having secrets, private codes, or rendezvous are damaging to your children because they learn to deceive and lie. They become confused, not knowing what is morally correct. If you have secrets with your children, stop immediately. You are hurting your children more than you know.

Using the Children as Spies Against the Other Parent

"Sadie, could you look in your daddy's top desk drawer and see how much his car payment is? I need to know for taxes."

Children get a damaging message that demeans the targeted parent when they are asked to spy or covertly gather information about that parent. The subtle message is, "Mom is bad" or "Dad is doing something wrong." These messages will cause the children to become suspicious of the targeted parent and pull away emotionally. If the alienating parent is clever, he may lead the children to believe they are playing a game while gathering the information.

There are many reasons why a parent would use the children to covertly gather information about the other parent. The parent may be sincerely concerned for their children's safety and welfare, or they may simply want to gather information that they can use later against the other parent. Whatever the reasons for spying, it is wrong. It teaches children to lie and sneak and, worst of all, to betray someone they love.

Roberta and Jerry

Roberta was worried that her ex-husband, Jerry, would allow their son to ride a four wheeler without wearing a safety helmet. She pleaded with Jerry to make Bobby use the helmet. Jerry was angry by Roberta's intrusion into "my business." He ignored her plea. He resented Roberta, "telling me what to do and having Bobby spy on me." Roberta had Bobby report back to her, telling her if Jerry was having him wear the helmet. Both parents were setting up a power struggle with Bobby in the middle. Bobby began to feel responsible for the arguments.

The example where Roberta was using Bobby to gather information because of her concern for his safety, put Bobby in the middle because of his father's refusal to cooperate. Roberta was correct in her assertion that Bobby should wear a helmet. Since Jerry was ignoring her pleas, Roberta's only choices were to either forget the issue, return to court, or teach Bobby proper safety regardless of whether his father required it. The latter choice is the most reasonable because going back to court is expensive and she should not ignore Bobby's safety. Unfortunately, this is an example where sometimes the children have to exercise more maturity and better judgment than the parent.

Gathering Damaging Information to Use in Court

Sometimes, a parent's motivation for having children gather information is not so noble. A noncustodial parent struggling with paying bills may want to know how his ex-spouse is spending his money. Or the custodial parent may have reason to believe that their ex-spouse is hoarding money rather then paying a fair share of child support. Drinking and driving, excessive punishment, allowing the children to engage in dangerous activities, or failure to supervise, are all reasons for parents to want their children to keep secrets because they know that some courts can restrict or even ban visits.

For a parent to prove an allegation, they often need the children's cooperation to gather information about when and where these questionable activities occur. A parent may think that if he or she can prove to the court that their ex-spouse is mistreating or neglecting the children during a visit, they can get a court order to restrict visits to daytime hours or eliminate it altogether. Such parents may believe the end justifies the means because they are so intent on restricting or eliminating parenting time.

The soliciting parent puts the children in a painfully awkward position because the children are asked to betray the other parent's trust. One example is a mother asking the children whether their father is having his girlfriend spend the night. If the allegation is true and the children are not bothered by the practice, the mother may unintentionally cause her own alienation. On the other hand, if the children are upset by the girlfriend's presence, the children may start feeling alienated from their father. Having to feed their mother information about their father's activities only adds discomfort. Even younger children learn that mother's inquiry has greater significance then just satisfying curiosity.

Before deciding to gather information, ask yourself, "Why do I need this information?" Is the information pertinent for a parental or ex-spousal issue? If the information has more to do with an ex-spousal issue than the children's welfare, do not ask your children to gather information.

Parents may have a strong opinion about the use of drugs. No reasonable person can argue that certain drugs are illegal and children should not be exposed to their use. Exposing children to drugs will cause most courts to ban parenting time entirely. However, there are those that believe marijuana should be legal and will smoke a "joint" in front of their children. They see nothing wrong with this practice, except they will ask the children to lie and not let anyone know what they are doing. These parents do not understand the dilemma in which they are placing on the children. Again, the children become confused about how they should behave and where to place their loyalties.

Drinking is a more complex issue because it is a legal activity. A parent cannot expect the court to restrict a legal activity unless it has been shown that the drinker has behaved irresponsibly in the children's presence. What the parent does when the children are not present is no one's business, unless that activity is illegal or a potential threat to their children's safety.

Using the Children as Witnesses in Court

A variation of gathering damaging information is using the children as a witness against the other parent. When a parent decides to seek custody, he or she realizes they are going to have to build a case against the ex-spouse to impugn their competency to parent. To do this, they know they must gather information. Boyfriends spending the night, drinking heavily, smoking in the presence of an allergic child, or using drugs are all arguments that have been used to force an involuntary change of custody. The parent drafts the children into service to covertly gather information against the other parent. The process of gathering information may be viewed by the children as a game. Together, they secretly develop strategies for gathering and exchanging information. While the process is occurring, an alienation evolves between the children and the targeted parent. Implied in the process is the belief that something is wrong with one parent, while the other parent is there for the rescue.

John and Tish

John used his children as witnesses of their mother's failure to cooperate with visits. John had custody of the two boys while Tish had custody of their daughter, Rosy. Because of John and Tish's fights, Rosy would refuse to visit her father and brothers. John did not believe Rosy's refusal to visit. Instead, he felt that Tish was brainwashing Rosy against him. To prove his point, John would come to pick up Rosy with the boys. Instead of going to the front door himself, John would sit in the car and have his sons go to the door to get Rosy. Rosy would have a fit and refuse her mother's encouragement to go with her father. Tish felt guilty for what she was doing to Rosy and angry because she knew she was being set up by John. She hated seeing her sons being used but knew she could not do anything about it. John reasoned that he could use the boys as witnesses against their mother to prove her lack of cooperation.

If the Children Volunteer Information

If your children volunteer information about what is going on in your ex-spouse's home, casually listen to what they say. Do not interrogate them by asking numerous questions. Instead, gently inquire and trust them to tell you if anything significant happens. If your child is upset by what happened they will spontaneously tell you when they are ready. Your children must feel comfortable and safe with you before they tell you anything they believe may upset you. Listen to what your children say without getting upset or making judgments or accusations. Otherwise, you will upset your children, causing them to temper their story.

Not knowing how to correctly ask your children questions can give you the wrong impression of what actually occurred. This can be dangerous and lead to false allegations. Parents are not properly trained to interview children. This is why a trained professional is needed to ask children questions about sexual abuse and other serious offenses. You should not ask your children questions about your ex-spouse's behavior that may impugn their character unless you have good reason to believe that your suspicions are true. Satisfying your curiosity is not sufficient reason to risk harming your children's relationship with the other parent.

If you have more questions, try to direct them to your ex-spouse rather than the children. When children tell you something that is inconsistent with what your ex-spouse has said, do not assume that your children are correct and your ex-spouse is lying. Your biased desire to believe your child is alienating and can cause tension between your children and their other parent. Without losing control, ask your ex-spouse to clarify your confusion about what your son or daughter is saying. Listen to your ex-spouse without blaming or attacking.

You can prevent problems by not asking your children or your ex-spouse about an alleged incident unless you have good reason to believe something actually happened. Having a vague feeling or sense that something may have happened is not a good enough reason to get everyone upset. One example is asking your children about whether or not their mother or father is using drugs when you have no reason to believe they are. Asking your children about such an activity, when you have no basis for your question, will raise doubts in your children's mind's about their parent's integrity. Your children may now have reason to feel suspicious and pull away from their other parent. Though you believe your reasons for asking the questions were innocent, you may have started an alienation between your children and the other parent.

Remember, your children's account about what happened will not always be accurate. This is because of their young age, their biased perception, and a limited vocabulary. Younger children will take short cuts explaining themselves because it is easier. Your children may agree with you before they really understand what you are trying to say. This happens frequently with younger children because they are usually more concerned about pleasing you than being accurate in what they are telling you. Asking your children, "Are you telling me the truth?" is meaningless because they will always say, "Yes." Have you known a child to say, "No?"

Before pursuing an issue raised by your children, ask yourself whether the issue is important enough to risk problems between you and your ex-spouse. If you decide the issue is not important, reassure your children and forget it.

7

The Importance of Symbolic Communication

"I don't know why you are making such a big deal of my forgetting Jimmy's birthday. I'll get a birthday gift before our next visit. He'll understand even if you don't."

During the latter months of a failing marriage, parents thread gingerly about the house, being sensitive to the silent nuances of each other's behavior, hoping to pick up any cues that may warn them of an impending skirmish. A tone of voice or a harsh stare serves warning to keep your distance. The tension will hover over the house until someone has the misfortune of triggering the inevitable quarrel. Once the fight begins, there is no retreat from the rapid escalation of hostilities. The skirmish never seems to get resolved. Instead, the hostilities slowly subside because fatigue sets in, or you retreat after feeling beaten down by the other's assault. With the return of uneasy calm, again you promise yourself to never again lose control. You may even rehearse in your mind a strategy for preventing the next battle, knowing in your heart that your attempts will fail. You are confused but still hopeful that another fight can be avoided.

It is a mistake to believe that parents will no longer argue once the divorce is final. Sometimes after the divorce, arguments between parents will actually get worse, though the issues will change. Parents continue to fight because old habits are hard to break, hurts continue to fester, and they continue to lack the necessary skills to talk out their differences. Another reason, which is rarely talked about and little understood, is the role of symbols that ignite hostilities. Skirmishes like those described above are often a clue that someone has triggered a symbolic issue. Symbolic communication is perhaps one of the more difficult concepts to understand, but is essential if you are going to prevent alienation.

What Is Symbolic Communication?

Everyday we rely on symbols to communicate with each other. The size of a tip tells the waitress how we value her service, foregoing a golf game to be with the family says "you are important," and wearing a black negligee suggests "I'm interested." These are all examples of symbolic communication. A symbol is any object or activity that has a special meaning and stirs an emotional reaction that is more intense than is warranted by the object's intrinsic value.

Symbolic communication and understanding boundaries (see chapter 3) can be confusing because there is sometimes an overlap in the meaning of the two concepts. Touching is a good example of the confusion. After a divorce, the old permissions to touch will change or be withdrawn all together. At one time, Robert's casual pat on Sandra's thigh was seldom noticed and had little meaning other than to suggest a friendly relationship. Now, Sandra could feel offended by Robert's familiarity, believing that he crossed over a boundary that he is no longer entitled. Robert's touch or intrusion into her personal space may also symbolize disrespect for her new founded independence. Ironically, sometimes an acquaintance or a first date can touch her leg in the same way as Robert and not be considered offensive because that person's touch has a different symbolic meaning. His touch may be flattering and symbolic of his desire for closeness. He is not violating a boundary if Sandra's smile or proximity gave him the permission to touch.

Symbols Can Be Irrational

While a family is breaking up, both the children and their parents learn that particular behaviors and various activities and possessions that were once taken for granted now have a new symbolic significance. Giving a rose to someone you love is an example of how an object takes on a symbolic meaning. For most women, and a few men, the rose is a symbol of love. Imagine instead, you decide to give the person you love five dollars because the money has more intrinsic value than the rose. After all, the rose will die. The receiver's reaction will be very different. Receiving the rose would bring the two of you closer together while the five dollars may actually be offensive or taken as a joke. Why is there such a difference in the way someone would react? The reason is that people in our culture have learned that a rose has a symbolic meaning beyond being a pretty flower. It symbolizes caring and love.

You cannot be expected to worry about everything you say. Instead, you can learn to recognize symbols and become more sensitive to the changes in your symbols and those of your ex-spouse. This will help you prevent a lot of confusion and hurt for the people you care about. To help you better understand and identify symbols, you may want to complete the following exercise.

EXERCISE: IDENTIFYING SYMBOLS

Remember the definition of a symbol: any object or activity that evokes an emotional reaction greater than the activity or object's intrinsic worth. Begin by remembering an incident when you or someone close to you had an intense emotional reaction that appeared to be out of proportion. Now, having the incident in mind, think about what the incident could have meant to the person having the emotional reaction. To help you, consider this example. Joyce got angry and began yelling when Terry offered to install her storm windows. Terry thought Joyce's reaction was out of line because she needed help and he only wanted to help her get ready for winter. Joyce's anger appeared out of proportion and suggested to Terry that his offer had a symbolic meaning for Joyce. At this point, Terry can only guess the meaning behind her reaction. She may have thought that Terry's offer was a put down, suggesting she can't take care of herself, or a reminder of her dependence on him.

List on a piece of paper other examples of symbols with your thoughts about the possible meanings behind them. After completing your list, think of new symbols that have come to light since the divorce.

This exercise, which I am sure you will agree was difficult, will make you more aware of possible reasons people emotionally react. Your ability to recognize symbols will cause you to pause and take a moment to think about how to react to someone's intense feelings. You may change your strategy or be more deliberate in what you say, either of which will help avoid an argument.

Symbols Are Learned

Beginning when a child is an infant, everyone learns a cluster of symbols that continually change with age and time. A mother's smile directed towards her child communicates approval. Father's pat on the back says, "I'm proud of you." Symbols vary from one culture and subculture to another. Much of the discomfort of beginning a new job or getting a divorce is having to learn a new array of symbols so no one is offended. You learn the symbols of power and authority, proper timing, and acceptable channels of communication. Even your dress has symbolic meaning. Ask any teenager about the importance of wearing brand-name tennis shoes.

A person's age, a change in circumstances, and timing all influence the symbolic importance placed on an object or an activity. A teenager will often feel slighted when they ride in a friend's car and are not asked to sit "shot gun." Somehow their symbolic status is demeaned by sitting in the back seat. Worse yet is the teen staying home on Friday and Saturday night. Not going out for the evening is symbolic of a lack of popularity. When the teen becomes an adult, staying home on Friday night is less important because the symbolism has been removed. The adult is now more concerned about his comfort than the status of sitting in the front seat of a car or the shame of not having a weekend date.

When a couple is newly divorced, both parents quickly learn that their unique clusters of symbols have changed. Behavior that was once acceptable may now be offensive. No longer can you safely assume that your ex-spouse will approve of your behavior.

The value or significance of the objects or activities are defined by the person's interpretation or thoughts about what is happening. Jessie sees her ex-husband take a piece of chicken from her refrigerator. Reacting to his action, Jessie immediately perceives them as inappropriate and offensive. She probably didn't care that much about the chicken but was offended by her ex-husband's presumption that he could go into her refrigerator and help himself. Going into the refrigerator and taking the chicken is the context that gives meaning to the chicken (symbol) and may symbolize for Jessie a lack of respect and an unwanted familiarity. Notice that this example demonstrates strong feelings felt by the person who is reacting to the symbol, in this case, Jessie. Her ex-husband's reaction is usually not to the symbol but, instead, a reaction to Jessie's intensity that is thought of as irrational or ridiculous. That is why is it so hard to win an argument with a person who is reacting to a symbol.

Learning to identify symbols is helpful in preventing alienation and resolving conflicts between you and your ex-spouse. Once you have identified a symbol, you must realize that you are not going to change how the person feels about the symbolic object or act. You cannot expect to change another person's symbols. Whether or not the symbol is irrational makes no difference. You will only make matters worse if you try to convince someone that their symbols are arbitrary and less important than they think. All you will do is cause the other person to get defensive and angry.

Instead, listen to what the person is saying and try to negotiate your difference of opinion. To keep the peace, you may have to compromise your position after realizing that the issue isn't that important to you. If you are lucky, you and your ex-spouse don't have the same symbols, otherwise you may need professional help or mediation to work out your differences.

Recognize that adult symbols can be confusing and difficult to learn. You can have some idea that you were reacting to a symbol when you later think back to an argument and can't remember what you fought about, or you conclude that was a stupid thing to fight over. When you figure out that you are fighting about a symbol, your best strategy is to back off and let the tensions cool because you will never win. At best, the two of you will beat each other down until one of you quietly surrenders. Of course, when this happens, the issue is not resolved.

If you listen carefully to an argument between two ex-spouses, you will often hear one trying to convince the other to change the value of their symbols. Ramone, feeling frustrated and angry by Mary's refusal to allow him to attend their son's birthday party, will think, "She doesn't want me around because she is jealous about my relationship with Jose." Mary in turn argues, "You don't live here anymore. Can't you get that in your mind? If you want, have your own birthday party but leave me alone." Because of Ramone and Mary's intense feelings, we know that Ramone's attendance at Jose's birthday party has a symbolic meaning for both. Ramone may think that not being at the party will make him a less of a loving parent in his child's eyes. Mary believes that Ramone's insistence is his way of controlling her, an attempt to deny that the relationship is over.

At times like this, parents must remember that children who watch both parents calmly communicate with each other have been shown to adjust better to the divorce than children who are consistently exposed to their parent's arguments. If Ramone and Mary are going to work out their differences, they must begin by realizing that neither one of them will back down because they agree with the other person's view. If they throw insults at each other because the other's symbols are irrational, or worse yet stupid, they will do nothing more than incite a fight. Instead, they must learn to tolerate the opponent's symbols and negotiate a compromise about whether Ramone should or should not attend the party.

TIPS ON WORKING WITH SYMBOLS

- Begin by recognizing a symbolic issue. You can tell when a person's verbiage is more intense than what seems reasonable.

- You cannot reason with a person until the person calms down and speaks with a normal tone of voice. Focus on reducing the tension rather than the issue. You may suggest, "Let's talk about this later."

- When tensions are calmed, try to find a compromise, knowing that neither of you will be completely satisfied.

- If the issue is important and there is no compromise, consider mediation.

Money Can Be Symbolic

Money is probably the most powerful symbol of power in our culture. Money, or the lack of it, is often a weapon that parents use against each other. This is seen in the number of times parents return to court because of child support.

Child Support: A Painful Battleground

Child support is perhaps the most sensitive issue parents will address before the divorce is final. The noncustodial parent, whether the father or mother, will be required to pay a determined amount of money to their ex-spouse monthly. Men paying support continues to be the norm. The amount of child support is an emotional issue. The size of the payment has both a symbolic and a practical significance to both parents. Both parents are keenly aware that their standard of living and the amount of their discretionary money will be dramatically reduced because of the divorce. Before going to court, the parents have heard horror stories of how both custodial and noncustodial parents have been shafted by the court. The parent, usually the father having to pay child support, may hear rumors that support has gone through the roof. These rumors evoke bitterness even before the parents enter the courtroom. The father imagines a future of living in a dingy three-room apartment while their ex-spouse and children continue to live in the marital home with a new car in the garage and the ex-wife's boyfriend mowing the lawn. To make matters worse, the boyfriend is probably using father's self-propelled, self-mulching lawn mower. These images may not have a shred of truth, but they provoke intense bitterness.

Support payments is not an easy issue for the custodial parent either. They have their worries too. They know that they will be financially dependent upon their ex-spouse for many years to come. They worry about whether or not their ex-spouse will lose their job, continue to pay support, whether the check will arrive on time, or if they will have money for financial emergencies. All these worries remind the custodial parent of their vulnerability and dependency upon their ex-spouse. They feel their ex-spouse's power from the threat that the money can be held back at any time. Each month when the check is due, there is that reminder of the past that they cannot shed.

Michelle

A unique tactic used by one mother, Michelle, to alienate her children from their father was to schedule shopping with the children on the day that the support check was to arrive. The shopping day became a ritual and was greeted with great anticipation by the children. They knew their mother was planning to buy them clothes or something special. If for whatever reason, the check did not arrive on time, the children were understandably disappointed because they could not go shopping. Of course, the father was to blame even if the check arrived just one day late. They learned from their mother that the reason they could not go shopping was "your father didn't pay support." The support check and the shopping trip became a weapon used against the father, and it taught the children to resent him. Sadly, for years their father didn't even know this was happening.

Society's Changing Attitudes Toward Deadbeat Dads and Moms

The courts are experiencing a dramatic change in attitudes toward the noncustodial parent's responsibility to help support the children. In years past, there was considerable variation between courts on how they determined a noncustodial parent's fair share of support. As recently as the early 1990s, it was not unusual for a noncustodial parent to pay as little as fifty dollars per month for each child. Anyone in their right mind knows that this amount of money was not enough to pay for a month's food or a good winter coat. Now, both custodial parents and society at large are demanding that non-custodial parents pay a greater share of money to support the children. The term "Deadbeat" reflects the common belief that there is something very wrong with people who ignore their responsibilities to their children. (Of course there are also Deadbeat Moms.)

With societal changes in attitude towards child support, no longer is a noncustodial parent able to gloat about not paying support without feeling ire from others. The taxpayer is angry for having to support children through federal entitlement programs such as Aid to Dependent Children and the Women, Infants, and Children (W.I.C.) program. Taxpayers are no longer empathetic toward parents who evade their financial and moral responsibilities. They are demanding action to reduce the tax burden.

State and federal legislators are responding to these outcries. There have been many changes recently in both state and federal laws mandating and enforcing child support payments. Millions of federal dollars are given to states and local jurisdictions to enforce child support laws. Even the Internal Revenue Service has gotten into the act by allowing the withholding of tax refunds to pay for arrears. Though there are still loopholes in the support system, it continues to improve.

Some improvising parents continue to avoid their obligation to pay support. One example is the interstate truck driver who keeps changing his address from state to state, thus preventing child support investigations from apprehending him. In time, the truck driver will be caught. The revised laws are to ensure that the court will place greater responsibility on the noncustodial parent to financially support the children.

"But You Spend It on Yourself, Not the Kids"

A custodial parent asking for more money is usually greeted with suspicion and distrust. In rebuttal, the noncustodial parent complains that the money isn't really being spent for the kids. Often a symbolic power struggle ensues with allegations flying back and forth. The noncustodial parent may accuse the other parent of greed and reckless spending. The custodial parent argues that the other parent has no understanding about how much it costs to raise their children. Parents will rarely agree on what it costs to raise children. There are always unforeseen expenses like braces, medical bills, school fees, and clothes that seem to wear out too soon. Rather than fighting, parents need to negotiate their differences. If you love your children and you don't trust how your ex-spouse spends the support money, there is no reason you can't pay some of the extra expenses yourself. After all, you could write a check to the dentist or take your kids out to buy a new winter coat. It is hard for me to understand how a parent can deprive their children of a necessity if they have the money.

A common argument or rationalization that some noncustodial parents use to justify not paying support is that the custodial parent is somehow cheating because they pool the support money with their other income into a single bank account. I guess the idea behind this argument is if the moneys remain in two separate accounts, their would be no opportunity for the custodial parent to spend the money on something other that what is for the children.

Of course, this argument is absurd. Parents do not separate the children's money from other family income because it is more expensive and inconvenient. They would have to carry two checkbooks and make separate deposits. This isn't as easy as it sounds. How would the noncustodial parent account for their contribution to the children's support? Would they have to take an equal amount of money from their personal account and transfer into the support account? Would they have to prorate how much of the child support payment goes toward the house payment and utilities. Parents demanding this type of accountability are only trying to harass the custodial parent because they are angry and bitter. Bills have to be paid regardless of the source of income. The noncustodial parent should not assume that depositing the child support payment into a single family bank account means that the custodial parent is using the money frivolously rather than for the children.

Feelings of Entitlement to the Same Lifestyle as Before

Many of today's young parents feel that they should not have to sacrifice or experience any financial discomfort after the divorce. When parents want to purchase something that they could have easily afforded before the divorce, they may feel bitter about waiting until they can afford the purchase. When parents have a responsibility to support their children, these narcissistic attitudes no longer work. Parents must realize and accept the fact that children cost money and this sometime means personal sacrifices.

During my interview with Judge Leven, he expressed the belief that much of the antagonism parents feel coming to court is due to their outdated belief that they are entitled to avoid their financial responsibilities to their children. This attitude is similar to the belief that one should do whatever is legal and necessary to avoid paying your income tax. The judge believes that once noncustodial parents finally learn to accept the fact that they will pay their fair share of child support, much of their resistance and animosity will stop. As long as noncustodial parents believe they can successfully avoid their financial responsibilities for their children's care, antagonism between them and the court will continue. Judge Leven is not suggesting that fathers will like paying child support any more than they do now, but he believes that strict and equitable enforcement of support laws will abate much of the antagonism between the parents.

Difficult Unanswered Questions

Though the child support system is in a state of change, there continues to be serious problems and unanswered questions. Some argue that allocation of financial responsibilities should change when parents remarry, start a new family, or have a severe financial hardship. Others disagree with this contention. They believe that parents must plan their financial future while considering their current obligations. A good example of this point is seen in the letter written by a father to his children in chapter 5. The father was asking for his children's understanding when he wanted to stop their support payments. He and his present wife needed the extra money because they had adopted a son. He was asking his oldest children to sacrifice their financial security so he could have the privilege of starting a new family. Most people would consider this father irresponsible and insensitive to his original children. The father's boldness for suggesting to his children that he stop paying child support is beyond a reasonable person's comprehension. Still there is no consensual agreement how this or similar issues should be resolved without hurting children. These problems will continue as long as parents are irresponsible and only consider their own comfort.

Possessions Can Be Symbolic

After a divorce, a child's possessions may take on a new symbolic significance for either parent. A toy or an article of clothing may have an emotional value worth far more than the intrinsic value of the object. The toy may trigger a parent's thoughts about betrayal, envy, or power. The idea that an article of clothing would stay at the other parent's home may arouse strong feelings that may appear irrational to an observer. In such instances, ask yourself, "What symbolic meaning does the object have for me?" There are many possible symbolic meanings that a child's possession may have for a parent.

A well-meaning parent is risking alienation if he buys the children expensive gifts without the other parent's support. The expensive gift can be a reminder to the other parent of her financial loss from the divorce or feelings of inadequacy for not being able to give a toy of similar value. Before making an expensive purchase, think about the consequences for your children and their relationship with their other parent. Giving the expensive gift may make you a hero in your children's eyes, but remember the illusion is short lived. Other consequences may last longer.

When your ex-spouse buys your children expensive gifts, don't agonize over the idea that he is buying your children's love. Unfortunately, there is not much you can do about the gifts. You will probably make matters worse if you try to stop the other parent. Instead, have more faith and trust the quality of your relationship with your children. When they feel your love and acceptance, the other parent will not destroy those feelings with expensive gifts. True, children can be influenced with possessions, but as they get older, the quality of relationships and experiences will mean more. Look back on your own fond memories of your parents. Which ones warm your heart the most?

Robert and Lisa

Robert bought his eight-year-old son a motorized dirt bike despite his ex-wife's objections. Though Lisa may have good reason for her disapproval, the bike was a symbol of Robert's contempt for her authority. She was angry and frustrated, knowing she was powerless to do anything about the gift. She knew she could not say too much to her son because he would either ignore her plea to not ride the bike or see her as the bad guy. Talking to her ex-husband was useless because he had already made his point: "I don't care what you think."

Children Taking Clothing and Toys on Visits

Parents have many arguments against children taking their possessions back and forth between households. "I bought the clothes, they stay here," says one mother. Some parents use the child's property as a ploy to hurt the other parent. Refusing to allow the child to take a favorite doll or coat may be an opportunity for a parent to say to the child, "He keeps the good clothes and returns junk." or "If you take that home, I'll never see it again," implying that the other parent is irresponsible. The child, hearing the allegation, is supposed to blame the other parent for not being able to take her favorite coat. Sometimes this alienating tactic will backfire, causing the child to feel estranged from the complaining parent.

Children do not want to be part of their parent's battles. Instead, a child should be allowed to transport toys or inexpensive clothing between homes as long as they are properly cared for and returned. Large toys, such as a bike, can be a problem and may not be practical to transport between homes. If expensive jewelry is likely to cause problems with the other parent or there is a fear that the jewelry could be lost, it may be best not to give the jewelry to the child until he or she is older. It is unfair to expect the other parent to be responsible for such a gift.

TIPS ON MANAGING TOYS AND POSSESSIONS

- Children should be allowed to have some choice about what they take to the other home.

- Do not blame the other parent for your decision to not allow your children to take a toy or clothing to the other parent's home.

- Do not give your child a toy or clothing that is not age appropriate. It is not fair to give the other parent responsibility for taking care of something valuable when they didn't agree it was age appropriate for the child. An example would be a motor bike for a three year old.

- If your children cannot properly care for a toy, do not have him take the toy on a visit.

- Do not have your children take a toy to the other home if it requires close adult supervision without first, getting the other parent's approval. An example is having your ten-year-old take chemistry set on a visit. The other parent may resent having to supervise the activity.

- If parents can't stop arguing over clothing, it may be a good idea for each parent to have their own set of clothing. Be sure to return the clothes they came in.

- In winter, expect your children to take their winter jackets or boots on a visit. Having two sets of outerwear does not always make sense for many families because of the expense.

- Your children should go on a visit and return home wearing clean clothes. If they can't because they will be returning from the beach or someplace where they will get dirty, warn the other parent about what they can expect.

Both you and your ex-spouse must agree to not ensnare your children in settling your differences about where they take their possessions. Parents should settle their differences about possessions between themselves without the children hearing an argument. It is fine to ask their opinions about what they would like to bring, but you may have to make the decision. Continuing to fight has an emotional cost to you and your children. It is not worth fighting about a dress, a blanket, or a Nintendo tape if you harm your relationship with your children.

Timing Can Be Symbolic

Timing is an important concept when trying to understand symbolic communication and alienation. An activity that occurs at one particular time may have an entirely different symbolic meaning at another time. To illustrate the concept, consider the effects of timing when teaching your children about good and bad touch. Parents will take the time to teach the children this concept when they are old enough to understand. The explanation is a warning to the children not to allow anyone to touch their "private parts." If anyone attempts to touch the private parts, they are instructed to say "No!" and immediately tell their parents.

Imagine how different the symbolic meaning of your teachings would have on your children if you initially instruct them on good and bad touch just before they go on their first visit with their father. Your timing could suggest to the children that there may be something seriously wrong with their father, that he is dangerous and should not be trusted. Although you are not intending to alienate the children from their father, your timing may have a symbolic connotation suggesting they are at risk.

Eleanor and Tom

"I wish you would say what you mean!" were Eleanor's departing words to Tom. Tom had bitterly left Eleanor's house before without the children. Tom persisted because he didn't want this to happen again. "I don't see what the big deal is if I'm a little late. I said I would be here at 4:00. It's 4:20, so what?" Feeling empowered, Eleanor stood firm. Tom was helpless because he knew, for now, he could not do a thing about Eleanor's tenacity.

"The custody agreement says four o'clock Saturday, not any time after 4:00 or when you feel like arriving," she declares. In turn, she informs the children that their dad must not really want to see them. "If he did," she says, "he'd be here on time."

When Tom retaliates by taking Eleanor back to court (for the fourth time in two years), she tells the judge that her ex-husband's lateness "upsets the children terribly" and brings along their daughter Angela to corroborate the claim. Her parting words to the nine-year-old as she goes in to testify against her dad are, "I know you love me and would never let me down."

Is Eleanor irrational? Why would she feel that twenty minutes is so important when her defiance will force a return to court and publicly reliving the animosities with Tom? The issue is not Tom being late, but his tardiness has a symbolic meaning for Eleanor. This is apparent because the intensity of Eleanor's feelings are greater than what most people would feel in a similar situation. True, Tom's chronic tardiness can be a nuisance and perhaps is inexcusable, but is it worth going to court? There are many possibilities about what Tom's tardiness could mean to Eleanor. She may feel incensed by what she believes is Tom's lack of respect for her time, his blatant refusal to comply with her demand that he be on time, or a reminder of his lackadaisical attitude that helped destroy the marriage. Anytime a person like Eleanor appears to be overly reacting to an activity or an event, the person, is probably reacting to the symbol rather than the activity or events intrinsic value.

TIPS ON WORKING WITH TIMING

- Being sensitive to timing will avoid a lot of arguments.

- Don't drop a bombshell on your children or ex-spouse and expect to walk away without any discussion. You are asking for trouble.

- When you ask a favor or a change in the parenting time schedule give the other person time to think about your request. If you expect an immediate answer to something that is important or requires sacrifice, you will likely hear a "No!" You are more likely to get cooperation if you let the person think about your request before responding.

- Give your children and your ex-spouse time to plan.

- Surprise changes in plans will usually cause problems for both your children and your ex-spouse. Being predictable and consistent will strengthen trust in you.

- You can expect trouble if you show up at your ex-spouse's home without an invitation.

Tony and Martha

Tony was excited about attending his son's sports banquet. He proudly attended most of Kenny's games and now wanted to share the spotlight with his son. Without thinking to give his ex-wife notice, Tony appeared at the banquet and started to sit down at Martha's table when he heard, "What the hell are you doing here?" Kenny, equally startled, wanted to crawl under the table. Recoiling from Martha's unexpected reaction, Tony, straining to keep his voice down said, "What the hell are you talking about? I have a right to be here."

"No, you don't. Can't you see you are embarrassing Kenny? Why don't you go and sit at another table and stop bothering us?"

Activities Can Be Symbolic

When the court dictates to parents, most specifically to noncustodial parents, how and when they are to spend time with their children, it is not uncommon for them to feel enraged because their power to choose when to see the children has been eroded. The court's declaration can be symbolically interpreted by the parent to mean that "I'm no longer important to my children." This message causes some parent's excruciating pain and bitterness. Blame for the decision is often given to the other parent even though he or she did not make the decision. To make matters worse, the noncustodial parent often perceives that the court has given the other parent all the power, the power to give or take away permission to see the children or attend their activities. No longer can the noncustodial parent come and go as they please in their children's lives.

The parent's relationship with their children is no longer equal or necessarily fair except on rare occasions when both parents have learned to coparent. Courts have sincerely tried to find ways of reducing this inequity by encouraging shared parenting, joint custody, or whatever other custody arrangement is currently in vogue. Regardless of the arrangement, the symbolic issues around the sharing of activities will not be dealt with by court orders alone. Courts cannot dictate a cooperative attitude, happy feelings, or a parent's sincerity in wanting the other parent involved in her children's lives. The recognition that both parents' need to be active participants in the children's lives must come from the parents themselves.

Take a moment and think about how Kenny and his father felt after Martha berated Tony publicly. What should Tony do? Insist on sitting at

Martha's table? Leave the banquet? Go to another table? What was Martha reacting to? Who has the power? What can both parents do to make things better for Kenny? Most importantly, what could have been done to prevent this confrontation?

Martha and Tony's confrontation is an example of how one incident can trigger intense feelings because of what the incident symbolizes for each parent. Tony's unexpected appearance may remind Martha of his presumption that he can do whatever he wants without asking. She feels his intrusion, thinking that he has no regard for how she may feel. She remembers the many times during the marriage when he tried to control her. "Tony would care less about my feelings. All he was interested in was doing what he wanted. Well, he isn't going to run over me again."

Tony also has his symbolic issues. He is hurt by Martha's abrupt rejection and the humiliating thought of sitting alone while his son is sitting at the next table. He is furious at Martha's reminder that she has the power to dictate where he is not allowed to sit. Rejection was not new for Tony. He recalls how "the bitch has always tried to interfere with the relationship with my son. Now I'm supposed to be happy relegated to a nobody."

The interaction between parents, when one has to ask the other for permission to see their children or attend an activity, can be a symbolic trigger that ignites old hurts and hostilities for both parents. The parent asking for an extra eight hours may think, "What right does she or the court have telling me when I can be a father to my kids?" He is reminded that some of the rewards of being a father can be taken away, like being able to spontaneously ask his kids, "Would you like to go and get an ice cream?" Worse yet is the belief that something is wrong with him because he wants to spend more time with his kids.

Exchanging the children or showing up unexpectedly at an activity are the times when parents are at greatest risk to trigger an intense feeling caused by some symbolic meaning the parent has about what is said or is occurring. Parents often sense this, even if they cannot explain it. Children, too, feel the tension. Parents need to realize that the exchange is a risky time that requires a concerned effort to not pick a fight and to make the exchange as pleasant as possible. They must remember that the children may also be uncomfortable because the exchange becomes their symbol of the divorce.

Courts recognize the importance of encouraging the noncustodial parent's involvement with their children. Children want both parents involved with their school or extracurricular activities. They want to believe they can hug and kiss both parents without them worrying about how the other parent will react. When the custodial parent interferes with the other parent's opportunity to share in the children's activities, the children may feel frustrated and bitter, perhaps thinking they have been snubbed or rejected. The children may falsely accuse the noncustodial parent of not caring. Parents refusing or forgetting to give the other parent advance notice of their children's activities are risking alienation. For specific strategies on managing children's activities, see chapter 9.

Understanding symbolic communication will take you a long way to understanding and preventing alienation. It is not always easy to know what to do when you see the emotional outburst that comes after violating something that is symbolically important to another person. It requires both you and your ex-spouse to be patient and forgiving of each other for the other's mistakes. Try to remember that attacking hurts everyone, including you but especially the children who are less able to control and emotionally defend themselves against the hurt.

8

Values and Discipline

*"I don't dare discipline my kids. If I do, they'll run to their mother and
complain about what a bastard I am. I'll never see them again."*

Both of these statements reflect the fears that many parents have about
parenting their children once they are separated or divorced. The custodial
parent, usually the mother, sometimes feels cheated because she thinks she
has majority of the responsibility for raising the kids while their father is
irresponsible, the "good guy" who can't do anything but show the kids a
good time. Mom has to be the bad guy, setting down the law. Dad is sometimes envious of the time his ex-spouse has with the children. Little things
like helping the kids with their homework, getting them off to school, and
taking them to the doctors are all activities that many dads would like to
do if they had the kids during the week.

Behind parents' envy for each other is often a distrust of their own
ability to influence the children and to remain loved by them. This is especially true when alienation is involved. The targeted parent becomes insecure because of their belief that they cannot overcome the damaging
influences of the alienating parent's brainwashing, especially when they see
the children only every other weekend.

I am sure that, like all parents, you want to trust your relationship with
your children. You want to be able to correct them, discipline, and if necessary, punish them without fearing reprisal. You want to know that your
children are not going to run to the other parent and complain every time
they do not get what they want. This chapter will help you toward these
goals.

Discipline Is Vital to Good Parenting

Let's be realistic. Sometimes children can be mouthy and defiant.
Sometimes you will respond in anger and say things to your children that

should not have been said. You aren't Mr. Rogers or Captain Kangaroo. Like all parents, you'll make mistakes. You'll lose your cool and hopefully step back to figure out how not to the next time.

Striving to improve your children's behavior is a big part of being a parent. It never really stops. When your children fall short of your standards for good behavior, you may think that you've failed as a parent. You haven't. You simply have more parenting work to do. And no one does it perfectly.

Approaches to discipline vary, and no psychologist can say with certainty that one method is clearly the best for all children. However, experts do agree that the goal of all disciplinary measures should be to teach appropriate behavior, respect for others, and self-control. Is your approach accomplishing this goal? Now might be a good time to rethink certain practices, especially if your parenting skills and ability to manage children without abusing them are being questioned by your ex, a court-appointed psychologist, or anyone else.

Discipline Is Both Parents' Job

Children need discipline from both of their parents. They need caring adults to set limits for them and put on the brakes when their behavior exceeds those limits. Without that safety net, that sense of someone older and wiser being there to keep them from going out of control, kids become frightened and insecure. Even though your rules and methods need not be identical, both parents are responsible for disciplining children.

Structure is important. Kids feel more secure in a home where there are rules and boundaries. They may not always like your rules; they may fight you on them or seem bent on blatantly disregarding them. However, if your rules are fair and consistently enforced, your children will not only adjust to them but also feel reassured that you care enough about them to keep them in line. It's possible to provide structure without being rigid about it. Bend the rules when the circumstances warrant it.

Don't Let Your Children Manipulate You

Children are expert manipulators. If they sense that you are uncertain or insecure, they can't help but take advantage of it. In the absence of clear limits, predictable consequences, and the caring, consistent parental guidance they need to feel safe and secure, children instinctively try to gratify their immediate desires. Without malice or much forethought, kids will nag, pout, throw tantrums, feign illness, or make it look as if they're about to embarrass you in front of half the population of your home town if they think that will get them what they want. They have an uncanny ability to threaten you with the very consequences you most fear.

Feeling powerless and frustrated by what appears to be their children's control over the situation, noncustodial parents worry that youngsters will refuse to visit. Custodial parents imagine their children asking to live elsewhere. As a result, they discipline tentatively at best. Some make weak threats that their kids know they won't carry out. Others let things slide for hours and then blow their stacks, or they appropriately punish youngsters, then feel guilty and "buy back" their affection with gifts or special treatment.

Don't succumb to those maneuvers. You are the grown-up, and your children are counting on you to provide them with structure, stability, and reasonable guidelines for living. Whether you're the parent in charge two days per month or twenty, you need to set aside your fear of being rejected by your offspring and learn to consistently and appropriately discipline them when discipline is called for.

Both custodial and noncustodial parents can be susceptible to their child's manipulations if they think that whatever they do with the child will be outweighed by what the other parent does better; they fear that the other parent is more fun, patient, and loving. Either way, the problem is your not trusting your own relationship with your children.

Children who see their parents calmly talk to each other about their welfare are less likely to manipulate them. They know that their parents will compare notes about what they are doing. In addition, you have the added benefit of knowing that your children will be healthier and better adjusted. This mutual dialogue needs to be your goal.

Why Many Noncustodial Parents Hesitate to Discipline Their Children

Discipline is difficult for many noncustodial parents. They want the parental responsibilities and yet feel threatened by the prospect of alienating the children. The child's words, "I'm going to tell Mommy on you," and the fear that the child will run to the other parent and tell horrendous stories about what you supposedly did can set the stage for manipulation. Don't let this threat intimidate you from disciplining your children.

What if angry children tell exaggerated tales that make reasonable attempts at discipline sound like abuse or neglect? You might not only suffer your ex's fury but quite possibly be investigated by social services at your ex's request. Again, don't let the children intimidate you. If you believe your discipline was appropriate and you maintained self-control, then trust the love and respect you and your children have for each other and do not be defensive. On the other hand, if you do lose control and have to defend your punishment, think about getting help. You could lose control again.

Many noncustodial parents think, "If I don't criticize or correct my kids, and if I make sure I befriend them and make every visit fun, they won't turn against me." They're in for a rude awakening. Parents are not doing their children any good by being their "best friend." In fact, be careful about being a best friend. Your kids have friends at school and in their neighborhood. They need you to be the parent they can depend on and look up to—especially when they are already confused by your divorce and unsure about how to behave in your presence. Treating your children as best friends tends to cause friction between you and your ex-spouse. You will probably also use your children as confidants and say more to the children than is good for them.

Sissy and Her Children

Sissy was an extreme example of a parent trying to be a friend to her daughter. She was a thirty-five-year-old mother of a son, Jason, age eleven, and a daughter, Becky, age fifteen. Sissy was enthralled with Becky's friends. She began dressing like a "biker" and "hung out" with Becky's teenage friends in the driveway until late at night. Neighbors began complaining to the police because of the noise. She was often seen riding around the community with a teenage boy driving the family car. Most of the time, Becky was nowhere in sight. When Sissy's husband, Andrew, was out of town for business, Sissy allowed as many as four teenagers to spend the night. Neighbors talked among themselves about all the cars parked in the driveway overnight. They complained to her and Andrew about the noise and the cars speeding down the street. Sissy was angry and contemptuous towards the complaining neighbors.

When Andrew realized that Sissy was not going to change, he felt responsible and concerned for the children. He had no choice but to get a divorce. Initially, Becky lived with her mother and Jason with his father. Sadly, Sissy embarrassed Becky and Jason by continuing to befriend the teenage boys. The children felt protective towards Sissy but were confused because they knew that her behavior was inappropriate. Sissy's behavior caused her to lose custody of her children.

Consistency Helps Children Feel Secure

Children need structure with predictable rules and consequences. Your children need to know what you expect from them and what they can expect from you. They need to see you react to various circumstances in a logical, consistent manner so that they can predict your future responses with a reasonable amount of accuracy and adjust their behavior accordingly. They need to realize that if they do X (misbehave), then they can expect Y (a negative consequence) will happen. When they learn to trust that Y consistently happens, they will likely refrain from misbehaving to prevent further punishment. The same goes for positive consequences. Kids learn to continue desirable behaviors in order to produce desirable responses from the parent who routinely rewards or encourages that behavior.

Also, remember that consistency does not require absolute uniformity. You don't have to respond in exactly the same way every time your ten-year-old talks back or your six-year-old shows you an arts and crafts project he made.

Children Need Consistency Within Parents, Not Between Them

Many parents worry that the children's psychological health depends on both parents being consistent in their rules and values. Their worry is unnecessary.

What troubles children are not that parents have different bedtimes or who requires them to clean their dinner plate. What troubles them is being told they are allowed to cross the street without asking permission and later being punished by the same parent for doing what they believed was permissible. In this example, the children cannot predict their parent's behavior. Whether or not the other parent allows them to cross the street without permission has nothing to do with the children's current dilemma. Now the children have good reason to feel anxious and fearful toward their inconsistent parent. They are learning to distrust what the parent tells them.

Outbursts that come out of nowhere, rules that are ignored one minute and rigorously enforced the next, rewards promised but not delivered, and other inconsistencies in one person's parenting methods can produce anxious, untrusting, insecure children—and adults.

Children Learn to Discriminate

Children learn to size up new situations and adjust their behavior according to each set of rules and expectations. They know to behave differently in school, on a playground, or at Grandpa's house. Making these discriminations healthy and necessary for them to survive in the adult world.

At school, they quickly figure out which teachers are strict and which are lenient. To stay out of trouble, they learn to adjust their behavior to suit each teacher's standards. They may initially challenge the rules and test the waters to see what they can get away with, but once they know that there are limits and that the consequences for overstepping them will be consistently enforced, kids generally settle down and obey. The same holds true when they encounter different rules or expectations in each of their divorced parents' homes.

In all likelihood, your children are already aware of the discrepancies between your value system and their other parent's. They know, for instance, that the consequences for certain misbehavior will vary depending on which parent catches them at it. They've figured out what they must do in order to stay in the good graces of the parent who is responsible for their care at a particular moment. And in order to feel at ease, they follow that parent's rules and routines and adapt to his or her feelings about neatness or roughhousing or back-talking while they are with him. They do the same for their other parent when they are with her.

The Secret of Building a Positive Relationship with Your Children

Both parents can cultivate the power to influence their children—and without degrading the other parent or causing the children to feel a divided loyalty.

Effective parenting begins with the power to influence your children's behavior and values. Threats and excessive punishment can influence your children's behavior simply because their they are afraid of you, but compliance because of fear is not long lasting. Rarely does such behavior influence a child to become a "true believer" in the values that you are trying to instill. On the other hand, if your child values your relationship because of what you do to cause them to feel good about themselves, your son or daughter child will be more likely to ascribe to your beliefs about what is right and wrong. Children should want to obey because they want to please and maintain a relationship with the people they love.

The difficulty with combating alienation is your not having any control on what the other parents does or says to your children. You are in a helpless situation, especially if you and your ex-spouse cannot talk to each other. So you may ask, "What am I supposed to do when I know that my ex-spouse is saying derogatory things about me to the kids?" The answer to this question is simple but for some parents hard to do. You must learn to trust and continue to build your relationship with your children. A solid relationship with your children is good protection against their other parent's efforts to alienate them. Although young children are easily influenced by what they hear, their critical parent's words will have less impact when their actual experience with you contradicts those words. Older children are even more likely to make judgments based on personal experience rather than hearsay.

The process of building a stronger relationship with your children, and with anyone for that matter, begins with a simple concept: People like to be with people who makes them feel good. Anyone who makes your children feel good about themselves has power. Here, I am talking about the kind of trusting relationship that is built over a period of time. It means more than treating the child to ice cream every night, heaping her with flattery, or saying yes when your good judgment tells you to say no. It means treating the child with respect and love but knowing how to establish limits.

Reward Your Children for What They Do Right

Discipline is more than punishing misbehavior. You also shape character, teach values, and motivate kids to do their best by rewarding what they do right. By praising their accomplishments, encouraging them to try new endeavors, correcting their mistakes without intimating that they are bad, and showing you love them no matter what they do, you help them feel good about themselves. The seeds of positive self-esteem you plant now will serve your children throughout their lives, enabling them to take risks, bounce back from disappointment, make healthy choices, and more.

Yes, you can still punish. Children need to know that their actions have consequences, and it's your job to teach them. But in the course of correcting your children's errors and teaching them proper conduct, don't lose sight of their positive qualities, their natural exuberance, their compassion, creativity, agility, adaptability, and other attributes. Take the time to admire your children for who they are and to appreciate whatever they do well at their present stage of development.

If you do this, you won't have to worry about disciplinary measures driving a wedge between you and your children. Your kids will still look forward to seeing you because, on the whole, they feel safe, loved, and appreciated when they are with you.

A Comparison of Two Families

To help you better understand the concept, let's contrast two fictitious families. The Discontents have a lot of problems with their children, who fight, disobey rules, and isolate themselves from the rest of the family. The children from the Glad family have their typical problems with growing up but for the most part are well behaved, like being part of the family, and obey the household rules. So what makes the Glads and the Discontents different?

If you could sneak behind the walls of these two families' homes, you would see quite a difference in the way that the parents relate to the children. If you could observe one hundred interactions between Mr. and Mrs. Discontent and their children, you could expect that about 70 percent of the interactions were negative or of a corrective nature while 30 percent of the interactions were positive. In effect, because of the amount of negative interactions, the children find that it is more comfortable avoiding their parents. The parents, in effect, lose power to influence the children. The circumstances with the Glad family are different. With these parents, 70 percent of the interactions are positive and 30 percent are negative or corrective. Parents like Mr. and Mrs. Glad have power to influence their children because they help them feel valued.

Now, you may ask, if Mr. and Mrs. Discontent wanted to become more like Mr. and Mrs. Glad, how could they ignore their children's misbehavior? They can't. Instead, such parents actually have to make an asserted effort to make more positive time with the children so they can change the proportion of positive to negative interactions. Discontent-style parents typically ignore the children when they are behaving themselves. They are not taking advantage of the opportunity to build a more positive relationship with their children.

Avoid Excessive Punishments

Causing bodily harm, isolating children for long periods of time, depriving them of food or water, or causing them to be degraded and humiliated are inappropriate and abusive.

Many child-rearing experts frown upon physical punishment under any circumstances. They believe that inflicting physical pain to teach children lessons about their behavior only teaches them that it's okay to hit or hurt people when you're angry. Parents who hit may get short-term obedience, these experts say, but they're breeding future violence and aggression. Besides, there are more effective ways to discipline.

Other psychologists, while agreeing with this last point, see nothing wrong with an occasional controlled smack on the hand or swat on the butt. Control is essential, however. Lashing out in a moment of fury or frustration doesn't build character. Hitting again and again because you've run out of patience or can no longer contain pent up emotions is abusive. If you lose control while spanking a youngster, seek help.

I'm always amazed to hear parents say they spanked their children because they wouldn't stop crying. Do they really expect a child to stop crying while they were inflicting pain?

If you must hit, don't use belts, paddles, switches or other weapons. Because you have no way of knowing how hard you're hitting, you're more likely to injure children. What's more, the only reason for using these implements is to inflict additional pain, and any parent who sets out to hurt their children needs to examine their motives and take immediate steps to change the way they parent. Threats, especially absurd ones such as "I'll get new kids who love me" or "You'll never see Grandma again," should also be avoided. Other than scaring your children, these threats serve no constructive purpose.

Some parents use threats and excessive punishments to scare their children into compliance. But fear is an ineffective teacher. Although it will keep kids in line on a day to day basis, they'll rarely become true believers in the values you're using fear to instill. In fact, they're apt to reject or rebel against those values the first chance they get. Because your children aren't internalizing your standards and adhering to them for their own sake, you're forced to continue threatening and punishing in order to get your message across.

It's more effective to capitalize on your natural power to influence children's values and behaviors. That power stems from the strength of your relationship with your children and their desire to please you. When you show your children that you love and approve of them, they meet your standards in order to maintain your love and continue receiving your approval. Your encouragement, praise, attentiveness, and unconditional commitment helps them feel close to you and good about themselves, and youngsters who feel that way are more likely to obey your rules and follow your lead on moral issues. Indeed, the more you do to build your children's confidence and sense of self-worth, the more you'll influence their behavior and values.

Know What Type of Discipline Is Appropriate for Your Child's Age

Make sure your expectations for your children, and your disciplinary measures, are compatible with your child's age group. Punishing a one-year-old for holding his spoon incorrectly is pointless. There is no incentive, threat, or bribe that can make him do what he is not yet developmentally ready to do. Likewise, having a fifteen-year-old sit in a time-out chair because she stayed out past curfew is ludicrous. Time out is a tool for helping young children learn self-control. Grounding, taking away a privilege, and charging a fine to be subtracted from their allowance are more logical consequences for out-of-line adolescents. Likewise, sitting down, discussing rules, negotiating penalties, and drawing up behavior contracts work well with teens and older children but not with younger ones who have a limited cognitive ability to plan ahead.

Good Relationships Are Built Deliberately

Building a relationship doesn't happen by accident. Most effective parents are conscious of what they are doing to strengthen their relationship with their children. They can tell you specific ways they build rapport and let the children know they are loved. The more support and praise you give another person, the more support and praise you will receive in return. This is true for both your children and your ex-spouse.

If your fourteen-year-old's father helps him with a scouting project, express your appreciation. Let your kids' full-time mom know how well behaved they were when you took them out to dinner or how terrific they looked when you came to pick them up for a visit. Making a conscious effort to give credit when it's due will improve the coparenting relationship you have with your ex-spouse. And that will rub off on your children. After all, former mates are human, and like all human beings, they're inclined to continue behaviors that are recognized and rewarded. Thus, praising positive parenting brings more of the same.

The point I am trying to make is important. Your effectiveness in strengthening your relationships will be greater if you know what you are trying to do. To help you become more conscious of what you are doing, I suggest you complete the following exercise.

EXERCISE: RELATIONSHIP BUILDING

Time yourself while completing this exercise. When you are ready to begin, write down five examples of what you consciously do to help build the relationship between your children and their other parent. If you have not completed your list in ten minutes, quit. Write the time you take to complete the exercise in the space provided at the end of your list.

1._____
2._____
3._____
4._____
5._____

Time: _____

After you finish reading this book, you might want to try this exercise again and list ten items instead of five. You will be surprised how much faster and more easily you will complete the exercise the second time.

Four Disciplinary Practices That Cause Problems for Divorced Parents

Divorced parents must deal with the same discipline challenges as all other parents—plus a few special ones of their own. These problems can lead to arguments and alienation if not handled carefully.

First Mistake: Trying to Impose Your Rules on the Other Parent

Remember our earlier discussion of consistency within the same parent versus consistency between parents. Does it logically follow that "My rules are better than your rules, so let's raise the children my way"? Such a statement may sound absurd, but it reflects how many parents feel.

Believing your rules and values are better than the other parent's will cause a power struggle with no winners. After the divorce is final, one parent does not want to be told by the other parent how they should raise the children. Doing so will cause a lot of resentment.

A parent who alienates this way generally wants total control over any situation involving her children and has a powerful need to dictate how they are raised. She also sincerely believes that her way of parenting is best. Of course, the targeted parent isn't easily convinced of this. And why should he be? Just imagine how angry and resentful you'd feel if your former mate made up a list of rules and disciplinary practices and expected you to follow them. Such an arrangement is unreasonable, unrealistic, and unworkable.

If you question your ex-spouse's parenting and you feel you really must say something, tactfully ask your ex-spouse it they would like a constructive suggestion. If the parent says "No," you should say no more. This can often prevent a fight.

You can ask diplomatically. For example, instead of just blurting out unsolicited criticism, try saying something like, "Sandy's really been argumentative lately, hasn't she? It's tough to deal with sometimes. But would you like a suggestion that I have found helpful?" Seeking the person's permission for the feedback gives him or her more of a sense of control and power. This way, your ex-spouse is less likely to get defensive and feel attacked.

Marge and Wally

"After a weekend with their dad," says Marge, the divorced mother of three elementary-school-aged sons, "my boys are completely out of control. At his house, they have no set bedtimes or mealtimes. They bathe if they feel like it, wear anything they want to, and don't have to pick up after themselves. Naturally, when they get home from their forty-eight-hour free-for-all, they're not the least bit interested in following my rules. All I hear is 'Dad lets us do this,' and 'Dad doesn't make us do that.' Wally's house is a full-service motel and amusement park. Mine's a prison. He's their pal. I'm the warden. I spend half the week trying to get the boys back on track, and when I finally do, they go on another visit!"

Second Mistake: Letting the Children Run Wild During Visits

As discussed earlier in this chapter, children need structure and familiar routines. They need limits and a clear idea of what to expect from you if they do or don't do what you expect of them. If you are the noncustodial parent, there is no faster way to make an enemy of your former mate than to impose no structure on your offspring during visits.

If you are a custodial parent who struggles to rein in your youngsters after visits with their noncustodial parent, you probably share Marge's frustration. You may picture your youngsters doing whatever they please during those visits and envy your ex's fun, fun, fun relationship with the kids. Or you may resent being cast as the bad guy when you try to settle them down. Perhaps you've started to dread parenting time.

If you feel furious at your former mate, it would certainly be understandable. After all, the entire burden of teaching values, socially acceptable behavior, and basic life skills shouldn't fall on your shoulders.

Helping Children Adjust after a Visit

Some children have difficulty adjusting to changes forced upon them by visits. Upon return, they may be restless and misbehave. Such behavior is not always the fault of the noncustodial parent. Some children have trouble adjusting to any change. They squawk about going to bed or getting off the couch. Nothing you can do will make them happy. To help lessen the blow, give your children a warning in advance that a change is forthcoming. Let them complain and moan. When the time comes to make the change, be firm but compassionate. You don't have to yell or get upset. Most important, stay calm and remind yourself that you do not have to always be responsible for their being unhappy at that moment. Many parents easily forget that your goal at this point is compliance and not happiness. If you remember this, you will get less upset by your child's whining.

Karl, the Weekend Drill Sergeant

Karl took his parenting responsibilities very seriously. He never missed a support payment or an opportunity to be with his kids. Every Friday Karl eagerly picked up his five children, who ranged in age from three-and-a-half to ten. The two oldest children started complaining to their mother about not wanting to visit. "Dad is mean. He calls us crybabies and stupid," said Vince. "He makes us watch the other kids," Jessica reports, "and if they're bad, we get punished." One weekend they both had to write "I will set a good example for my brothers and sisters" one hundred times. "We couldn't eat supper until we were finished," Vince states. And when Jessica complained, their father took away the sentences they'd already written and made them start over.

The mother, Jamie, was angry and felt protective as her children tearfully described their ordeal. Immediately, she was on the phone with Karl, angrily attacking his insensitivity. Karl counterattacked, feeling defensive and sincere in his love for the children. He acknowledged that he was strict because of their mother's laxity. "You let them get away with anything." The fight escalated until Jamie threatened to take Karl back to court. She hung up while Karl was still talking. Karl was angry and scared of the threat but was willing to fight her in court.

Third Mistake: Being a Harsh Weekend Disciplinarian

Problems also arise when a noncustodial parent believes his ex is a lax disciplinarian and tries to compensate by being extra strict during visits. Whether the strict parent is terrified that his kids will grow up to be criminals or convinced that constant vigilance and harsh punishments are proof of parental love and competence, he devotes virtually every moment of his parenting time to breaking his children's supposedly bad habits and teaching them to behave properly according to his unusually high standards. In his mind, the urgency of his mission—to shape character in the brief amount of time available to him—seems to justify the severe and ceaseless disciplinary measures he employs. "Sure, making Joey scrub the entire bathroom with a toothbrush is a little harsh," this sort of parent says, "but letting him become an inconsiderate slob who forgets to wipe out the tub after showering would be worse. This will teach him."

Unfortunately, there's a good chance it will also alienate him. If you try to compress a year's worth of discipline into two weekends a month, you're apt to come off as harsh, rigid, hypercritical, and barely human. Your kids could very well learn to hate you.

Certain that he's doing what's best for his youngsters, this drill-sergeant type of parent is perplexed and hurt when the children start complaining about him and refusing to visit. Such parents are blinded by their good intentions. He's sure his kids know how much he loves them. ("Why else would I devote so much time to setting them straight?" he asks.) He also believes he deserves thanks, not rejection, and accuses his former mate of turning the children against him when the truth is that he's alienating them himself. He can't see that he is overly critical and punitive, and he gets angry when someone points out how the children are reacting or someone questions his parenting skills. In his eagerness to raise perfect children, the superstrict parent loses sight of the fact that no one, young or old, likes to be around someone who constantly criticizes them.

Although children need structure and limits and consistently enforced consequences, that's not all they need. And if all they get is rules, restrictions, lectures, threats, and punishments from a parent who can't seem to be anything but harsh and critical, they'll want to avoid that parent. After all, children are not stupid. They will naturally gravitate towards the parent who—through a mixture of encouragement and instruction—helps them to feel confident, competent, and good about themselves.

Be realistic. You are not going to cram all of your values and discipline into your children during two weekend visits a month. They should leave the visits feeling good about you and the time they spent with you, not thinking, "Boy, am I glad to be outta there!"

In the example of Karl and Jamie, neither parent took the time to think about how the children would feel about them fighting over disciplinary issues. The children were caught in a dilemma with many unanswered questions. Should they continue to visit their father or stay home? How will the two oldest children feel the next time they see their father? Will the other children go on their next visit? What do the children do with their guilt for saying something to their mother? Maybe the children would have been better off if Jamie had thought of some of these questions before making her phone call. Though her feelings were understandable, she and the children might have been better off if she had first calmed down and thought about how she and Karl could work together to solve this problem.

Fourth Mistake: Blaming Your Ex-Spouse for Everything Your Child Does Wrong

Finally, divorced parents tend to be quick to blame their ex-spouse for any undesirable changes in their children's behavior. "If you weren't so critical (lenient, busy at work, wrapped up with your new boyfriend, etc.)," they claim, "then Billy wouldn't be fighting on the playground (failing French, wetting his bed, picking on his sisters, and so on)." Naturally, the accused parent feels attacked, becomes defensive, and retaliates in some fashion.

Always blaming bad behavior on parenting or the divorce itself has a similar effect. Believing in these explanations not only blinds you to other reasons your children might be acting up but can also lead to totally unnecessary arguments. You could even end up back in court only to discover that the changes in your child's behavior were typical for his age and not signs of post-traumatic stress or mistreatment by your ex.

As your children mature, you'll witness many changes in their behavior. They'll go through relatively placid phases when they're compliant and eager to please, as well as tumultuous stages when they're more often moody and defiant than not. You'll tangle with tantrum throwers, toddlers who say no to everything, argumentative adolescents, and more. In fact, it will sometimes seem that just when you've adjusted to one set of quirks, your children take on an entirely new cache of bewildering characteristics.

That's how children are. All children. As a child development expert who influenced my early counseling (and parenting) career once put it, "even under the best of circumstances, kids go a little nuts every six months or so." Coping with their ever-changing needs, interests, and sensitivities comes with the territory of parenthood.

Learning About Childhood Development Can Prevent Misunderstandings

Kids go through predictable developmental stages. If you learn about those developmental milestones, you'll know what you can reasonably expect from children of various ages. Reading books and attending workshops on child development or effective parenting can teach you many things:

- When children begin to understand the difference between right and wrong
- How five-year-olds express emotions
- Why an eight-year-old might tell lies
- How much household responsibility a twelve-year-old can handle

They'll also show you that some problems aren't anyone's fault.

In addition to helping you differentiate between behavior that's normal at a particular stage of development and problem behavior that requires special attention, books and courses on child development usually offer a lot of sound advice and may even have suggestions for handling special circumstances such as divorce.

Parents are usually good about taking time to learn about their children's development when they are infants and toddlers. However, after the children turn five or six, many parents spend less time learning about their children's development. This is the reason there are so many baby books and few books about older children, particularly about adolescence. When problems start to occur, parents are quick to blame the other parent rather than trying to learn if the misbehavior is typical for their child's age. Trying to learn about a child's normal development can prevent a lot of mislaid blame on the other parent. If these readily available resources don't provide the answers you're seeking or if your children's misbehavior persists and begins to cause family problems, I recommend getting professional help.

TIPS ON DISCIPLINE

- Listen to yourself. Do you express to your children some of your excitement and pride in them at least once a day? Children thrive in an atmosphere of enthusiastic love.

- Praise your children more often than you criticize them.

- If you must criticize, comment on behavior, not character. (For example, "Melissa, you know better than to eat ice cream with your fingers," not "Oh, Melissa, you are such a disgusting slob!")

- Do not call your children derogatory names.

- Do not make negative comparisons between your child and their other parent. (For more about this, see chapter 5.)

- Always make up after a punishment. Praise your child when they have complied with your punishment.

- When you must punish or discipline, complete the punishment at least two hours before they go to the other parent's home. Never end a visit during a punishment because the punishment, rather than the good times, is what the child will remember until the next visit. The child may even refuse to return.

- During visits, don't expect to compress all your teachings and discipline into a weekend. This is not only impossible, but it is good reason for children to dread the next visit.

- For better or worse, children are always changing. Their changes are not always caused by the divorce or what happens in the other household.

- If you see your child behaving in a way that you don't understand, try talking to your ex to see if they see the same behavior. Rather than blaming, speak with concern and a desire to understand the behavior. Decide how you can work together to change the behavior.

- Regularly ask yourself, "How effective is my discipline? Is it producing only short-term results or actually teaching my children to be more responsible, socially conscious, acceptable, and accepting human beings?"

Be a Mentor to Your Children, Not Just a Disciplinarian

All parents have an idealized image in their mind of the perfect child. Then there is reality, which often falls short of your ideals. As a parent, you must accept your children and offer them loving guidance. The children must believe they are valued for who they are rather than feel inadequate for not living up to your ideals.

Children are frequently faced with new and unique situations that they don't know how to handle because they lack maturity and experience to respond appropriately. Because of their inexperience, children will make poor decisions that could make it appear to you as if they deliberately misbehaved. This can be confusing for both you and your children.

Parents must be mentors to their children. A mentor is a teacher who leads by example. Take time to explain and interpret confusing and troubling events to your children. Mentoring is an excellent occasion for creating closeness between you and your child. It will help them grow and make sense of the world. Above all, try to set a good example by your own behavior.

Elise and Carrie

Carrie is a usually well-behaved ten-year-old, but today was different. Elise could see from Carrie's expression that something was wrong, but Carrie obviously wasn't ready to talk. Elise patiently waited until Carrie finally confessed, "Robin and I got into trouble today and we were sent to Mr. Troy's office." Elise was shocked. "What happened?" Carrie's voice quivered while she slowly started to explain. "Mom, I didn't know that Robin had taken money off Mrs. Malloy's desk. I didn't see her take it." "Carrie, calm down and tell me what happened." "We were in the lunch room and Mrs. Malloy was coming over to our table when Robin put the money in my hand. Mom, I didn't know what to do! Mrs. Malloy caught me with the money and I didn't take it. Robin gave it to me. We had to go to Mr. Troy's office, and he said he was going to call you. I think I'm supposed to get a detention."

Elise had to make a decision about what to do with Carrie. Should she punish Carrie for having the money or take this occasion to give her some advice about what she should have done when Robin gave her the money? Elise knew that Carrie needed her understanding and help. Carrie had been in a unique situation that she didn't know how to handle. She knew she was in a bad situation and Robin had done wrong.

Wisely, Elise decided that Carrie needed mentoring and help rather than punishment. She took this opportunity to instruct Carrie and strengthen their relationship.

Give the Gift of Acceptance

Children deserve to be valued for who they actually are and not made to feel inadequate for failing to live up to an ideal that probably came into existence before they did and doesn't account for their uniqueness. This sort of acceptance, along with your loving guidance, is the greatest gift you can give your children. It enables them to grow and develop into healthy, happy, well-adjusted adults.

Janet and Peter

Janet is very conscientious about her parenting. While trying to be sensitive to her children's needs, she expresses strong opinions about what is best for them. "No one gave me the values and self-esteem to make smart choices when I was growing up," she explains. Jane is determined that things will be different for her girls, Valerie, fourteen, and Natalie, ten. Because Janet is a recovering alcoholic, she insists that Valerie attend Alateen. Valerie complains bitterly, but Janet is unyielding.

Visits with their father, Peter, had been going well until Janet learned that Peter had been taking the children to a truck stop for dinner. Janet did not believe the truck stop was a proper setting for her children. "They shouldn't be exposed to the truckers' filthy mouths and see the way those poor waitresses are pinched and harassed," she said. Janet was also upset about Peter keeping *Playboy* and *Penthouse* magazines in his night table drawer, "where anyone could find them." On another occasion, Valerie mentioned to Janet that her father allowed them to watch a movie that Janet knew had an explicit love scene. She was enraged by Peter's lack of morals and sensitivity. Janet lectured Peter on the proper way to raise the children and demanded that he change his ways. When he didn't, she requested the court to limit Peter's visits, firmly believed she was protecting Valerie and Natalie. The court denied her request.

Values: Who Has the Right to Judge?

Religion, nutrition, sex education, household rules, neatness, when and how to punish children. In these and other areas like them, parents tend to have a strong personal sense of what's right or wrong, and a limited tolerance for anyone who doesn't share their point of view. This is a frequent source of heated conflict between parents. There may be differences in religious beliefs or what is considered safe recreation. One young father made national headlines when he sued for custody because he believed it was wrong for his son to be in day care while the boy's mother attended college courses. I've also known mothers who were prepared to go to court because dad allowed their son to listen to heavy metal music and dads who wanted mom declared unfit because she hired a babysitter with streaked hair and a nose ring.

Their responses may sound like overreactions. But extreme behavior is commonplace when moral or ethical matters are at stake. Wars have been fought over them. Protesters have been carted off to jail because of them. Fueled by righteous indignation, people throughout the ages have fought with all they had for what they believed were worthy causes. And what cause could seem worthier than making sure your children are raised with the right values or sheltered from the wrong ones?

For example, Janet sincerely believed that she, and not her ex-husband, was best suited to teach the children proper values. She believed Alateen would give the children proper guidance about alcohol abuse and that eating at truck stops would subvert their morals. Unfortunately, Janet's insistence that the children follow her values ultimately backfired, causing them to feel alienated from both her and her ex-husband.

Janet implied that Peter's values were demeaning toward women and damaging to the children. The girls could see that their mother had a point, but they saw her obsession as vindictive and fanatical, and they pulled away from her. Since they were unwilling to put their faith in or emulate either parent, as the girls got older, they took their cues from other sources, most notably their peers who seemed to think that smoking and drinking were perfectly acceptable. This was precisely the opposite of the message that Janet had wanted to impart to her daughters.

Values Conflicts: A Major Source of Alienation

Value differences escalate into value conflicts when one or both of you believe that your values or methods for teaching children right from wrong are best and try to force the targeted parent to act in accordance with your moral code. Value conflicts lead to alienation when you attempt to convince your children that their other parent's values are wrong, bad, perverse, or dangerous.

Like Janet and Peter, you and your former mate may have decidedly different opinions on at least one personal value or moral issue. Perhaps you attend church regularly and expect your children to do the same, but your ex-spouse, who places less emphasis on religious training, lets the kids sleep in on his Sundays. Or maybe one of you is a recent convert to low-fat cooking who carefully monitors the children's diets, while the other is a junk-food junkie who considers bologna on white bread, corn chips, and ice cream the perfectly balanced meal. Or your standards of modesty may differ. I've had clients who were appalled because their ex walked around in his underwear or allowed her children into the bathroom while she was showering. The presumably perverse parties saw nothing wrong with their behavior, and in fact, wondered if their "ridiculously uptight" accusers might be damaging their kids psychologically.

It probably is not news to you that you and your ex-spouse have these sorts of values differences. In some instances, arguing about moral and child-rearing issues may have contributed to the dissolution of your marriage. Those old conflicts often continue with added emotional intensity once you've been through the heartache and upheaval of a divorce. In other cases, more recent changes in your own or your ex's belief systems create new values gaps—and new conflicts. Whether you've returned to your Baptist roots or embarked upon a recovery program, embraced a new-age philosophy or gained the confidence to speak up when you disagree with someone, the attitude upgrades you've made since your divorce can put you and your ex on a collision course. But no matter where or how long ago the conflict originated, when deeply held beliefs or strong convictions clash, the ensuing battles tend to be loud and long. They can also be alienating.

Although no one can fault you for wanting your children to grow up with a healthy set of values, criticizing your ex-spouse's values in front of your children or badgering them into agreeing that yours are better is counterproductive. It leads the children to needless anxiety and confusion, as well as a cloudy sense of right and wrong.

Just witnessing your arguments and power struggles over whose beliefs are better and which behaviors are morally preferable causes children considerable distress. They feel pulled in opposite directions, pressured to choose sides, and miserable about the possible repercussions of their choice. No matter what they do, they will end up disappointing one of you—and young children in particular have a powerful need to please you both.

At some point, your children will make up their own minds about whose standards and values they will follow as adults. But while they are still dependent on you and their other parent to clothe, feed, shelter, love, and protect them, they have no choice but to try to make you both happy (or at least neither of you angry.) The last thing they need is to have either or both of you make them feel bad or guilty for being good by their other parent's standards.

TIPS ON VALUES

- Values are often passionately held. Don't expect to change your ex-spouse's values. You can't.

- Do not try to convince your children that your ex-spouse's values are worse than yours. This will cause alienation and confusion.

- It does not harm children to be exposed to more than one set of values as they grow up. They are exposed to different values at their friends' homes and every time they turn on the TV.

- Make it clear to your children what your values are and how they are expected to behave when they are with you. As they reach adulthood, they will choose their own values. The more positive your relationship with them, the more likely they will be influenced by your values.

It is tempting for targeted parents to retaliate against the alienating parent with defensive allegations and counterattacks when their values and standards are attacked. The targeted parent must try to avoid the temptation. So instead of taking the offensive and laying on guilt, acknowledge your kids' dilemma. Convey empathy for the confusion or anxiety they're apt to feel. And then, to reduce that anxiety, make your rules and expectations clear. Whether your standards are strict or lenient or somewhere in between, stand firm about what you will or won't accept from your children when they are with you. Assure them that it's okay that they live by different rules when they are with the other parent. And you don't have to be in sync with your ex-spouse 100 or even 10 percent of the time. Exposing children to two different moral codes or methods of discipline will not necessarily harm them. And once again, have faith in the strength of your relationship with your children. It cannot be emphasized enough that a powerful deterrent to alienation is your children seeing you as a source for building their self-confidence and self-esteem.

9

Parenting Time and Children's Activities

"I don't care if you are only fifteen minutes late. When the court says you are to be here at 6:00, it means 6:00, not fifteen minutes later or earlier. Now would you just leave! We have to be somewhere."

Parenting time (or visitation) is important. The amount of time children spend with their noncustodial parent is often a barometer of alienation. Those who have regular contact and meaningful relationships with both parents benefit in many ways. This is why courts encourage frequent visits, providing the tensions between parents don't harm the children.

But parenting time can be messy. The transfer of children from one parent to another and phone calls to make or change visiting arrangements provide the perfect breeding ground for conflicts and power struggles.

A question frequently asked is, "Why wouldn't a parent want to visit his children?" Dudley (1991) examined the reasons why eighty-four fathers had infrequent or no contact with their children. He learned that thirty-three fathers identified the relationship with their former spouse as the major obstacle, twenty-two described personal reasons (substance abuse, job demands, girlfriends), thirteen said the children were too old or too busy to visit, and the final twelve complained that the children lived too far away. Of the thirty-three fathers whose spouse was the major obstacle, eleven complained about the court's failure to enforce or increase parenting time.

For parents, just seeing each other can stir strong feelings that they know must be controlled for the children. The tension grows when the alienating parent begins scrutinizing the targeted parent's words and actions during the preparation for the visit. Sensing the scrutiny, the targeted parent becomes defensive. Both become overly sensitive and ready to pounce on each other.

Now you need to learn about the different ways visits are used to cause or reinforce alienation and what tactics you can use to prevent or resolve these problems before they become insurmountable. Unfortunately, there are a lot ways for one or both parents to use parenting time as a weapon against the other parent. As you will learn, even the children can get into the act and cause problems.

The Courts Do Not Equate Parenting Time with Child Support

When courts make decisions about parenting time, they begin with the assumption that all children should have an opportunity to have a healthy relationship with both parents and nothing or nobody should interfere.

Implications for Custodial Parents

"He doesn't pay his support on time, so why should I worry about his visits?" is the battle cry often heard to justify a parent's refusal to allow the ex-spouse to visit. Courts do not accept this argument. In most jurisdictions, you cannot withhold visits because your ex-spouse is behind in child support. These issues being separate, your must continue to allow visits and discuss with your attorney about what to do about the child support.

Because child support is an issue between you and your ex-spouse, your children should not have to hear about your ex-spouse not paying support, just as your children don't need to hear all about other financial problems, such as credit card debt. True, children should have a basic, realistic understanding about family finances. They need to hear, "We can't afford to buy . . ." but not, "We can't afford that because your father doesn't give us enough money." The children, like you, must face the reality that divorced parents don't usually live as well as when they were married

Implications for Noncustodial Parents

Parents have asked "Why should I continue to pay child support if I can't see my kids?" The argument against this logic is that the money is for the children's care, which continues regardless of whether or not parenting time is occurring. The children still need to be fed and clothed. The court views withholding child support under these circumstances as punishing the children rather than the uncooperative parent. Unfortunately, the court does not have effective sanctions when a parent refuses to cooperate with visits. Ideally, any sanctions should not harm the children or the children's relationship with either parent.

Some states have laws allowing for an involuntary change of custody when a parent refuses to allow parenting time. There is no research on how an involuntary change of custody affects the children's adjustment and their relationship with both parents. Potentially, an involuntary change of custody is risky. The risk lies in not understanding how the children perceive and feel towards the new custodial parent when forced to live with them. When the new custodial parent receives custody, it is essential for that parent and the children to receive counseling together. The children and parent are likely to have problems integrating into a new family. This is especially true if stepchildren are involved.

Managing Visits

Most cases of alienation involve some problem with parenting time. Parenting time is a commodity that has value for both parents as well as the children. The time spent with either parent is much like a rubber band that is pulled in opposite directions by both parents and is ready to snap. Someone will win and someone will lose the struggle. Strength has nothing to do with who has the power. Instead, the power rests with the parent or child who says "no."

"I Don't Care About Your Business Trip. The Court Says You're Supposed to Take Jackie That Weekend!"

Many problems with visits would be eliminated if parents followed the court order. Ideally, time and activities should be negotiable between both parents—and the children will sometimes request schedule changes for their own reasons. In practice, most courts do not care what parents do with visits as long as it is legal and everyone agrees. If parents cannot agree on parenting time, the court has no choice but to order a rigid schedule.

Parents who rigidly follow the court ordered parenting time schedule may often do so to satisfy their own needs rather than those of their children or ex-spouse. A request for a change in the schedule may be met with an angry rebuttal, "Why should I let you bring Tracy home late? You wouldn't give me the same courtesy." The rejecting parent may feel a sense of power in being able to say "no" to the other parent's request.

Conversely, making excessive requests to change scheduled parenting times is often disruptive and should be avoided.

Watching parents argue about changes in the parenting time schedule can remind your children of past fights. They will silently sit back, hoping that neither parent will notice their presence. The children learn to dread the question "Do you want to visit this weekend?" The children are now feeling uneasy because they know they must choose a side. Whatever side they choose, someone will be disappointed. The children's desires get lost. The children may even think that the fights are their fault because they have done something wrong. To keep peace, the children learn to keep quiet and not ask for any changes in visits. They learn that requests for changing a visit have become a trigger for more fighting. They know they cannot be late returning home or give in to offers to go someplace special on a weekend different than one already scheduled. Sadly, the children learn to keep their desires to themselves.

TIPS ON CHANGING THE PARENTING TIME SCHEDULE

- If you want to reschedule a visit or bring the children home late, clear it with the other parent first before asking your children about it. Don't get them excited over a special event that will be vetoed when the other parent doesn't agree to change the schedule.

- Don't get your children involved in fights over visits. Don't make them feel caught in the middle.

- What seems to you like an important reason for changing the parenting time schedule may seem unimportant to your ex-spouse. Don't assume that your ex has to agree with your opinion.

- It's okay to ask for your children's input but not in a way that makes them feel that they must choose one parent over the other. Be aware of how your voice or choice of words can influence your child's feelings.

- Asking whether the children would rather see their other parent this weekend versus next weekend is different from continually trying to discourage them from visiting. Also, as mentioned in chapter 5, frequent requests for schedule changes can be viewed as a harassing intrusion in your ex-spouse's life and can stir considerable resentment.

- Don't tempt your child with a fun activity that conflicts with a scheduled visit before getting the okay from the other parent.

"I Don't Want to Visit, and You Can't Make Me!"

The most common symptom of alienation is the child's unwavering insistence on not wanting to visit the targeted parent. Behind the child's cutting words is often an obsessed alienator who has many reasons for refusing visits. Some of their reasons may sound reasonable while others are ridiculous. A teen in love would rather be with the boyfriend than seeing Dad, or an important ball game perhaps conflicts with Mom's weekend. Even good reasons for changing visits should only be an occasional interruption to a consistent pattern. When the excuses become a pattern, or you can reasonably expect that someone is trying to alienate you from your children.

The noncustodial parent has good reason for being suspicious when the other parent cancels visits frequently. The cancellations are a reminder of the noncustodial parent's power over the time he or she spends together with the children. Non-custodial parents fear an abuse of power because there is little they can do about it other than file an expensive contempt charge against the custodial parent for failure to cooperate with parenting time. The noncustodial parent must trust the custodial parent's motives and judgment for canceling a visit. For example, they have to believe that a child's illness was serious enough to justify canceling a visit. (For guidelines on how to judge whether a child is too ill to visit, see chapter 10.) If you and your ex-spouse distrust each other, reasons for withholding visits may be seem like excuses.

"Sweetheart, Do You Really Want to Visit Daddy This Weekend?"

Courts differ on the matter of how much control a child has on deciding whether or not to visit a parent. Some courts insist that the noncustodial parent's right to have a visit has precedence over the wishes of the child. Other courts argue that children who have reached a certain age, say sixteen, know what they want and should exercise greater control over parenting time. Still other courts are vague about the child's power to decide. The important point is that the children's right to decide should be part of the court order and not up to the discretion of the custodial parent. If the court order is vague, mediation can help resolve the dispute and is less expensive than going back to court.

Courts maintain the position that you should not offer your children choices that are contrary to court orders. Doing so sabotages the court's authority. In fact, many judges will take your defiance as a personal insult. They will reject your argument that you cannot force your children to visit. The court may remind you that children have no choice about attending school. You do not ask your children if they want to attend school; you tell them to be up at 7:00 to catch the bus by 8:00. So why should your authority be any less in demanding parenting time?

As a parent, it is difficult to know what to do when your children start complaining about visits while the court insists you follow through with the parenting time order. You may want to support your children's wishes while knowing you could be held in contempt for not enforcing the court order. Your desire to please your children and your frustration for having to enforce the parenting time order will incite your anger. Your anger may be inappropriately directed toward your ex-spouse for insisting upon seeing the children at the court-ordered time. However, to avoid the possibility of alienation, do not give your children a false impression that they have a choice about parenting time when, in fact, there is no choice.

Imagine you are told by the government that you have a choice about whether or not to pay taxes for a year. The reason for the government's offer is to stimulate the economy. Initially you feel excited by all the ways you can save or spend your money. Later you learn that the government rescinds the generous offer. All your dreams fade while you feel disappointment and anger toward the government. You may realize your feelings are irrational because you really have not lost any money. In fact, you may have thought that the idea of not paying taxes for a year was bad considering the budget deficit. Regardless, you are resentful because the government has taken away your choice to not pay taxes.

Your children will experience similar feelings if they are given a choice about whether to visit and then that choice is taken away. Suppose the noncustodial parent gets angry about not seeing the children and brings the other parent back to court. Now the children must adhere to the parenting time schedule. They understandably become angry and resentful. They may unfairly blame the noncustodial parent for wanting to see them and taking their choices away. The visits may be strained and uncomfortable for both the children and the parent. This can cause alienation.

If you are the custodial parent, you have a responsibility to ensure that this does not happen. The message is worth repeating: Children who are actively involved with both parents are more likely to be better adjusted than alienated children.

"If The Kids Don't Want to See You, What Can I Do?"

Rather than taking responsibility for interfering with visits, many alienating parents place the blame on the children. Do any of these tactics sound familiar?

- "Isn't it a shame that the children don't want to visit you?" The alienating parent pretends to be a sympathetic harbinger of bad news.

- "My son knows what he wants. I'm not getting involved." This is a passive attempt to alienate. The alienating parent appears neutral and uninvolved, denying any responsibility for the child's behavior.

- "I can't force them to visit! If they don't want to go, that's their choice." The alienating parent professes lack of control over the children's wishes.

- "Nobody, not even the court, is not going to tell my children they have to visit you. They have rights too." The alienating parent doesn't believe they need a court order to do what they want. In fact, the alienating parent is often self-righteous in their belief that they are defending their children's rights, so they feel justified in defying the court orders.

This final stand-off between parents usually occurs with the obsessed alienator because nothing anyone does or says will change their position. They get angry when anyone, including the court, challenges their authority to make this decision. How the targeted parent feels is completely unimportant to them. The targeted parent is now helpless because he usually can't get his point across to the alienated child, and the alienating parent has made her position clear that she is not going to do anything to help. The only choice the targeted parent usually has in this situation is to return to court.

"Mom, I Had a Great Time with Dad!"

Children like to talk about what a good time they had on a visit after returning home. They will do this only if they know they are not hurting their mom because they had fun with their dad. They may be excited about recounting their weekend. Yet hearing their stories about their good time can cause a parent to feel envious of the children's weekend and the relationship they have with the other parent. Though the parent tries to hide the hurt, children are sensitive and may see a disappointed look or the forced smile on the parent's face. Children sensing there is something wrong learn to watch what they say. When your children notice your feelings, they may become cautious before expressing any more enthusiasm about the visit. They do not want to add to your hurt.

Children will react differently when they sense your reactions to their having a good time. They could feel guilty, thinking that your pain was their fault. Or they could get angry, blaming their other parent for hurting you. Whatever the reasons are for your reaction, the children should not have to dampen their excitement and lose out on sharing their good time with you. Your children should be expected to have a good time during their visit and should have the right to express their pleasure about a visit without feeling guilty for hurting your feelings. If you find yourself feeling jealous or hurt by your child's account of their weekend, rather than lying about your feelings assure your children that you are glad they had a good time on a visit but you also feel sad that you couldn't share the good time with them. Children will learn to understand how you can have two conflicting feelings. Give your children support. Let them know that having a good time on a visit is important to you. Let the children spontaneously tell you about their visit, but do not pump them for information.

Feeling jealous of the time your children spend with your ex-spouse is miserable. There is no fixed deadline after which you should no longer feel jealous about your ex-spouse's activities. If you are not healing and you continue to feel hurt or bitter by your children's account of their visit, you should consider getting counseling. Your children should not be stifled because you are not healing.

Lynn and Jacob

Lynn was remarried and had two stepchildren. Her son from a previous marriage, Jacob, was scheduled to visit his father on Labor Day weekend. Lynn was bitter about Jacob's visit because her family had a traditional family picnic on Labor Day weekend, and she knew her ex-husband would refuse her request to change the visit. Though Lynn did not want to hurt Jacob, the family decided to have the picnic at Sea World. Unfortunately, her stepchildren teased Jacob about not going to Sea World. Jacob was hurt by the stepchildren's teasing. He no longer wanted to visit his father, but instead wanted to go to Sea World. Jacob started complaining to his father about feeling bored and not wanting to visit.

"Dad, I Can't Go to Disneyland. It's Mom's Weekend."

Both parents should know the children's parenting time schedule. The schedule outlined by the court will allow you an opportunity to plan vacations and spend recreational time with your children. There should be no confusion where the children are going on any particular week or weekend.

Parents know how easy it is to entice children to spend time with them. They know that their children will want to go anywhere they think will be the most fun. A parent dangling a temptation like a trip to the amusement park or the beach will knowingly cause the children to feel torn between wanting to go and wanting to spend time with their other parent. This is a common alienating tactic. Children will typically not empathize with their targeted parent's dilemma. Instead, they are driven by their immediate desire to have fun. The children are frustrated and angry when their parent insists on the visit that interferes with something else they would rather do. The parent who tells the children they cannot go will be vilified while the other parent is adored. Unless you intent to alienate, do not invite your children on a special activity when you know it interferes with the other parent's time with the children unless you ask the parent first. I wouldn't even say anything about the activity to the child until to talk to your ex-spouse. If you say something to your children first and the other parent says "no," you are setting her up for your child's wrath and hurt. This is not fair to either your ex-spouse or children.

Jacob's dilemma is a common occurrence for children of divorced parents. He wants to experience a feeling of family unity by participating in family gatherings and traditions. Lynn and her ex-husband could have prevented Jacob's distress by asking him what he wanted to do that weekend. Jacob's father would have had to set aside his feelings and place his child's needs before his own; Jacob could have visited him a different weekend instead. Lynn could have been more sensitive about planning such an exciting event on a weekend when Jacob was not home. Lynn could have argued that not going to Sea World would have been unfair to her stepchildren, but this would have been a groundless argument because there are always other weekends.

Parents rarely think about hurting their children when making a generous offer for a weekend activity. They justify the invitation by saying they are just thinking of the children. They may criticize the other parent, arguing that he or she is the one who is being selfish and insensitive to the children's needs. The targeted parent is in a no-win situation. Whatever the parent does, allowing the children to go for the weekend or insisting on the parenting time, he or she loses.

Alienation occurs because the offending parent sets up a temptation that interferes with a visit. This puts a strain on the relationship between the children and the nonoffending parent. If the nonoffending parent insists on having the entitled visit, the children may feel resentful. If that parent allows the children to go for the weekend, he or she will miss the time spent with the children. This would not be so bad if the parents agreed to make-up the time. Very often, however, this is not what happens. Frequently the offending parent will not trade weekends. Instead, he or she blames the nonoffending parent for the trouble they are causing.

Whether your children are home or on a visit, both parents should know if your children are leaving town for an extended time. For example, if your son or daughter was going on a class trip to Washington D.C., telling the other parent is a courtesy.

Special occasions require parents to work together by negotiating changes with visits. The parent's animosity should not interfere with the children's desire to attend a special function. Your children should be given an opportunity to express their feelings about attending the function without interference or coaxing from either parent. The parents should not get into a fight trying to convince the children what to do. Both parents need to support the children by either negotiating an exchange of weekends or leaving well enough alone. For your children to feel comfortable about their choice, their parents must set aside theirfeelings and consider their children. Otherwise, the children are again victimized.

"I Have a Date. Why Do I Have to Visit Dad This Weekend?"

When children become teenagers, their social lives become more independent from their parents. Visits can become an annoyance when it interferes with their social life, especially when they fall in love. Almost any teen would rather be with a boyfriend or girlfriend than with a parent, especially if they don't have access to their friend because of distance. Parents need to empathize with their children's desires and not take personally what appears as rejection. Instead, the noncustodial parent needs to be flexible and willing to negotiate. If you start fighting about the visit, you may get your visit, but what have you won if your teen's attitude makes the visit miserable? Most often there is no reason why a son or daughter could not leave for a date from Dad's home.

"Mom, Will You Come Get Me? I'm Bored."

Rescuing is a subtle alienating tactic because the rescuing parent appears to others as a concerned and caring parent who is only trying to do what's best for the children. Any responsible parents knows of their responsibility to protect their children from potential harm or threat to their safety, even if the threat is from the ex-spouse. When parents believe they have reason to be concerned, they will be vigilant and listen closely for anything that is a potential threat or sounds out of the ordinary. At the same time, wise parents realize that their children's account of what happens on a visit may be misunderstood or distorted. They will be cautious before reacting to what children say.

As children grow older and mature, they are allowed greater freedom and discretion over their behavior. Though a parent becomes less protective as the children grow older, the responsible parent continues to maintain a vigilant eye. Children, at any age, should sense their parent's supervision even if they don't literally see their parents watching them.

A parent going through a bitter divorce has a lot of hurt that will influence their perceptions about the children's safety, the other parent's competencies, or the child's sense of responsibility. This is particularly true when the parent has been abused and questions whether or not the children are safe and properly supervised by the other parent. The embittered parent may believe that there is a threat to the children's safety when they are with the other parent.

Sensing the parent's apprehension, the children may also start to fear being with the other parent. They approach the visit with a critical eye, looking for any fault in the visiting parent. Their demeanor is reserved, judging the parent's every move. They may be looking for you to make a blunder: drinking a beer, having a girlfriend over, or getting angry. In the most nightmarish cases, kids panic at the thought of visiting; they shriek, cry, run away, or call home begging to be rescued. Most often, however, the only fault your children find with the visit is boredom. As soon as they feel uncomfortable, for whatever reason, they call home asking for their mother to pick them up. Mom, sitting home worrying, is quick to jump into her car and come to the children's rescue.

Upon mother's arrival, she frantically walks up to the door. Seeing her children, mom is quick to reach out to comfort them. The children immediately feel relief from any discomfort, reinforcing in their minds that something was wrong. Consequently, the children are alienated from their father. Yet if left alone, the child would usually have calmed down and adjusted to the situation within a short time.

A good example of this occurrence is when your children start daycare.

Remember the guilt the first time you dropped your children off at day-care? You may have had to pull your son or daughter off your leg. Most parents know that feeling of walking guiltily away from the daycare believing that you are leaving your children in a hysterical frenzy in the arms of strangers. Later, you call the school expecting to hear the worst. Instead, you hear the teacher's reassuring voice, saying your child is doing fine. Now suppose that, when your child got hysterical about being dropped off, you decided to take your child home rather than having them stay at the center. Immediately, your children calm down and feel relieved as they leave the daycare center. Their immediate relief reinforces in your children the desire to avoid the center. The next time you return to the center, you can expect your children to have greater difficulty leaving you and staying at the center. Without intending to do so, you have made the problem worse because you rescued the children when there was no threat to their safety.

If you are too quick to rescue the children, you will make their fear of staying with the other parent worse. Taking such a drastic action can cause alienation. For this reason, parents should not rescue their children from the other parent unless there is a real threat. The children wanting to come home because they are bored is not a reason for rescuing.

If your ex-spouse and child have an argument, you should let them work their problems out and not interfere. How can your children develop self-confidence when they are swept away every time something goes wrong? Interference sends the message that something is wrong with the father and your child isn't capable of taking care of himself. Neither of these messages are good for your child's relationship with his father. Most of the time, they will do fine if you do not interfere. If they continue to have problems, I am sure you will hear about it from someone.

Sometimes parents have problems with their children and want the other parent to come and get them. In effect, the parent is asking to be res-cued. This practice should also be avoided. Parenting involves handling discipline and making some tough decisions with your child about what is acceptable behavior. Another concern is if you ask the other parent to pick up the chuldren because you can't handle them. This could later be used against you in court.

EXERCISE: IS YOUR EX-SPOUSE REALLY A THREAT TO YOUR CHILDREN'S SAFETY?

If your history with your ex-spouse gives you reason to worry about your children's safety, you may want to complete the following exercise. To assess your ex-spouse's potential threat to your children's safety, answer the following items "yes" or "no."

1. Has your ex-spouse ever lost control while physically punishing the children?
2. Has your ex-spouse ever caused welts, bruises, cuts, or any other injury when he/she was physically punishing the children?
3. Has your ex-spouse failed to keep promises to never physically hurt you or your children again?
4. Has your ex-spouse ever threatened or assaulted you in your children's presence?
5. Has your ex-spouse ever been charged and convicted for assault?
6. Does your ex-spouse use drugs or become obviously intoxicated when drinking in front of your children?
7. Do you often feel that you must "walk on egg shells" to avoid a fight with your ex-spouse?
8. Has your ex-spouse ever brandished weapons during a fight?

If you answered "yes" to any of these items, you need professional or court assistance in helping you to outline specific ways of controlling your ex-spouse's behavior. Keep in mind that you cannot assume that your ex-spouse will get violent because your answered "yes" to some of these items. It only means that there is reason to be concerned and further evaluation by someone qualified is recommended.

"One of These Days, I Know He's Going to Hit Me Again."

Sometimes there is so much bitterness between the ex-spouses that the mere sight of an ex-spouse's face may trigger intense rage. Whether or not the rage is justified is beside the point. The alienating parent will always have a reason or a rationalization to explain the anger. When parents cannot control their anger and be civil with each other, contact between the parents may need to be limited to a public or a supervised setting. There may need to be a restraining order or a neutral location designated by the court for picking up and dropping of the children after a visit. Keep in mind that, in many jurisdictions, a restraining order expires after thirty days. After thirty days, you may have to re-file or appear in court to justify a continuation of the restraining order. The renewal of the order is not automatic.

A restraining order is most effective with people who respect the law. If there is a restraining order and you invite the restricted party onto your property, you may have negated the order, making it unenforceable. Before inviting the restricted party onto your property, consult your attorney.

A restraining order is no guarantee of your safety, although it is more helpful than harmful. People not intimidated by the legal system may ignore a restraining order because they do not believe you will call the police or sign the complaint. Unfortunately, this happens quite often. Police and counselors at battered persons shelters will attest to their frustration because a spouse will make a complaint and not follow through with prosecution. In time, your ex-spouse, as well as the police, will come to believe that you are just bluffing and you won't follow through with your threat.

Some courts have developed programs (Garrity and Barris, 1994) to work with high-conflict parents and monitor high-risk parent's behavior. These programs are effective. Parents are more likely to behave themselves if they know their behavior is being watched. Secrecy increases your risk of future abuse.

Managing Children's Activities

Courts could help prevent a lot misunderstanding if they were more specific in outlining the parent's rights to attend their children's activities. Many parents would be less confused. Often, the noncustodial parent has the perception they must have the custodial parent's permission to attend the children's activities. Having to ask permission sets up a potential power struggle between parents. To avoid a possible fight and the humiliation of losing the argument, the noncustodial parent will refuse to ask permission. They just don't show up. Unfortunately, the children do not understand this. They may assume that their noncustodial parent does not want to attend. Now the children are hurt by the parent's obvious rejection, even if the rejection is caused only by the custodial parent's refusal to cooperate with the ex-spouse. The noncustodial parent misses the opportunity to see their children perform. Everyone loses, except the alienating parent.

Court orders outlining parental rights should include a statement encouraging the noncustodial parent's participation in the children's activities. If possible, a parent should not have to ask the other parent's permission to attend the children's activities. Both parents should have equal rights to attend athletic events, school parties, teacher conferences, graduations, recitals, or scouting events.

For more on the symbolic aspect of parental battles over children's activities, see chapter 7.

"Mom, Why Can't Dad Come to My Game?"

Children who are not alienated from either parent will want both parents to attend their social activities. They want to show off their talent at sporting events or recitals so they can revel in their parents' applause. Only after the children have experienced alienation will they comment about not wanting both parents to attend. (This is discussed further later in this chapter.) A custodial parent who refuses the other parent permission to attend an event or "forgetting" to give the other parent advance notice of their children's activities are encouraging alienation, usually for their own self interest.

Noncustodial parents are as eager as custodial parents to watch their children play baseball, sing in a school concert, or have them leave from their home for a date. To squelch unnecessary suspicion and distrust, the parents must tell each other their children's schedule. This allows both parents the opportunity to choose whether or not to attend the activity.

At this point, you may be thinking that you do not want your ex-spouse to attend your children's activities. You may think of their presence as an intrusion into your private life or a hassle you would rather avoid. If you feel this way, you should consider whether you are reacting to your own self interest or what is best for your children.

Having both parents attend their children's activities together can be awkward for everyone. If you anticipate too much tension between you and your ex-spouse, consider attending the school open house at a different time or rotating the ball games. When both parents attend an event simultaneously, you should expect to sit apart. The parents do not have to socialize with each other, though they must be civil and polite for the children's sake. When your children feel tension between you, they will usually feel guilty and ashamed, thinking it is their fault. Do not subject your children to this ordeal. Do not ruin their special event.

TIPS ON MANAGING ACTIVITIES

- The courts should be explicit in encouraging the noncustodial parent to attend the children's activities.

- Both you and your ex-spouse should plan your children's social activities together if the activities are expensive or may potentially interfere with visits.

- Do not schedule your children in too many activities. The courts will suspect alienation if the numerous activities interfere with scheduled visits.

- Custodial parents have more power than noncustodial parents because they have physical possession of the children and can say no. However, the noncustodial parent should not have to ask permission to attend one of their children's activities. Otherwise, the other parent has too much power, which can be abused.

- Remember, your children's activities are for everyone to enjoy. If need be, put your feelings aside and support your ex-spouse's desire to attend school activities, ball games, or recitals. Your children will feel better having your support.

- If you tell your children you will come to an activity, you must make every effort to keep your promise. Otherwise, you can cause your own alienation by not showing up. Remember, children are quick to believe that your agreement to attend an activity is a promise to be kept.

- Don't let your children dictate who attends their activities. Often children who say "I don't want Dad to come to my ball game" really mean "I feel the tension between you and Dad whenever you are together."

- Parents do not have to sit together at their child's functions. Don't expect your children to sit with you during an event if it is not your weekend or the children are not in your care. Parents should be polite and focus their attention on what their child is doing rather than on each other.

- Make a conscious effort to give you children permission to greet the other parent when you both attend the same activity. As discussed in chapter 3, the children should feel your assurance that they can hug or kiss the other parent in your presence.

- If the parents live a reasonable distance from each other, there is no reason why your children should not leave for a social activity from the noncustodial parent's home.

"She's Got Gymnastics or Swimming Every Weekend. You Can't Expect Her to Visit."

In recent years parents seem to be doing whatever they can to get kids enrolled in many outside school activities. There seems to be this belief that healthy, well-rounded children must be very busy. Young children may start in dance, gymnastics, or karate. Older children are busy with music lessons, soccer, or scouts. Parents frequently complain about the time spent chauffeuring children from one activity to another. Running around is exhausting.

Some parents describe feeling guilty and rushed because of the children's limited time to do homework or sit down and eat dinner with the family. One mother explains, "I often feel worse for her than for me because I believe she is overextended." Despite your children's cramped social schedules, time has to be set aside for the noncustodial parent. How to orchestrate time is a challenge that can fray one's nerves.

Children should not be scheduled in so many activities that visits becomes impossible or restricted. Overscheduling is an act of alienation that causes stress caused to the children and inflicts damage to their relationship with their other parent. "If your father really cared about you, he wouldn't expect you to choose between scouts and visits. He should understand there are times when you are too busy to visit." This is a statement that rationalizes a parent's attempt to alienate. In essence, the parent is saying that the children's activities are more important than any relationship the child could have with the other parent.

Ideally, when the children are younger, you and your ex-spouse should plan your children's social activities together. When doing this, don't schedule your children in too many activities. You and your ex-spouse need to find a balance between your child's desires, time, visits, and nondiscretionary time like school. Try not to overwhelm your children.

Most children know when they are involved in too many activities. They complain of feeling tired or will give you a hard time about going to the activity. If you have to nag or cajole your children to attend a specific activity, you may want to question why your child's participation is so important. Are you more interested in satisfying your own needs than those of your children? If you hear yourself say, "I know what's best for my children. They will thank me later," you need to question your motives. Maybe you should take a moment and listen to what your children are telling you. It is possible they want to slow down and feel less stress.

Scheduling children in too many activities is usually motivated by a parent's desire to live vicariously through the children's successes. Parents may have an unconscious need to enhance their own self-esteem through their children's successes. They hope for bragging rights to embellish their own sense of self-importance. They appear to others as driven in the quest for their children to succeed. They are usually the parents who yell the loudest at ball games, are visibly angry when a referee make a bad call, or are quick to publicly criticize their children for a less-than-perfect performance.

Both parents want their children to be active and well-liked by their friends. Noncustodial parents do not want to feel that their time with the children takes away from the children's social life. On the other hand, they do not want to be seen as a meddler or a nuisance who must be patronized. This loss of status is demeaning. Instead, the noncustodial parent wants to feel as important in their children's lives as the custodial parent.

One option is to volunteer to transport your child to and from the activity. There is no reason why you cannot be as actively involved as the other parent or why your child could not leave for a social activity from your home. True, if your child lives some distance away, the transportation could be time consuming, but that's the cost of living a distance from your children. Taking over some of the chauffeuring could even give your ex-spouse relief from a hectic schedule. These responsibilities are part of what parenting is all about and are often welcomed by the noncustodial parent.

There is a price to pay for passively waiting when you are denied time with your child. Precious opportunities are lost. Alienating parents rarely see what they are doing, and if they do, they usually don't try to make amends by allowing make-up visits. Instead, the victimized parent is usually forced to go back to court and ask that limits be placed on the children's activities. Unfortunately, this may give the children the perception that you are the bad guy, especially after the alienator explains to the children why they are returning to court. A more effective and less expensive approach is court-ordered mediation, starting with the assumption that the victimized parent is entitled to the standard order of parenting time.

"But You Promised You'd Be There!"

A problem frequently occurs when the parent does not understand that, for many children, saying you will attend an activity is considered a promise. In your child's mind, not attending the activity is the same as breaking a promise. If you tell your children you plan to attend a sports or social event, you must live up to your promise. If you don't, you better have a good reason; otherwise, you are creating your own alienation.

People often misunderstand the word trust. Trust has nothing to do with liking a person. It simply means the ability to predict, meaning you do what you say you are going to do. Parents must learn to teach and demonstrate trust to their children. One way to do this is to keep the promises they have made. If you value trust, the only way trust is going to be built is to be consistent and predictable with your child and your ex-spouse. If you develop a pattern of not keeping your promises, you are heading for big trouble with your children. They will learn that your word is meaningless. Or worse, they may think of you as a liar. Either way, you are seriously damaging your relationship with your children.

If you want to make amends, you must start by becoming predictable. You must do what you say you are going to do. Whatever you do, you cannot expect your ex-spouse to keep making excuses for you or mend your children's hurt. This is your responsibility. After all, the damage is your doing, not your ex-spouses. If you do nothing to stop your children's hurt, they will learn to emotionally defend themselves by not caring. That means not caring about you. This is a terrible price to pay for something that you have control over.

Roger and Johnny

Roger meant well when he told his son, Johnny, "I'll be at the park this weekend to watch your tennis match." Johnny, sounding almost apologetic, said to his father, "You don't have to, Dad. I know you're busy." Roger persistent in assuring his son that he would be at the match. Later Sunday evening, Roger called to apologize to Johnny. "I'm sorry, Johnny, It couldn't be helped. I got called in to work." Protesting, Johnny said, "But you promised to come. You said you would be there." "Johnny, I didn't promise. I did say I would be there." "Yes you did! You lied to me! I don't want to see you anymore!" Roger sat there listening to the dial tone.

Johnny's father knew why his son was angry. What happened later came as a surprise. As the weeks past, Johnny no longer wanted to visit his father. For whatever reason, Johnny's anger was not healing. Somehow, his anger is being fueled, perhaps by his mother or someone else close to him. Johnny is angry and reasons that he is punishing his father by refusing to visit. This is giving Johnny too much power. If Johnny's mother remains passive to her son's behavior, she is encouraging his perception that he is entitled to make these decisions. Johnny learns that his anger is justified and has the right to dictate Roger's behavior. This perception is not healthy for Johnny or either of his parents.

"You Don't Care Anyway."

Many children eventually reject a parent who frequently disappoints them by breaking promises or canceling visits. This was definitely true for Roger. Johnny retaliates with a rationalization proclaiming, "Dad never cared; otherwise, he would have come to my tennis matches." He wants to hurt his father by rejecting him. Johnny's reaction is not hard to understand. Children, like adults, will often not tell another person of their hurt. Instead, they hold in the feelings until their hurt turns to anger. Now they share their anger rather than their hurt with such statements as, "I don't want you to come. You don't care anyway." He reacts with the only power he knows: rejecting his father. Sadly, Johnny pushes his father away when he really needs his father's reassurance that he cares.

Johnny should be able to tell his father about his hurt, but he should not think he can dictate his father's behavior. Such a mistaken belief will cause Johnny, in time, to become more demanding and resistant to both of his parents' authority. When listening to children like Johnny, one will usually hear the arrogance in their voice. This attitude is not healthy for children. Johnny should not think he has the right to demand that his father not attend his tennis match or not to visit his father. Both parents can expect Johnny to become more arrogant and demanding.

One method to break this impasse is to encourage your children to share their hurt rather than their anger. They must learn that sharing hurt is okay and not a sign of weakness. In fact, they may be surprised to learn that sharing their hurt will get a different reaction from the other person than if they started yelling. This really works. Try it the next time you get angry. Try sharing your hurt if that is what you are actually feeling.

"I Hate You! You Don't Deserve to See Me Play!"

Alienated children often think they have the authority to decide whether a parent can attend one of their social activities. They feel the parent's presence as an intolerable intrusion. Sometimes, unlike Johnny above who had a specific reason for being angry at his father, such children cannot give you a sensible answer when asked why his feels this way. Remember that unjustified anger is a good benchmark that alienation has occurred. You should suspect alienation when your children cannot tell you why they do not want you or a family member to attend one of their activities. "I don't know," should not be an acceptable answer for something as important as parenting time. True, your child may be too uncomfortable to answer your questions, but you should be patient before taking any action to change visits. Unfortunately, you also have to contend with a parent who is probably reinforcing the idea that your child has the right to make these decisions.

Often children who say "I don't want Dad to come to my ball game" really mean "I feel the tension between you and Dad whenever you are together." If you believe your children are afraid that you and your ex-spouse will fight, reassure them that you will do whatever you can to prevent an argument. This should not mean that Dad cannot attend the game, but it probably means that you and he should not sit together.

If your child gives you some other reason, like "Dad criticizes my playing too much," then reassure your child that you will try to solve the problem. Ideally, if you can talk calmly with your ex-spouse, pass along what your child has said and gently suggest that your child would love to hear more supportive comments. Or perhaps you can suggest that the child discuss this with the other parent directly.

Some overzealous parents get critical about how their child is playing ball. During a game they take every opportunity to tell their son or daughter how to improve their performance. Their criticism, and often yelling, drives the kid nuts and takes the fun out of playing. When this happens, the child will frequently complain, saying, "Dad, I don't want you to come and watch me play." The father is insulted and hurt. He immediately thinks that his ex-spouse is behind his son's attitude; he can't imagine that his behavior, not hers, has caused his son to feel this way.

Parents must remember that children play ball to have fun. They want to succeed and do well for their parents and teammates. They don't want to hear someone yelling and criticizing every move they make. Whatever you do, let your children know that you are proud of them, even if they make mistakes.

"Surprise, I'm Here!"

There are two fairly common circumstances when parents can make a surprise visit. The most frequent occurrence is when a parent decides to come to a sporting event or other special event without either the parent or the child having any prior notice. All of a sudden you look up and, "Dad's here." The other circumstance is when the parent hasn't been around in months, or perhaps years, and out of nowhere shows up at the door. Either of these situations can be uncomfortable, but there are ways to deal with such surprises.

Advice to Custodial Parents

To begin with, have realistic expectations. As emphasized above, many courts will write into the divorce decree a provision stating that either parent has the right to attend any of the children's social or educational activities. If this decree is in your shared parenting plan, you should not be surprised if your ex-spouse shows up. If you are surprised by your ex-spouse's appearance, the time to discuss why he's there is not during the ball game or open house. This could cause a scene and make everyone uncomfortable, particularly your child. Instead, stay calm, be polite, and discuss it later.

If it has been years since you have seen your ex-spouse and he's suddenly at the door, you will certainly be surprised. The most important thing is not to panic. As discussed in chapter 3, people emotionally react to their own thoughts and conjectures, which may not be the same as reality.

Calmly talk to your ex-spouse about his intentions and try to work out a plan together that will be most comfortable for the children. Remember that your ex-spouse still has a right to see them unless there is a court order stating otherwise. Even if you are not thrilled to see your ex-spouse standing in your doorway and wish he wouldn't complicate your children's lives, remember that you do not have the authority to disobey a court order. If you any have questions, consult your attorney before taking any action. If you are in contempt for disobeying a court order, your attorney will have to defend your behavior, which is a situation you should try to avoid. You are better off going to court being on the offensive rather than having to be defended for contempt.

Most children who are not alienated are happy to see their father after many years. They may at first be a little apprehensive because they don't know how to react or what to say. I remember when my father came to see my brother and me after many years and my brother asked me what to call our dad. By this time, he was calling our stepfather "Dad," so it felt funny for him to call his biological father "Dad" as well. If the relationship between child and the absent parent hasn't been close, your son or daughter may not know whether to hug or kiss their father. You may have to give your child some reassurance about how they feel and let them know "it's okay if you are not comfortable hugging your dad." It is also a good idea to remind your ex-spouse that the children "may feel a little awkward about seeing you and not know how to react, so please be patient."

Advice to Noncustodial Parents

If for whatever reason you haven't seen your children in a while, you shouldn't just show up unannounced. You could make everyone uncomfortable because they don't know how to respond. Your child could be caught off guard. Before doing anything, it is only polite to let your ex-spouse and children know your intentions. If you expect problems or resistance, that is even more reason for not showing up unannounced. Begin by talking with your ex-spouse and if there are any problems, discuss this with your attorney or mediator if you have one. Whatever you do, don't do anything rash. Instead, think ahead of time about what you want to do and how your children will feel.

It is hard on your children if you have not seen them for a long time and out of the blue you show up at your children's door, proclaiming your right to visit them. The custodial parent now has a dilemma. They may know that you are legally justified to see your children, but they also have to be concerned for your children's feelings. The custodial parent may actually welcome the idea of you re-establishing a relationship with the children. At the same time, the custodial parent is feeling uneasy because they are afraid that you will get enmeshed in your children's lives and again disappear. Your ex-spouse will naturally want to protect your children from being hurt in the future. They may also resent picking up the emotional pieces after you left the last time. There is no longer any trust because the custodial parent has no idea about what you will do in the future. All of these concerns are frightening to the custodial parent. They want to protect the children and, at the same time, may believe that you and the children should have a healthy relationship.

Caught in this dilemma, the custodial parent often does not know what to do. The two of you will need to be patient and take time to rebuild mutual trust. If you have not seen your children in a while and you want to see them again, initially plan short visits until your children get comfortable. Allow your children to have some input in setting the pace for extending the length of the parenting time. When children feel that they have some control, it helps to reduce their anxiety. Because children want to avoid any situation that is uncomfortable, you may have to do a little supportive coaxing.

What if your ex-spouse refuses to let you see the children, even though the most recent court order gives you parenting time rights? If all your efforts have failed, you may consider filing a contempt charge against your ex-spouse. Though this sounds like a reasonable solution, you must be realistic in your expectations. Sometimes courts have limited power to enforce a parenting time order when the other parent doesn't really care about the consequences of his or her actions. The obsessed alienator may be entrenched in her belief that her position is correct and is consequently willing to defy the court's authority.

This causes problems for the court because much of the court's power comes from the perception of authority and the threat of locking up the uncooperative parent. Putting the uncooperative parent in jail is a problem because the children will likely blame you for sending their mother to jail. Now the children feel more estranged or alienated from the noncustodial parent than ever. The custodial parent, sitting in jail, becomes a martyr for protecting the children. The courts see this dilemma and try to avoid putting anyone in jail. They know that jailing a parent does little to change attitudes or bring families closer together.

Advice to Step-parents

Sometimes step-parents become uncomfortable when a biological parent shows up after years of absence. They are threatened because they have by now developed a loving relationship with their stepchildren and don't like the idea of "this guy just showing up and thinking he can disrupt our lives. How dare he act as if everything is the same, as if he never left?"

Step-parents may have strong feelings, but unfortunately they have few rights to determine what will happen with visits. Remember, the last court order is still in effect unless the custodial parent has returned to court and changed the order. If you have questions, call your attorney. The step-parent needs to sit back and be supportive of the spouse's efforts to work things out. They should not get too involved, especially in talking with the other parent about visits and their rights to see the children.

I have found that all hell can break loose if the step-parent, rather than the biological parent, gets too involved in discussing visits or how to reintroduce the parent into the children's lives. The returning noncustodial parent gets angry, questioning, "Who is this guy telling me whether I can see my own children?" This can be a delicate situation because it is easy for the step-parent to start alienating the children against their father. Many step-parents feel threatened that this man is going to come back into their lives and try to resume his paternal responsibility and, in effect, push the step-parent aside. This can be scary. However, remember that if you have built up a strong, loving relationship with the children, they will continue to love you as well as their biological father. For more about building relationships, see chapter 8.

10

Health and Safety

"Why is it that every time the kids have a runny nose you have to take them to the doctor's office and tell me I can't see them? You're just making excuses to keep the kids from me."

Parents' first responsibility is to protect their children's health and safety. No one, including the court, will excuse any parent who neglects the children's health or allows them to be put in a hazardous position. Sometimes, however, knowing what is safe takes more than common sense because parents have different values or ideas about safety and health.

Also, many health and safety threats are unique for this generation of children, so that the parents cannot rely on their own experience to know how to deal with it. An example is having to teach young children about HIV and AIDS. If you are like most parents, you probably felt strange watching Linda Ellerby and Magic Johnson demonstrating the proper use of a condom to younger children. Unfortunately, today's children do need to know about safe sex and HIV. In addition, our children are also more likely to witness violence in school or on the streets. School officials report an increase in the number of children carrying weapons to school. Hearing about teenage shootings on television causes every parent to wonder about their children's safety. Parents have also developed a pervasive fear about their children being abducted or molested. School-age children are taught "good touch and bad touch." For many children, they can no longer feel safe in their own neighborhood. They, as well as their parents, have had to become more vigilant, watching for any threat. Parents are caught in the dilemma of needing to alert their children to dangers without making them timid and paranoid.

Simple Decisions Can Get Complicated

A child's age or maturity can make a difference about what he or she should be allowed to do. A six-year-old riding a bike in the streets is different from a fourteen-year-old doing the same thing. Even where the parent lives can make a difference. Seven-year-old Billy may be perfectly safe riding his two-wheeler on Dad's dead-end street, but riding on Mom's busy street would pose a serious threat to his safety. Mom would be expected to use her good judgment about what Billy is allowed to do on her street.

Not everyone will agree about what is safe for children. Dad may see nothing wrong with his ten-year-old riding a dirt bike, while mom panics over the vision in her mind of her son's bloody body under the mangled bike. Both parents may have strong feelings about what is safe. When Mom tries to say something, Dad may resent the intrusion, complaining, "I don't have to do what she tells me. She's just trying to control me the way she did in the marriage." On the other hand, Mom may resent her ex-husband's carelessness and insensitivity to her fears. Now the groundwork is laid for a power struggle to see whose will is stronger.

Fights between parents can ignite from simple disagreements about what is a reasonable effort to keep children safe from harm; sincere concerns about a parent's ability to care for and protect youngsters; and mistrust, disdain, or an interest in criticizing and controlling disguised as sincere concern for a child's welfare. Overprotective parents are usually seen by targeted parents as being aggressive because of the frequent complaints and harsh judgments about their parenting. Both parents have their own beliefs about how children should be raised. When differences occur, parents must temper their feelings and appreciate the wisdom in learning how to cope with each other's beliefs. There must be room to negotiate and compromise. Otherwise, the children are trapped between the parent's demands and their desire to please both. When children are caught between opposing parents, they are often forced to lie to keep peace. This isn't the message you want to give to your children.

Health

How sick does Billy have to be before he sees a doctor? When should you cancel a visit because he doesn't feel well? Is it child endangerment if you smoke cigarettes in his presence or allow him to ride his bicycle without a helmet? Can someone with no experience taking care of children ever really be trusted with children? These are just a few of the health and safety issues divorced parents grapple with that sometimes turn into World War III.

In most states, the custodial parent is responsible for the children's health and medical care. If there is a shared parenting plan or joint custody, the parents are expected make health-related decisions together. Cooperation is an absolute must; otherwise everyone's life will be miserable. If the parents don't have a shared parenting plan or joint custody, the court usually gives the custodial parent the responsibility of selecting the children's physician and deciding when and how they will receive medical, dental, and any psychological treatment. This parent, in effect, becomes the medical-care coordinator who will delegate, instruct, and communicate the physician's orders to the other parent. Ideally, and for the child's best interest, the two parents can do this without resentment and animosity. This should be a simple and straightforward arrangement, but often it is not.

The Decision Maker versus the Bill Payer

A problem with this arrangement is that the custodial parent has total control and power to direct the children's health care, while the other parent has to pay the medical bills. This arrangement can be humiliating to the other parent, who may feel obligated to bow to the controlling parent's demands; otherwise the custodial parent can retaliate by cutting off the flow of information, or worse yet, stopping visits. To make matters worse, there are instances such as the child needing braces or some treatment that is not a medical necessity but would enhance the child's appearance or self-esteem. When the bill-paying parent has no money, he or she can get angry and defensive when accused by the other parent of being selfish or insensitive to the children's health needs.

When Children Become Ill

Children get sick. There is little a parent can do about it other than take reasonable precautions to keep the children healthy and care for them when ill. The problem occurs because parents have different opinions about how to keep the children healthy. Some of these opinions, though well meaning, are based on old wives' tales or are not supported by the medical community. Many parents continue to believe that children can catch a cold if they get their feet wet or play outside in cold weather. These unfounded beliefs can lead to arguments that are never resolved.

Parents cannot be expected to be medical experts or always know how best to care for an ill child. There are too many differences of opinion about preventative health care and treatment. Even religious beliefs can influence a parent's ideas about good health care. So how do two parents come to some agreement about taking care of their children's health?

Before answering this question, we must begin with the assumption that both parents are equally capable of caring for a sick child. True, some parents are better caregivers than others. But that is not to say that a poor caregiver can't learn to be a better one.

Not all sick children need to see a physician. Children can get colds, skin their knees, cut their finger, or have a stomachache without having to stay home from school or go see their doctor. Recently I was surprised to learn that children with mononucleosis can continue to attend school. Parents always have to make a judgments about when to get treatment or keep their child home. The problem arises when having to decide to keep the children from going on a visit.

When Should Visits Be Canceled Because of Illness?

A good guideline for when to cancel a visit because of illness is to use the same standards that you use for deciding when to keep your child home from school. If you are told by your child's physician to keep her home from school or in bed, the same standard could apply to a visit unless the doctor says otherwise. Sometimes the physician will see no problem with the child recuperating at the noncustodial parent's home if the child remains quiet and rested. Whatever is decided, the physician's orders must be law. Both parents must follow the doctor's orders.

Parents who work well working together are able to share medical information and instructions without animosity or defensiveness. The noncustodial parent is able to converse with the children's physician without any threat of offending the other parent or putting the physician in a awkward position. Cooperation and amiable discussions with the other parent must be your goal. Courts may need to be specific in stating that both parents are to have access to the physician and medical records. Otherwise, you can expect to see more animosity and distrust.

There are many opinions about when a child should stay home from school or not visit because of illness. I found it interesting that there are no medical standards to help you make this decision. After talking to several pediatricians, I have gathered some guidelines that may helpful. These guidelines do not address all the possible circumstances that may arise. The most important guideline is to follow your physician's or pediatrician's instructions.

YOU SHOULD KEEP YOUR CHILD HOME FROM A VISIT IF HE:

- Has a temperature over 100 degrees.
- Starts an antibiotic for an infection. For some infections, the physician may order the child to remain home for the first twenty-four hours after starting the antibiotic. Ask the child's physician when your child would be healthy enough to leave the house or visit.
- Has had active vomiting or diarrhea during the past eighteen hours.
- Has dizziness, weakness, or flulike symptoms.
- Has any physical pain or discomfort that immobilizes the child. This may be reason to keep the child home. Your family doctor should be called for any unexplained physical pain.
- Has observable physical complaints or symptoms requiring immediate medical attention.
- Has a contagious disease, such as measles or mumps. The physician may advise you to keep your child isolated from others while the disease is in its incubation period.

Medication

If the child is on a medication schedule that cannot be given by the school nurse or staff, the child may not attend school but could go on a visit providing the noncustodial parent agrees to give the medication on schedule. The custodial parent should be given written instructions that includes proper dosage and times when the medication is to be administered. Following the physician's order is critical. If you don't, the court may think you are neglecting your child's care.

When you decide to let your child visit, you have the responsibility to give the other parent the doctor's instructions and an amount of the medication that will last the duration of the visit. You should not expect your ex-spouse to buy the child's medication because you are too stubborn to share. This can be too expensive and impractical if the physician has written a single prescription. If you are the noncustodial parent, you are expected to continue your child's treatment while he or she is under your care.

One Sick Child with Healthy Siblings

A common alienating tactic that stirs bitter resentment is keeping all the children from going on a visit when only one child is sick. If one child is ill and the others are healthy, there is no reason why the healthy children should not go on the scheduled visit. Do not keep all the children from the visit unless all of them are ill or were recently exposed to a contagious disease, seriously enough so that the physician judges that they might pass it on to others. Again, if there are any questions about what is best for the children, express your concerns to your ex-spouse and consult the child's physician.

Medical Emergencies

Medical emergencies can happen anywhere and anytime, even when the child is with the most cautious parent. If your child is hospitalized or has a medical emergency, you should assume that your ex-spouse will want to be told immediately. After all, your ex-spouse has as much emotional investment in your child's health and care as you do. Nothing gets a parent angrier than feeling excluded from knowing about their child's medical emergency. Withholding information will remind your ex-spouse of the power you have. This is very humiliating, especially when he has to either lie or tell your child why he didn't come to see her at the hospital. In addition, your ex-spouse will learn that you can't be trusted.

After telling your ex-spouse of the emergency, he or she will decide whether or not to go to the hospital. Sometimes, when the parent fails to visit, this puts the other parent in a awkward position with the child. Now the parent feels obligated to make excuses for the other parent for not coming to visit. This isn't really necessary. Your child may be hurt or disappointed, but it's up to the other parent, not you, to explain why he didn't show—and decide how to make it up to the child.

Larry and Karen

Larry and Karen were never married. When James was born, Larry assumed that Karen would raise their son while he had regular visits. Larry was a compulsive sort of guy who was thrilled about being a father. He was devoted to his visits, never letting his interests or anything else interfere with time with his son. Shortly after James turned

---

five, Larry and Karen learned that James had severe allergies requiring weekly shots and a smoke-free home environment. The list of requirements provided by the allergist was extensive. Karen was supposed to have plastic covers over James's pillow and mattress, allow no pets or stuffed animals, and give him an air-conditioned bedroom. Unfortunately, Karen was a smoker and very messy. On Friday nights, she had her usual ritual of having friends over to party. When Saturday morning came, the house was filthy and filled with the stench of cigarette smoke. The ashtrays were often full, and the trash can overflowed.

Larry badgered Karen to stop smoking and to clean her messy home. Though Karen tried to keep the house clean, there were piles of laundry on the damp basement floor, a family cat, and an array of clutter scattered about the house. Larry would see the mess when he picked up James. He was angry about Karen's insensitivity to their son's poor health. Larry would enter the home with the eyes and nose of a drill sergeant. He would smell for cigarette smoke and look for dust or anything that violated the allergist's instructions.

Karen naturally became defensive, waiting to be chastised at every turn. She learned to dread Larry's arrival, knowing that she was going to be lectured by "this self-righteous bastard." James watched his father lecture and humiliate his mother. He felt the tension between his parents, believing the arguments were his fault. James, like most children trying to cope with a bad situation, became withdrawn and quiet when his parents were together. Blindly, his parents went on with their power struggle, unaware of how James felt. Larry, feeling that he was getting nowhere, filed for a change of custody. He argued that Karen was neglectful of James's unique medical needs because of her addiction to cigarettes. She argued that Larry was excessively critical and her home was not a hazard to her son's health. She denied smoking in James's presence though the dirty ashtrays betrayed her. The case is still not settled.

Differing Opinions About a Healthy Environment

Parents may have different values or ideas about what they consider a proper lifestyle and a healthy environment. Such differences in opinion are frequent sources of conflict. For example, one parent may be a strict vegetarian while the other depends on feeding the children fast foods. Or one ex-spouse may ignore the children's severe allergies and smoke cigarettes in front of them. Nonsmoking parents may feel appalled by the smoking parent's lack of sensitivity. These parents have been known to seek a change of custody because they believe that smoking is a serious threat to their children's health. Since smoking (particularly passive smoke) has become a hotly contested issue, I wouldn't be surprised to see it come before the court more often. If this happens to you and you're a smoker, your personal bias may not be enough to persuade the court to allow you to keep custody.

One parent nagging the other parent about not smoking or eating properly does nothing to help the relationship with your ex-spouse. Though you are sincerely concerned for your child's health, your ex-spouse does not have to agree with you. Furthermore, your nagging is not likely to change your ex-spouse's mind. Instead, you are creating a climate of alienation because your children will learn to dread when their parents are together. They do not want to hear your fighting.

Many problems between parents can be avoided if everyone agrees that the physician is to mediate any disputes about the children's health care. For this to happen, both parents must have equal access to the physician and the children's health records. You should be sure that your attorney includes in the divorce or custody papers a provision that both parents are to have access to the physician and medical information and that the physician will have the last word about the children's medical treatment. If you and your ex-spouse find that you cannot agree, there should be a provision that will allow either parent to get a second opinion. Either way, remember that courts have little tolerance for parents who ignore a physician's order. Don't use your children's health as an excuse to get back at your ex-spouse. The only ones you are really hurting are your children.

There were two problems facing James, the boy with severe allergies. His parents had different values about cleanliness, and his mother wasn't sensitive to his allergies. Your children, like James, have little choice but to adjust and survive with the difference in values between you and your ex-spouse. Do not criticize or badger your spouse about whose standards are correct. In time, children will make up their own mind about whose values they will later follow. For now, they have no choice but try to please both parents. Rather than argue with your children, try to empathize with their dilemma.

Today's parents are more health conscious. More parents do not want their children exposed to passive cigarette smoke and are insisting that they wear safety belts when riding in a car. Whether you like it or not, you must follow community standards for proper safety and health care. Otherwise, you are jeopardizing your visits or custody.

Safety

Parents do not have to agree on what is a safe activity or environment for their children, providing it is legal and proper safety precautions are followed. Your children should not be without proper supervision in any activity where they are physically or mentally at risk. Some communities require children to wear safety helmets while riding their bicycles. If your child is injured and you violated community standards for safety, you will have little defense if you are taken back to court to defend your behavior. Remember, regardless of your standards, the judge will use community standards—and usually take a conservative position—when making a judgment about your child's safety. Everyone by now should know the laws about wearing seat belts, using car seats, and having children under the age of twelve ride in the back seat. If your children are in an accident, you have no defense for not following proper and usual safety practices.

Calculating Risks

During your children's growing years, there will be many times when you and your spouse have to make decisions about whether your child is mature enough to take on a new risky activity. When toddlers are learning to walk, you will empathetically flinch when they fall and hit their head. Playing outside without close physical supervision, crossing the street, leaving the block to visit a friend, swimming, strolling the mall, going out on a first date, and—oh yes, the fear of all fears—driving all are examples of activities where parents may disagree about what is safe. A wise parent knows that they have to let their children take new risks in order to grow, although the parent will try to make sure the children do not get into a situation that is over their head.

Making the decision to allow your child to do something new and risky will depend on your child's age and their sense of responsibility. Because there are no rules about when a child should be mature enough to do a particular activity, you have to use your best judgment. This is scary because you can learn later than your judgment was wrong. What can make matters worse is someone over your shoulder reminding you were wrong. After a lot of nagging and trepidation, you will finally give in and pray that you made the right decision.

Because you have to depend on your judgment to allow your child to do something that months earlier was too risky, it's possible that your ex-spouse will not agree with your decision. This can create quite a problem, especially because your child will side with the more lenient parent. Your history with your ex-spouse can also add to the problem, especially if the two of you have always had problems coming to an agreement. Unfortunately, two battling parents are as likely to argue after the divorce as they did before the divorce. In many cases, increasing age and maturity—and both parents getting on with their own lives—will temper the hostilities.

Parents should try to work out their differences of opinion if they can do it without fighting and yelling in front of the children. If not, safety can become an issue that serves as a catalyst for a power struggle. The children become victims because they do not know what is the right thing to do. They are pulled between their own desires, having to please the opposing parent, and the fear that they will get into trouble. This is not fair to your children.

Tammy's Trip to the Mall

After months of nagging, Tammy, a rambunctious ten-year-old, was finally allowed by her father to cruise the mall with friends. She couldn't wait to get back home and tell her mother about her new adventure. She felt so grown up and excited! But Tammy didn't get the reaction from her mother that she expected; her mother was furious. "I don't care what your father says. I told you are not to walk in the mall without your father. I expect you to do what I tell you. If anything ever happened to you, I don't know what I would do." Tammy felt deflated.

Whether you agree with Tammy's mother or father isn't the issue in this example. Both parents had to make a judgment about Tammy's maturity and the risks involved with her walking the mall with her friends. Tammy's father did nothing that was illegal, though some may question his judgment. The problem now is with Tammy. She is trapped between wanting to walk the mall with friends, her father's permission, and her mother's demand to do what she says, suggesting that otherwise she will be in trouble. What would you guess Tammy will do? If Tammy complies with her mother's demand, her father could get angry because his ex-wife is trying to control what she does during his visit. He could take his ex-wife's demand as a criticism of his judgment and parenting. Again, the battle line is drawn and the ground is fertile for alienation unless the parents come to some understanding. One parent mandating the other parent's safety standards will surely cause problems for everyone. Rather than mandating standards, the parents should discuss the issue calmly or accept the ideal that both parents have an equal right to set safety standards even if the other parent disagrees. If the activity is legal and meets community safety standards, the disputing parent must learn to accept that there is nothing he or she can do. It is important not to keep your child trapped in the middle of your dispute. You cannot expect her to comply with your demands while she is with the other parent.

Deciding what is a safe activity is not easy because there are no definitive rules. Parents have to use their judgment. When differences occur between you and the other parent, take a moment and think about the dilemma this is for your children. How are they supposed to feel? Which parent should they obey? Crossing the street without supervision and swimming are examples of activities where parents may disagree as to what is safe. Parents must try to talk to each other if they are to resolve their differences.

Another concern you may face is when your child tells you about something you consider dangerous that he did during a visit. Before reacting to what you are told, remember that children—especially younger children—may not understand or communicate accurately, so take their account with a grain of salt. Your child's description of what happened may be unintentionally wrong or distorted. Rather than just reacting and making a rash judgment to restrict or deny visits, make an effort to get an explanation from the other parent. If you get no satisfaction, consult with your attorney or mediator before considering stopping or restricting visits. Otherwise, you will be asking for a lot of trouble, like having to return to court.

11

Allegations of Sexual Abuse

"Sweetheart, I know you have a good time when you visit your daddy, but I need to ask you a question. Has Daddy or anyone ever touched your privates?" "Uh, Daddy touches my pee pee."

These are words that every mothering dreads hearing: "Daddy touches my pee pee." Immediately mother is in a panic, not knowing whether to ignore what is heard or to call the attorney the first thing in the morning.

How you handle allegations of sexual abuse depends on whether you are the parent hearing your children's accusations for the first time or the parent being accused. Hearing the allegation of sexual abuse for the first time while a divorce is in process is devastating for both the alleged abuser and the children. The divorce process is thrown into turmoil because the allegations typically have to be addressed before the divorce can proceed. The outcome of the investigation can have a baring on custody and parenting time.

How Courts Handle Allegations of Sexual Abuse

Courts are becoming more suspicious when allegations are heard for the first time during the divorce proceedings. In years past, the common belief among attorneys, prosecutors, and mental-health workers was that children don't lie. The validity of this doctrine is now being challenged. Experts now recognize that the issue of telling the truth is more complex because of various ways that children can be manipulated and deceived by a parent to think that something bad happened when, in fact, nothing happened. Manipulation isn't always caused by a sinister parent wanting to get back at an ex-spouse. Well-meaning parents who are frightened by what they understand or think happened can unintentionally manipulate or reinforce in the child's mind that something awful happened. Children's perceptions and interpretations can be manipulated by both parents, lawyers, and unqualified mental-health workers. That is the reason professionals investigating sexual abuse require specialized training. Damaging for everyone is the unqualified investigator or mental-health worker who uses the allegations to further their own personal agenda.

The investigation is typically assigned by the court and conducted by the children's services agency. Every state has an agency responsible for conducting investigations, but they're called different names. Some families have complained about investigators who come across as friendly and caring and then gather information that the prosecutor can use against them, leaving them feeling trapped and betrayed.

The court has a dilemma when someone makes an allegation of sexual abuse: Whose rights have precedence, the alleged victim's or the alleged abuser's? Courts will typically, and rightfully so, protect the alleged victim by asking the alleged offender to leave the residence until the investigation is completed. This is to protect the children's safety from the chance of further abuse and to prevent the children's story from being contaminated by the parent's questions and possible intimidation. The parent remaining with the child is expected to cooperate with the investigative agency and keep the children from the spouse. Parents who do not cooperate with the authorities and allow the accused back into the house can be seen as more worried about their own needs than their child's. The parent is expected to demonstrate a greater loyalty and concern for the child's welfare than worry about how the spouse feels. If the investigative agency believes that you will not keep the child from the alleged offender, the agency may decide to remove the child, and sometimes all the children, from both parents. The children are usually placed with a relative or in a foster home until the case is resolved.

States have varying definitions of sexual abuse. Common among most states is the distinction between sexual contact and sexual penetration. Sexual contact refers to "any contact with intimate body parts including genitals, breast, buttocks, or mouths" (Bensel, Arthur, Brown, and Riley, 1985). Sexual penetration is the insertion of a finger, penis, or an object into the rectum or vagina. When penetration occurs, including oral sex, a charge of rape could be forthcoming.

Most often sexual abuse will be reported to the authorities before the offender progresses to intercourse. Usually the complaint will describe a progressive seduction from seemingly innocent playfulness and touching to not-so-innocent sexual fondling. In some cases, the progression may takes months or even years. A question often asked is "How far would the perpetrator have gone if they were not caught?" Of course, no one is certain of the answer. Investigators and the court will usually assume that it is only a matter of time before the perpetrator would rape the child.

Fixated Offenders versus Regressed Offenders

When most people think about an abuser, they have a picture in their mind of a stranger hiding behind the bushes and grabbing your children. Though this happens, it is very uncommon. Most sexual abuse is done by someone who already knows the child. Dr. A. Nicholas Groth (1979) makes a distinction between the fixated offender and the regressed offender.

The primary sexual orientation of fixated offenders is toward children. They typically target their victim and plan their seduction, which can occur over a period of time. They are usually single but will make a point to be around children. They can be volunteers, youth leaders, or coaches. It is not uncommon for them to be well liked, even by parents. That is one reason everyone is upset when they learn of the offender's behavior. He is often a person that others have learned to trust and like. These are the offenders that most parents worry about. Their prognosis for a favorable response to treatment is questionable. They require psychotherapy, monitoring, and frequently medication.

Regressed offenders prefer same-age adult sexual partners, not children, as their primary sexual orientation. These individuals may have never had a sexual encounter with a child until a stressful event precipitates a serious temporary lapse of judgment when they sexually offend. Their behavior is more impulsive than premeditated and usually directed toward a member of the opposite sex. After the offending, they feel guilty and ashamed. They know what they did was wrong and will do most anything to convince the victim to not say anything. From this point on, they live with the fear of being discovered. These offenders, once their behavior is disclosed, are responsive to treatment providing they get beyond making excuses and take responsibility for their misbehavior. What's important for the regressed offender is that their offense may not be seen by the court as being any different than that of the fixated offenders. Both can go to prison for many years.

I didn't explain the differences between the fixated and regressed offender to scare you or make you an expert. My intent is for you to understand that sexual abuse and the abuser are complex, and a qualified specialist is needed to investigate any allegations. If your family is faced with the revelation of sexual abuse, the entire family may need therapy.

Sexual Abuse and Divorce

While a marriage is falling apart and a divorce becomes more imminent, there is an increased chance of one parent accusing the other parent of sexual abuse. Unfortunately, the risk of sexual abuse increases because a parent may become emotionally needy and vulnerable. This is what happens with the regressed offender. Occasionally the parent, usually a father, begins to put the child in the role of a surrogate wife or intimate friend. The father begins confiding in his daughter about his hurt and loneliness. In turn, the sympathetic daughter offers her love and comfort. Feeling lonely and insecure, the father begins a slow progressive seductive process of holding, touching, and in time, sexual fondling. The regressed abuser may, in time, try an overt sexual act. This usually occurs in a context where the parent is trying to be nurturing and kind. What the parent does not realize is the confusion and fear that he instills in his child. Often the offending parent does not believe that he is doing wrong because, in his heart, he does not want to hurt the child. He may rationalize the abuse by thinking that he is not hurting the child because sex is pleasurable.

Stacy and Her Dad

Stacy had just turned seventeen when she learned that she was pregnant. She was confused and scared because she had not had sex with her boyfriend. Unknown to the rest of the family, Stacy and her father had been having intercourse for the past three years. The sexual fondling began when Stacy was about four years old. She and her father had kept their little secret through the years, until Stacy knew she had to talk to her mother about the pregnancy. Her mother, of course, had a fit. A complaint was made to the Children's Services Agency, and charges were later filed against her father. Stacy was angry towards her father and the legal system. She complained that the investigator from Children's Services and the prosecutor had lied to her in order to charge her father. She felt that all her power had been taken away by the legal system. Now she is waiting to see if her father goes to prison or is placed on probation. She is hoping for probation because she knows that her mother has no way to support the family. Stacy is afraid that she may lose her chance to attend college. She resents her father "for not letting me have a childhood."

Don't Jump to Conclusions

Stacy's mother was understandably outraged by her daughter's pregnancy. In general, however, parents must be cautious before making allegations of sexual abuse. An example is a mother witnessing her seven-year-old son masturbating and then remembering that he and his father had on one occasion slept together. At the time, there was no evidence to suggest any impropriety by the father. Mother became frightened and immediately filed a motion to restrict the father's parenting time. Upon inquiry, the court learned that much of the child's behavior was normal and found no reason to believe that the child had learned from his father how to masturbate.

This case demonstrates two important points that can lead to alienation:

1. Mistrust can escalate into damaging allegations.
2. Ignorance of normal psychosexual development can stir intense feelings in an unknowing parent.

The incident might have been avoided if the mother had understood that young children will explore their bodies and stimulate themselves for pleasure. A proper investigation by a qualified professional could also have prevented the mother from panicking. Instead, she reacted with fear and a desire to protect her son. The mother's motivation is understandable but she must learn to think, control her feelings, and request an investigation from the proper authorities. However, if you really believe that sexual abuse took place, you are obligated to report it to the children's service agency.

Children are sexual little people from the day they are born. They are curious and able to experience sexual pleasure at any age. Modesty, inhibition, boundaries, values, and guilt are not innate qualities. These qualities are learned, usually vicariously by watching peers, parents, and, of course, television. If you want to be an active participate in what your children learn, you need to talk openly and frankly about sex. They need to know that talking about sex is not taboo but instead an important part of life. For your children to ascribe to your family values, you have to talk with them. They need to feel comfortable coming to talk to you about sex. If they can't, how will your children ever be able to come to you and tell you "Uncle Charlie asked me to touch his pee pee"?

A frequent allegation during a divorce is that some family member has sexually abused a child. If the rumor is true, a parent should naturally be concerned. In this situation, the question is, "How can I ask my children about the alleged abuse without harming their relationship with the suspected family member?" Rather than making a specific allegation about the family member, ask your child, without mentioning names, to tell you when someone touches them. Teaching your children about good touch and bad touch is more helpful than saying, "Tell me if Uncle John ever touches your privates." Saying someone's name implies that something is wrong with that person and that they should be feared.

How Facts Get Exaggerated without Malice

Children can lie or give an inaccurate account about what happened without being malicious. Very young children can be confused about what is appropriate sexual behavior. Take for example a young child who says that someone touched his or her private parts. The facts may show this was true. The problem now is understanding the context in which this happened and the intent of the person doing the touching. This is where young children have a problem. They don't understand the importance of intent and context. When a child gives an account about what happened, they may not know that anything was wrong. Especially if the touching was pleasurable and not painful. They may not understand the social significance of the touching until many years later. So the child looks to the parent who is hearing the story to put their account into some context and give the act some meaning about whether the act was right or wrong. The child's account may be accurate, but it's often the parent who ascribes the intent of the perpetrator and the context of the act. This is where serious alienation can happen. Now the angry mother has every opportunity to embellish the story and nail the alleged offender. What is frightening for the father is not even knowing that anything is happening. Once the allegation is made public, he is labeled and on the defensive.

You can't blame a naïve parent for embellishing the child's account of what happened. That is why she is not an expert. She will do what comes naturally: interpret to the child the significance or meaning about what had happened. Now, the risk is if the mother's interpretation of the events is incorrect or if she reacts before hearing the whole story. The parent's reaction is seen and heard by the children, which is then incorporated into the children's story. So what was originally "Daddy touched my penis" is now "Daddy played with my penis." The latter statement has greater significance for the investigator. Yes, the change in the connotation between the two statements may have more to do with the mother's interpretation rather than an accurate account of what happened. What is more devastating for the father is that his child will come in time sincerely believe their own false or exaggerated allegation after someone has given them an interpretation of intent and context.

What Is Your Child Too Young to Know?

When children are interviewed and judgments are made about whether a child was sexually abused, a common criteria used to make that judgment was whether the child has a knowledge of anatomy or sexual behavior that is too advanced or sophisticated for a child of that age. True, there are some things that very young children wouldn't be expected to know. Young girls, say under the age of five or six would not usually know about erections. Both young boys and girls would not know about the vaginal canal. Young girls usually think of their vagina as a hole where urine comes from, not an anatomical structure for intercourse or putting something in it.

Even with these examples that I just described, there is a problem because I have to make some assumptions about the ages children typically learn about their anatomy and sex. The fact is, we don't know. Today's children are exposed to sex and language unlike previous generations. This confuses children because the frequent viewing of sexually suggestive or explicit material gives them a confused sense of what is right and what is wrong. They don't learn what are appropriate boundaries unless they are specifically taught. It is for these reasons that young children can be taken advantage of and sexually abused. With what children are exposed to on television and even their own parents' conversations, experts do not know at what ages children learn about explicit details of their body or sexual conduct. There are no studies saying whether Susan, age five, should or should not know about erections, oral sex, or intercourse. These are assumptions that child welfare workers or professionals use to support an allegation of sexual abuse.

What to Do If You Are Accused of Sexual Abuse

It is horrifying to be accused of sexual abuse, but this occurs too often in divorces. Whether you are guilty or innocent, you will be immediately looked upon with suspicion. For many, the assumption still exists that children do not lie and you are guilty until proven innocent. The reasons for this hard attitude are, first, to protect your children's safety and, second, to protect your children's testimony.

If you are accused of sexual abuse, immediately notify your attorney. It is important to act fast because you don't want to waste precious time while the other side is gathering information against you. Ask the attorney if they have had experience in both criminal and domestic law. If not, ask for a referral to a more experienced attorney. You may even ask who he would hire if he were accused.

When you initially meet with your attorney, you must be completely honest and cooperate to the fullest. Though you are feeling scared and maybe angry, your feelings do not matter. Once the disclosure is made, a series of events will happen. The local children's services agency will conduct an evaluation. You, your children, and their mother will be interviewed. You may even be asked to submit to a psychological evaluation, which I think is interesting since psychological evaluations are not valid for identifying a sex offender. If the children's service agency beliefs they have a strong case against you, they could go to the county prosecutor or district attorney and file formal charges against you. In the meantime, your attorney will work with you, review the merits of the investigation and prepare your defense. This process can takes months and can be very complicated. Without proper legal council, you could make a lot of mistakes that will later hurt you in court.

After contacting your attorney, see about having your child independently evaluated as soon as possible. Have a qualified and respected expert interview and evaluate the apparent validity of your child's testimony. You will probably need your own attorney to get the evaluation done. However, after the investigation is done, follow the advice of your attorney.

Experts who investigate sexual abuse allegations cannot always tell if the child or parent are lying. There are no simple questions or techniques that assure honesty and accuracy of what the child and parent are saying because, remember, the child and parent could sincerely believe in the allegations. Children want to believe what their parents tell them. To get at the truth, experts in the field use a complex process for gathering what they hope will be valid and accurate information. The process is time consuming and, as mentioned earlier, requires specialized training on the part of the investigator. Even this process is not foolproof. That is why you want the most qualified investigators and mental-health professional involved, whether you are the accused or the frightened parent.

Sadly, some parents will need special help because the allegations are true. These parents are encouraged to stop what they are doing and get help. Their excuses and rationalizations do nothing but further victimize the child.

What If the Court Finds the Allegations True?

Very often, convicted sex offenders get probation or will be released from prison on parole. There is no easy way for the other parent to handle this. The convicted parents may want to see their children again. If this occurs, you may need professional assistance to evaluate your children's feelings. It is most important that abused children feel some confidence in deciding what they want to do. If there is parenting time, the court could require that the visits be supervised.

Repressed Memories

During the past few years you may have heard on talk shows or read in the newspapers of people claiming they recalled memories of sexual abuse when they were a child. These revelations usually came about during psychotherapy where a therapist was using a therapeutic technique called guided imagery or hypnosis. Part of the treatment advocated by the therapist to help the patient work through any residual feelings was to confront the parent and maybe even file suit. This has destroyed a lot of families and hurt a lot of innocent people. There is no scientific documentation that supports the validity of repressed memories. This therapy can be dangerous and should not be used as the bases for an allegation of sexual abuse.

Bertha and Margaret

Bertha, a particularly vindictive mother, told her daughter Margaret that Margaret's father, Sam, had sexually abused Margaret when she was very young. The disclosure may or may not have been true. Most important is that Margaret may have no memory of the incident. If she remembers, her recall of the abuse is probably distorted by time and by what other people have told her. Margaret has little choice now but to trust her mother's story because she would not want to think that a parent who loves her would lie. So Margaret is immediately conflicted between wanting to believe her mother and not knowing how to react toward Sam. She wants to see her father but is afraid of him.

Bertha sees that Margaret feels torn and comes to the child's rescue. She tells Margaret that she is not old enough to decide for herself whether or not she wants to visit Sam. Of course, Sam is unsuspecting and cannot explain the change in Margaret's attitude. Neither Bertha nor Margaret will tell him anything. Instead, Margaret feels uncomfortable, begins to avoid her father, and resists visitation. The alienation progresses as Bertha planned.

Alleging Sexual Abuse to Alienate

False allegations are hard on children because it drags them through the process of investigation and forces them to make public statements that hurt the other parent. It is malicious, and many people believe that it should be a criminal act. If you are consciously trying to use a false allegation of sexual abuse to get your ex-spouse out of your life, you need to get therapy immediately and think about the cruel long-term consequences of your actions for your children. Whatever your rationalizations or excuses, you are wrong in trying to destroy people's lives, including your child's.

12

Significant Others

Grandparents, in-laws, step-parents, and new romantic partners can all get involved in the problems between two parents. This creates a perfect breeding ground for alienation because often all these significant others believe that they have to take a side, especially when custody is an issue. Grandparents want to support their son or daughter, friends and in-laws have their opinions, and step-parents are always involved because of how custody will affect their lives. At the same time, each parent seeks support and affirmation about what they are doing. What should you do to keep alienation in control when everyone makes their opinions known to your children?

These family members usually care about the children and what happens, but what should you do when all this caring gets to be a bit much? How should you deal with grandparents who want to give advice and maybe even want to take over your life?

When couples separate, it isn't always easy to know how their siblings will line up. Sometimes your brother or sister will actually be more supportive of your ex-spouse than of you. There are many reasons for this. Depending who left whom, the sibling may hope that you will get back together. Your ex-spouse and your brother may have been friends years before you married or they may have been fishing buddies or coworkers. Sometimes siblings have their own issues with you or your ex, which continue to stir resentment.

Whatever the relationship, your siblings and in-laws should not get caught up in the conflicts or make an issue about who should have custody or how visits should be arranged. These issues are none of their business, and their involvement will usually cause more animosity. This is especially true if your sibling begins talking directly to your ex-spouse.

The best advice I can give to members of your extended family is to take a low profile and let you and your ex-spouse work things out between yourselves.

New Romantic Partners

"Dad has a new girlfriend"

New romantic partners can cause difficulty between you and your children-and between you and your ex-spouse-even if they do their best not to meddle in your business.

Introducing a New Romantic Partner to Your Children

How can you introduce your children to your new boyfriend or girlfriend without risking alienation? Your children may feel enormous conflict—a divided loyalty between you and their other parent. Often, they may not know how to feel or react toward you or your friend.

The issue of introducing your children to a new romantic partner is probably more of a problem with the noncustodial parent because the time they have to spend with their children is limited. A new partner will feel more like an intrusion for the visiting child. Of course, the custodial parent also has to be sensitive to how much time the partner is around them and the children. Since living together is now considered by many to be acceptable, these parents have to remember that their home is also their children's home. Having a friend move in and take over can be a terrible imposition on the children. They can get angry because the new partner is shoved down their throat and they have no power to do anything about it.

There are many issues facing children when meeting your new friend. Many of the issues are the same for both custodial and noncustodial parents. If they like your friend, they may feel guilty thinking they are betraying their other parent. The illusion that their parents may someday get back together again also is endangered. Your children are again faced with the reality of the divorce. Memories of the divorce are renewed and their grief is rekindled, especially for younger children. They may not be able to tell you how they feel because they do not want to disappoint you.

Judge Mann has learned from his years on the bench that the risk of alienation is greatest when a parent introduces a romantic friend to the children. Special caution must be taken by the parent to consider how the children will feel about the introduction. The children may not share your enthusiasm.

Children learn early that their parents will date and have other adult relationships. Some children will even encourage their parents to date. If you are dating more than one person, don't feel you have to introduce all of them to your children. Your will just confuse them. Don't introduce your friend until you know that you are fairly serious about the relationship.

TIPS FOR MAKING THE INTRODUCTION MORE COMFORTABLE

When it is time to introduce your children to your friend, prepare them before making the introduction. When you are alone with the children, let them know you are dating and would like to introduce them to your friend. Tell your children a little about your friend's interests and family. Take time for your children to express their feelings about your dating and your friend. Encourage them to ask questions.

The actual introduction is usually a tense moment for everyone, even when your children are prepared. Scheduling a structured activity like dinner or a theme park will help everyone to feel more comfortable. Structured activities will help to prevent those uncomfortable lulls in the conversation.

To help your children feel more comfortable, do not pressure them to like your friend or be too demonstrative. Asking your children to "kiss Annie good-bye" before they are ready is offensive. You must be patient. Your children need time to develop their own relationship with your friend without your interference. You may have to back off and be patient. Perhaps you need to let them set the pace for when they share their time with you and your friend.

During a visit, your children don't want to feel that they are the third wheel. This is very uncomfortable. Having the children sit in front of a television set while you are entertaining your friend is not visiting. It is saying to your children that they are not important, or at least, less important than your friends.

If you and your friend have to physically cling to each other, it is too soon for you to introduce the children. Children can feel awkward when they watch a parent hold hands, hug, and kiss. You may think this demonstration of affection is cute, but your children will not agree. You and your friend should not act like two high school lovers in front of your children. Instead, when all of you are together, you should sit closer to your children than to your friend. This will give them the feeling they are with you and not outsiders.

In addition, remember that visits are for being with your children and not your friend. If you think that you always have your friend with you during visits, you need to question your motives. Maybe you are not that interested in seeing your children.

Do not have your friend with you during the entire visit. Spend time alone with your children, especially at the end of the visit. All of you need this time alone to exchange your feelings in private before your children go home.

Having a friend spend the night during a parenting time weekend is a difficult situation. Some kids will care less while others will be troubled. Think hard before having your friend spend the night while your children are visiting. Many courts frown on this practice and feel justified in restricting your visits or ordering you not to have your friend present during a visit. You should also consider your children's feelings before deciding. If you have a good relationship with your ex-spouse, she may be able to give you some idea about how your children will react. If your ex-spouse is angry with you and believes your friend spending the night will hurt the children, he or she could sabotage your children's future relationship with your friend. That is why you might consider talking to your ex-spouse first. If you expect problems and can't talk with with your ex-spouse, you will have to rely on your own judgment. Whatever you do, move slowly. Also consider the moral lesson you are giving your child by having your friend spend the night. If your friend does spend the night, spend some time alone with your children before they return home.

Consider Your Ex-Spouse's Feelings

Before introducing the children to your friend, you may also need to consider how your ex-spouse may feel. You may rightfully believe that your ex-spouse should not influence how you manage your private life, but unfortunately, you are wrong. You must consider your ex-spouse's feelings because she or he may have to handle the fallout with your children and thus has a right to be prepared.

For the most part, parents expect their ex-spouse to date and eventually remarry. The problem occurs if the parent is struggling with ex-spousal issues and believes the new person is being introduced to the child too quickly. Perhaps they have no legitimate reason to complain, but that does not negate the strong feeling that the parent will have when hearing the news. If you anticipate having problems with your ex-spouse when you share your news or they learn the news from your child, maybe you need to think twice about whether your timing is appropriate. You could be pushing things along faster than need be. If the relationship is serious, you will need to be sensitive in conveying the news and not get defensive or angry if the other parent gets upset.

In addition, your new relationship could trigger old wounds or jealously that could interfere with your ex-spouse's support in helping your children adjust. His or her feelings could influence what is said to your children about you and your friend. The ex-spouse's hurt or sense of loss may be inappropriately focused on the new friend. The hurt is most intense when the ex-spouse knows the children are introduced to the friend. The offended parent may feel threatened by the mental image that the friend is a competitor for their children's affection. Feeling powerless, the offended parent waits, hoping there are no problems.

It is easy to blame your children's refusal to visit with your new friend on the custodial parent. You may want to accuse the custodial parent of, "brainwashing" the kids or make an equally absurd comment such as, "He is just angry because he still loves me." These alienating statements often perpetuate the noncustodial parent's irrational belief that the other parent is the cause of the alienation. The noncustodial parent is naïve in believing the children should automatically feel comfortable with his new friend.

Mary and the Bimbo

Mary was adjusting poorly to her divorce. She often felt lonely, believing she would never again find someone to love her. Though she publicly denied having any feelings for her ex-husband, she continued to love him. When asked, she expressed contempt for her ex-husband because he left her for a "bimbo" twelve years her junior. When John introduced their three daughters to his girlfriend, Mary was enraged. She knew, for her children's sake, that she had to control her feelings.

Mary was surprised to learn that John's girlfriend, later his fiancée, was actually an asset to her children. Mary had worried about John being too lax and insensitive to the girls' welfare. John allowed the girls to "run wild around the neighborhood" without supervision. He was lax about their hygiene. On occasion, the girls would go without baths and come home without once changing their underwear. Sometimes the girls slept in the living room with their clothes on. Mary knew that she could do nothing to restrict parenting time. Nonetheless, she worried every time the children went to visit their father.

When John's girlfriend came into the picture, Mary noticed an improvement in the girls' appearance after they returned from a visit. The girls were cleaner and appeared more relaxed. They became more enthusiastic and animated when describing the visit. Mary learned from the girls that their father's friend had a young daughter who was usually present during the girls' visit. Mary surmised that John's fiancée was taking an active part in caring for the girls and supervising their play. Much to her surprise, Mary felt more relaxed when the girls had their weekend with their father, knowing that the girls would be given proper care by the girlfriend.

Significant Others as an Asset

Mary learned an important lesson. She learned to not be too quick to judge John's fiancée harshly because she actually became an asset for both her and the children. Sometimes this happens. I find it's not unusual for girlfriends to empathize with their boyfriend's children. It's like the maternal instinct kicks in when needed.

Theresa expressed her feelings well when she stated, "I think my children feel a stronger bond with their stepmother than they do with their father. Cathy pays attention to them while he just sleeps." Theresa recognized the importance of having a positive relationship with her ex-husband's wife because they could calmly talk to each other about what was best for the children. In time, Theresa learned to trust Cathy. Theresa knew that Cathy would not let anything happen to the children. Theresa, like many parents, has learned that a step-parent or a friend can be an asset to her and her children.

Asking Children to Spy on the Girlfriend or Boyfriend

Spying as a means of alienation was discussed in chapter 6, but it is worth mentioning here in this specific context. A parent may want to know who an ex-spouse is dating because he or she continues to feel hurt and jealous. As irrational as this practice appears, some parents have a masochistic fascination of wanting information that serves no other purpose than to hurt themselves. Instead of ignoring or avoiding information that causes hurt, they tantalize themselves by dwelling on how to gain more information. The reason one would do this to themselves is not important. What is important is not to use the children to gather information to gratify a need to hurt.

Grandparents

"I know that I agreed to take care of my grandchildren until you got your life together, and I will, but I don't think you're ready yet for the responsibility."

Children need and want a loving relationship with their grandparents. This remains true after a divorce. Grandparents strengthen the grandchildren's sense of family by passing on family history, values, and traditions. They give the grandchildren a historical perspective on where they come from and a vision for the future.

Most grandparents are well meaning, but they too can get caught up in the alienation cycle. This can happen in many ways.

Grandparents Should Not Help Unless Asked

Grandparents do not always trust their own children to parent competently-and sometimes with good reason. They can be critical of their son or daughter's parenting, constantly looking over their shoulder, ready to criticize and correct them. Whatever they do, the parents never do it well enough. Of course, the grandparents say, "We're only trying to help." Well, they should not be helping unless asked. Grandparents are forgetting that the parents have a right to raise their children, just as they did. They may have different opinions or values about raising children, but when did different generations always agree about child rearing?

A parent's right to parent needs to come before the grandparent's right to parent. Grandparents should resist any temptation to take over the parenting of the grandchildren. Most parents like an occasional helping hand with the children. And children like their grandparents around, but let the parent have control of when and where you can help. Despite their good intentions, grandparents who get too involved demean their children and shake their children's confidence in their parenting skills. It will cause conflict for everyone if the grandparents are seen as an unwelcome intrusion.

A Parent and Children Moving In with Grandparents

After a divorce, many parents return to their parents' home, taking the children with them. Often the grandparents take care of the children while their mother is working or going to school. Sometimes the grandparents get involved with issues of visits and in-laws, leading to possible alienation.

Grandparents in this situation must cooperate with court parenting time orders and make it a point not to convey animosity in front of the children or even the mother.

Grandparents Rescuing a Parent in Trouble

Some parents have serious problems that tempt grandparents to come to their son or daughter's rescue by helping care for the grandchildren. This is noble and sometimes necessary for the grandchildren's welfare. Problems occur when the grandparents become overly assertive and controlling. Though they mean well, these grandparents take over everything. They tell the parents what and when to do whatever needs to be done. Sometime they get their leverage by threatening to withhold financial assistance or saying, "If you don't do what I tell you, I will just leave and get out of your lives. You don't appreciate me." Sometimes the son-in-law, who may feel capable of caring for the children, is pushed aside.

When grandparents, usually the grandmother, are invited to help care for the grandchildren, they should try to give as much responsibility as possible to the parents. After all, this arrangement is supposed to be temporary and the parents should understand this. Over time, and as the parents become more responsible, they should have additional responsibilities while the grandparents back off. In addition, the grandparents have to be careful about how they explain to the grandchildren about what is happening with their parents. At this point, the grandparents could easily cause alienation, especially with a parent not living at home.

When grandparents see problems with their son or daughter and ex-in-law, they should try to remain neutral and let them work things out on their own. Grandparents should not be responsible for solving the family problems.

Grandparents Serving as the Grandchildren's Full-Time Caretakers

For many reasons, parents will ask the grandparents to care for the children temporarily because they are unable to do so themselves. Typically, the grandparents and their son or daughter agree that the grandparents will take care of the children until the parent wants the children returned. The problem with this arrangement is the parent believes that he or she can get the children back anytime he or she wants and the grandparents assume that the children will be returned after they decide the parent is ready to resume parental responsibilities. I have seen many families return to court because the parent and grandparents didn't agree about when the children should be returned.

A Formal Written Agreement Is Essential

If you are considering having your parents take care of your children until you can get back on your feet, there are a few things that you can do to avoid trouble later. To begin with, get an understanding in writing, with an attorney's help, that outlines each other's expectations and conditions for when the children will be returned. Such an agreement may not be legally binding unless it has been signed by a judge and filed in court.

You should also include a provision that you and the other parent can see or visit with the children anytime you want. If you don't see your children or you wait a long time before asking for their return, it will be harder to get them back. The worst thing you can do is not visit your children and show little interest.

Sometimes the grandparents and children form a strong bond with each other. In this situation, the children either do not want to return to their parent's home or the grandparents set such an unrealistic standard for when the children are to be returned that the parent has no chance of ever getting them back. When this happens, the grandparents don't say it, but they really don't ever want to return the children. They like raising the children and wish the parent would just back off. When this happens, everyone returns to court.

Many problems can be avoided or solved if you use a court-ordered mediator or a family specialist. For example, if you want your parents to temporarily care for your children, you could use a mediator to negotiate the terms of your agreement. Then you could use a counselor to monitor how you, your children, and everyone else are doing. Whatever you do, plan ahead and get expert advice. You would be amazed at the problems that can occur that were not anticipated.

Grandparents, Getting Too Attached

If your parents are willing to be responsible for taking care of your children, make arrangements to guard against over-attachment on the part of your parents. This may sound ridiculously obvious, but always keep in mind that you may suddenly want your children back and that it may not be as easy as you think. You have to be emotionally prepared for this possibility. Take your children out or spend the day with them—it is not only good for the children and you, but is also good for your parents. If your parents know that you are actively involved with your children, it will prevent them from getting overly attached because they are reminded of your interest.

Your parents may have concerns that you are not capable of caring for your children because of emotional problems or substance abuse. They may in fact, require counseling as a condition for taking care of the children. If you refuse and your parents have reason to believe that you are neglectful or abusive with the children, they should report this to your local children's services agency and consult their attorney. If the children's services agency agrees with them, your parents can volunteer to take temporary custody. This way, everyone knows the process is legal. Now the children cannot be returned without a hearing and possibly a recommendation from the children's services agency. Your parents are looking out for you to get you the help that you may need. But there's a fine line between this and over-attachment to their grandchildren. Whatever happens, make it clear that the grandparents will not be raising them to adulthood. They will be disappointed, but if the parent's home is stable, the best place for the child is with his or her mother or father.

Why Some Grandparents Alienate Grandchildren

With few legal rights, grandparents may think that getting the grandchildren to reject their parents is their best chance of keeping the children and protecting them from a situation they sincerely believe to be unsafe. This tactic can ultimately hurt the children, especially when they get older and realize that you were alienating them from their parents.

Some grandparents blame themselves for the way their own children turned out. Now they want to make amends with their conscience by seeing to it that their grandchildren don't follow the same path. To steer them down the straight and narrow, they may use the absent parent as a negative example, playing up their faults and drumming in the notion that they are a bad person. This puts the children in a terrible position. They want to love even an absent parent without anyone's interference. Again, if you are a grandparent in this situation, keep your opinions to yourself. Let the children, over time, get to know their parents.

George and Missy

Like many couples whose marriage is failing, George and Missy decided to move from Ohio to Florida, believing a new start would save the family. Soon after the move, they realized this was no simple cure for their marital problems. Before their divorce, Missy decided to remain in Florida while George and their son Terry, age five, and daughter, Tracy, age sixteen, returned to Ohio.

Upon their return, George and the children stayed with the maternal grandparents. For a while, all went well until George decided to move into his own home with the children. The grandparents understood George's desires but felt a loss and emptiness when the children moved out of their home. In the beginning, the grandparents had frequent visits. Arrangements were made for Missy to return from Florida to visit the children. However, this arrangement was not working because Missy's finances prevented her from traveling back and forth from Florida. In time, Tracy and her brother felt abandoned by their mother's insistence to stay in Florida rather than return to Ohio. Since the children could not direct their anger towards their mother, they took their feelings out on the grandparents.

The grandparents could see Tracy's resentment grow. In turn, they became defensive of Missy's behavior. They made excuses to the children for her decision to remain in Florida and reminded them how much Missy loved them. The children did not accept their arguments. Each time the grandparents reminded the children of their mother's love, they got angrier. Eventually, the children refused to visit the grandparents because they were tired of their grandmother telling they should be understanding. Their comments made Tracy felt like there was something wrong with her for feeling angry with her mother. Tracy's refusal to visit was the only way she knew how to get back at her mother and grandparents. Tracy even refused to accept the grandparents' birthday and Christmas gifts.

The grandparents blamed the children's rejection on George's recent remarriage. George and the children denied the allegation, saying they could decide for themselves not to visit. The frustrated grandparents were successful in getting a court-ordered parenting time, which can be had in many states, because the children's mother decided to stay in Florida. However, George did not follow the court order. He continued to make it clear to the grandparents that he supported the children's decision about not visiting. He remained passive, waiting to see if the children changed their minds.

Grandparents, Be Careful about Defending Parents

Conversely, grandparents need to be careful when they defend their son or daughter's behavior to the grandchildren. If you are too pushy and insist that your grandchildren forgive their parent, you could be alienating the children from you as well as from your son or daughter. Children, like anyone, will make up their own minds about how they feel without your help. Rarely have I seen a grandparent successfully defending their child when the grandchildren's experience is contrary to what they are being told. If there is a serious problem with the children's feelings, the parent and not the grandparents need to repair the damage. Otherwise, the grandparent's good intentions could backfire, causing even more problems.

In the complex tangle involving George, Missy, Missy's parents, and the two children, several people had the power to intervene.

- George could have helped by reminding the children that the grandparents had nothing to do with their mother's decision. He could also have told the grandparents that the children were getting angry and gently suggested that they back off and not be so defensive of Missy. Finally, he could have encouraged the children to obey the court order and maintain a relationship with the grandparents.

- The grandparents' defense of Missy was understandable, but they would have had fewer problems if they had been less persistent about it.

- Missy, and not the grandparents, needed to defend her decision to live in Florida. She should maintain verbal and written communication, continue to acknowledge holidays with gifts, and make it a point to visit the children whenever possible.

- Tracy needed to learn to separate her feelings toward her mother from her feelings about the grandparents. Tracy and her brother needed their father's support to have an ongoing and loving relationship with their grandparents while knowing they could still feel hurt and angry about their mom's decision.

The sad irony of their quarrel was that the children did need a relationship with their grandparents. Unfortunately, the grandparents became a symbolic extension of the mother and a target of the children's anger.

Grandparents Can Be the Alienators Behind the Alienator

Some grandparents actively participate in their offspring's campaign against his or her ex-spouse and perhaps are even instigator. Their contribution might include egging their child on with insinuations and innuendoes against the mother and inviting their son and grandchild to live with them after they get custody. It is understandable that grandparents want to support their son or daughter's efforts to get custody if it appears justified. It is another issue to use your children to satisfy your own desire to raise your grandchildren.

Targeted parents need special help dealing with alienating grandparents because of the risk that any retaliation will alienate the children from them. Children usually have a special relationship with their grandparents and any interference with the relationship by the targeted parent will be interpreted by the children as alienating. If you are not careful, your children can actually learn to resent you and become aligned with the alienating grandparents. This is when you need a mediator to step in.

A Final Word to Grandparents

Most adults have fond memories of the times spent with their grandparents. Your grandchildren should be no different. They need your love. If necessary, you should exercise your grandparent parenting time rights in states that have such laws.

You can be an invaluable source of support for the whole family. Just remember to let your children do the parenting unless they ask you to help. But love your grandchildren and stay involved with them over the years. They will love it.

13

Working Successfully with Attorneys, Mediators, and Counselors

In going through a divorce—and especially a custody case—you will need professional help from several people. This chapter offers useful information on how to work with a qualified attorney who can represent you in court, a mediator to resolve family conflicts, and a counselor to help you or a family member resolve other problems.

In each case, it important to get the most qualified person you can afford to be part of your team. Competent representation can make the difference between a functional and dysfunctional family. After all, the decisions made will affect you and your children for many years to come.

Selecting an Attorney

Judges have their own biases and their own criteria for deciding a case. They will put more weight on some criteria than others, which makes it hard for you to outguess the judge. That is why you need to select a qualified attorney who knows the court and judges.

You may be tempted to represent yourself in court, but this can be risky because you don't know the laws or the procedures used by the court. Some judges or magistrates will automatically have a bias against you. If you decide to represent yourself, find someone to give you advice that has already gone through the process in the same court that will be hearing your case. You should be tutored, hopefully by an attorney. In general, I don't recommend anyone to represent themselves because they usually do so for reasons that have nothing to do with getting custody of their children. Representing yourself can become an issue that clouds the real purpose of being in court: the custody of your children.

Selecting the right attorney involves more than finding someone who will win the case. After the divorce is final, your attorney may continue to be a resource for helping solve future problems between you and your ex-spouse. For this reason, it is important to select the right attorney from the beginning—who is skilled and takes an interest in your case. Changing attorneys can be expensive because of the time needed to give an update on your history and explain the merits of your case. You may want to consider the following guidelines before selecting an attorney. These will give you an idea of what you can realistically expect from your attorney. This should help to reduce some of your frustration and confusion about how most attorney's work.

TIPS ON SELECTING AN ATTORNEY

- Always look for an attorney who is experienced family law. Though the competent attorney's hourly rate is usually higher, I have learned that by the time the case is completed, the competent attorney's costs were usually cheaper.

- Remember that you are paying for good representation and not specific results. Be suspicious of any attorney who makes promises about the outcome of your case.

- Select an attorney who has a proven track record in the county where your case will be heard. Ask how many divorce cases they have had in the past year.

- Usually a friend who has had experience with a case similar to your own is an excellent source for getting the name of an attorney.

- The local bar association will help you by giving you three names of local attorneys. Keep in mind that the bar association will give you names of attorneys specializing in domestic relations and who have an office close to where you live or work. The names do not take into consideration the attorney's reputation or competency.

- Be cautious when hiring a big-name attorney for a divorce case. Such attorneys usually specialize in criminal law, are usually expensive, and may show little interest in your case.

- You should interview the prospective attorney before deciding to hire him. After all, the attorney will be interviewing you to see if he or she can work with you and if you have the money to pay your bill.

- Look for an attorney who is interested, empathic, and knowledgeable of the law.

Going through any litigation is stressful, even if you are the plaintiff. To lessen the stress, you may want your attorney's reassurance that he or she will win your case. Though your feelings are understandable, your attorney can only represent you on the strength of the evidence and not guarantee that the judge will decide in your favor.

Because you are angry, you may think that hiring a big-name attorney will intimidate your spouse or the other attorney. This rarely happens. Most experienced attorneys know each other and are not intimated by the opposing attorney. Any intimidation is usually the client's illusion and not shared by the attorney.

Know in Advance How Fees Are Determined

The least expensive hourly rate is not always the cheapest attorney. Ask the attorney about their hourly fees and what your are getting for the money. Many attorneys will charge for their time on the phone, doing research, or standing in line to file papers. You should know ahead of time what you are paying for so you are not surprised.

My corporate partners and I once had the occasion to seek legal advice about franchising our clinics. We received estimates from local attorneys averaging around $40,000 for legal fees. We learned from our discussions with these attorneys that they would have to do considerable research to complete the franchising disclosure statements. Not one attorney said they were qualified and referred us to someone else. Because franchising can be complicated for an unqualified attorney, we decided to find a firm in Cleveland who had extensive experience with franchise law. Their hourly rate was double the estimates that we had received locally, but they did the entire job for around $4,000 or a savings of $36,000. The lesson we learned was that costs are not always what they appear. This is also true for domestic cases.

Most attorneys maintain a running invoice where they record the time and cost of your phone calls, interviews, consultation, research, preparation, and court appearance. I have no problem with this practice except I believe the client should know beforehand how costs are determined. Properly preparing a case can be time consuming. Remember that your attorney may be friendly, but he or she is in business to make a living. Also, they know more about contract law than you. After all, the agreement between you and your attorney is a contract and should be written to avoid later misunderstanding.

Some attorneys will quote you a flat fee for an uncomplicated dissolution or divorce. The attorney may later add costs if the circumstances of the case become more complicated. This is not unusual, especially when a peaceful divorce is later contested. When this happens, you can expect to see an increase in the fees. Understand beforehand what the circumstances are that could increase the cost of your litigation.

Remember, you, and not your attorney, will gather most of the information for your case. You will avoid a lot of disappointment if you understand that you will be doing most of the legwork gathering all the necessary documentation. You know better than your attorney does where and how to find the material needed to support your case. If your attorney does the legwork, you will pay dearly for that time.

Do not trust all attorneys to be honest about their knowledge of domestic law or the workings of the local family or domestic court. Some will present themselves as knowledgeable when they are not. Others may say they can handle a case assuming it is a simple divorce or dissolution. If the case becomes complicated or the attorney encounters trouble, he or she may charge you for their research time to get themselves out of trouble. This is expensive and usually unnecessary if you initially select a qualified attorney.

What to Expect from Your Attorney and the Court

The legal system moves slowly. In some jurisdictions, it may take a year to schedule a contested case for a full-day hearing. Typically, the individual who wants the legal proceedings to move slowly is the one who has the most control. This is because it is easier to slow the legal process down than it is to speed it up.

Your attorney will present evidence in a way to support your arguments. The judge then has the responsibility to sort out the truth and make a judgment on the case. You will lessen your hurt and disappointment if you understand that attorneys are not bound to tell the truth in court. An example is an attorney representing a murderer. The attorney may know the client is guilty, but their ethical responsibility is to give a good defense and instill a reasonable doubt in the juror's minds so they can get an acquittal. The truth and the defendant's guilt have little to do with the morality of the defense. This is also true in domestic court. Don't be surprised if the attorney for the other side distorts what you consider the truth. There are two sides to every story, and if you and your ex-spouse agreed on everything, you would not need to be in court.

Try not to take what is said too personally. Instead, help your attorney by being honest and maintaining your self-control. Never place yourself in the position where your attorney has to defend you or your behavior. By maintaining self-control and compliance to existing court orders, you allow your attorney to take an offensive rather than a defensive posture. This strengthens your position with the court.

Never lie to your attorney. When he or she learns the truth, they may get angry and feel embarrassed if they learn that you lied about the facts surrounding your case. Your attorney can do a better job if they know everything before going to court, even if the information is embarassing to you. The courtroom is not the place to begin telling your attorney the truth or details about your case. You may feel embarrassed telling your attorney everything that is relevant to your case, but you have to put those feelings aside.

Often decisions are made quickly at hearings. Do not allow yourself to be pressured into a decision until you are ready and understand the consequences. You must try to take some control over the pace of the events.

TIPS ON WORKING WITH ATTORNEYS

- You naturally feel passionate about your case. Do not feel offended if your attorney does not share your enthusiasm. After all, your case is one of many.

- Don't be outraged if the attorney for the other side distorts what you consider the truth in court. There are two sides to every story.

- Do not make any agreements in court that you cannot live with for a long time. Once an agreement is made and approved by the court, changing it will require legal representation and possibly another court hearing.

- Do not lie to your attorney. He or she can do a better job for you if armed with all the facts before going to court.

- Remember, you and not your attorney will gather most of the information for your case. Otherwise, you will pay dearly for your attorney's time!

- Although you will probably hear things in court that anger you, stay honest and self-controlled. This will help your attorney make a case in your favor.

Providing Emotional Support Is Not Your Attorney's Job

Parents frequently complain about their attorney not returning phone calls. Often an attorney perceives phone calls from their client as a nuisance unless they have new information to give them or they are waiting for their client to return their call. Clients often turn to their attorneys for emotional support. Most attorneys do not see themselves in the role of a counselor and do not feel qualified or comfortable in a supportive role. When a client calls to get a status report, most of the time your attorney will have nothing new to say. Consequently, the attorney may try to avoid taking your call.

A parent wants to believe that his or her case is the most important in the world; but remember, most cases are ordinary and they do not require special attention. Your attorney has many cases and will usually ignore your case until the hearing is scheduled and the date is approaching. This may offend you, but a good attorney is busy and has to prioritize their time.

It is not uncommon for a parent to make his or her case a personal crusade. This is noticeable when they carry a large briefcase of files and documents. You may make frequent calls to your attorney with new or additional information about your case. Though your voice is filled with excitement and you expect your attorney to share your enthusiasm, you may find your attorney busy and unavailable. Feeling disappointed, you may keep calling until you get through. When you finally reach your attorney and share your information, you may be disappointed by your attorney's lack of excitement and failure to praise your labor. Your disappointment is understandable. However, realize that your attorney cares about your case but won't necessarily share your passion. Most crusading parents tend to overkill on the amount and relevance of the information they give their attorney.

Motions and Court Orders

Parents not familiar with the courts often misunderstand motions and court orders. When you and your attorney agree to submit a motion before the court, your attorney will write out the motion and leave room for the judge's signature. The motion is then given to the judge at a hearing or privately in chambers (the judge's office). Both attorneys are not always present when the motion is presented and signed by the judge. Sometimes an ex parte order is signed without the other attorney's knowledge. The reason for the judge's action, without the benefit of the other attorney's presence, is that the judge must make an emergency order because the children's safety is allegedly threatened. The judge must act immediately and schedule a hearing soon so the offending parent can present evidence to vacate or remove the emergency ex parte order. If the offending parent fails to present convincing evidence to vacate the ex parte order, the children will remain with the other parent.

There are occasions when a parent, through the attorney, files an emergency ex parte motion for a change of custody that is predicated on false allegations. This practice is an abuse of the judicial system. Unfortunately, the judge, or even the parent's attorney, may not know whether or not the allegations are true until the case is heard at a later date. In the meantime, the judge may feel they have little choice but to act on the emergency order. The first thing judges want to do is to protect the children.

A written agreement between two parents, or between parents and grandparents, may not be legally binding unless the court has approved it. Remember that a person's intentions may change with time. What you once believed was an agreement may not be true later. The only agreement that counts is one signed by the judge and filed in the court.

Similarly, a motion is not an ordered motion until the judge signs it. Parents frequently complain about hearing the judge make an order at the conclusion of the hearing and later finding out that the order was never put in writing and signed by the judge. Consequently, the order had no legal standing. When you hear the judge or the attorneys agree to a motion, be sure that the motion is written out by your attorney and includes all the details agreed upon. Sometimes court orders are not put in writing by the judge because he or she assumes that one of the attorneys will write it out for his or her signature. Sometimes the attorneys assume that the other attorney will write the order and, consequently, nothing happens. Attorneys can get lazy and not want to write out the order for the judge's signature. Do not let this happen.

To help ensure the accuracy of the court order, you should write down on paper what you understand are the judge's orders given at the conclusion of the hearing. Then, ask your attorney if he or she will write the order for your review before getting the judge's signature. Remember, by the time the judge has to sign the written order, he or she may not remember the specifics of your case. Again, if the order is not written and signed by the judge, it is meaningless. Good intentions do not count. You must interpret a court order literally. Do not infer a conclusion that is not written in the order. If a point is not written in the order, it does not exist.

Have your attorney, rather than the other attorney, write out motions or court orders that have been agreed upon by both parents. If the order is complex, do not rely on the other attorney to write the order for the judge's signature. The final order may appear different from what you understood was the agreement. When this happens, you can expect a lot of animosity later. Instead, ask your attorney if you can review the written order before it is given to the judge for signature. Be sure the order is accurate and includes all the points agreed upon. Ask your attorney to clarify any points that are ambiguous.

Working with a Mediator

I think there will be a time in the future when all parents going through a divorce will be expected to have a family mediator to help resolve conflicts. The process makes sense because going to court is too expensive, attorneys are biased for their client, and parents usually don't have the skills to resolve serious conflicts without some help. This is why most parents got a divorce in the first place.

What Is Mediation?

Mediation is a cooperative effort between divided parents and a neutral third person to help develop healthy ways of settling difference about the care of their children. After a history of fighting and an inability to solve differences, mediation may sound like a fantasy, but it does work.

Unfortunately, having a neutral professional is expensive, time consuming, and not even available within a reasonable physical proximity to many families. However, when it is available, mediation can accomplish a great deal in less time than family psychotherapy and more cheaply than going to court.

Early detection of alienation requires an understanding and an ability to recognize the symptoms. This is sometimes difficult to do because of the parent's intense emotional involvement with his or her own case. Whether it is their own or their ex-spouse's behavior, the parent has a personal bias about how they perceive and interpret the alienating behavior. Their judgment will be clouded by their own rationalizations to justify their behavior. Sometimes an unbiased third party that is specially trained can better recognize and understand the alienating process.

The neutral third party may be a counselor, attorney, or a psychologist who has received specialized training in mediation. When looking for a qualified mediator, ask the individual whether they are a member of either the Academy of Family Mediators or your state association. You should be leery of someone who puts out a shingle, calling themselves a mediator without documented qualifications and references. Requirements for becoming a mediator vary from state to state. To play it safe, you may want to rely on a mediator recommended by your local domestic court or attorney.

Mediation Ordered by the Court

Sometimes family mediation is ordered by the court. In this case, ask your attorney to review with you the motion for family mediation before it is filed with the court and signed by the judge. Make sure the motion contains the following information:

- The name and address of the mediator.
- The names of all the family members ordered to mediation. This list could include the names of the step-parents, grandparents, or anyone that is actively involved with the children. Though a family member's name may be listed in the motion, the mediator or counselor will have the choice to decide who needs to attend the sessions. If the name of a family member is not on the list, the mediator may have no authority to require the member's participation. This can cause a delay if the attorneys have to return to court to modify the original court order.
- How the services are to be paid for and who is responsible for payment. A court order cannot mandate an insurance company to pay for the services if the services are not part of the insurance benefit package. Instead, the responsibility for payment should be assigned to a parent or parents and not an insurance company.
- A description of the services to be provided.
- A description of the mechanism for reporting back to the court. This may include a letter by the mediator describing the services provided, naming the participates, and outlining recommendations. The mediator or counselor will be careful to respect the participant's confidentiality.

How Does Mediation Work?

Participating in mediation and going to court are not the same thing. Going to court involves one person filing a formal motion or complaint against another. The complainant is saying to the court that he or she has a difference of opinion with the defendant that they cannot resolve without the court's help. Both sides present their arguments and evidences to the judge or the referee, who then delivers a judgment.

In mediation, the issues may be the same. How can the two parents work together to make life better for the children? The parents and the mediator meet together so agreements can be made on how they can best take care of the children. The initial session begins with a discussion of the mediation process and the parents explaining their concerns for the children's schooling, social activities, health care, safety, parenting times, and rules. The emphasis is on the parents making decisions together that will benefit the children. The mediator will discourage the parents from making accusations or laying blame. Little emphasis is made on looking at past mistakes. This is because parents usually do not agree on what happened in the past anyway. At the completion of the first session, the parents and the mediator decide whether to continue the mediation process. If they agree to continue, another session is scheduled.

In the following sessions, usually five or six, the parents share in a cooperative process of learning and making decisions. Together, the parents outline their points of agreement and then begin learning ways to work together to settle their differences. This is a give-and-take process where the mediator may have to remind the parents about what is best for the children. The mediation usually concludes with a written agreement between the two parents. The plan, which may be submitted to the court, includes only those points of agreement.

Confidentiality

Mediators are bound by an ethical code assuring the parents confidentiality. What they report to the court is limited to the signed agreement between the parents. The mediator may ask the parents to agree not to repeat what is said in mediation to anyone else. However, if the mediator has reason to believe that one parent may physically harm someone, confidentiality could be forfeited. During the initial session, you should discuss with your mediator the state laws that pertain to confidentiality.

Using a mediator to help parents from divided homes resolve differences is becoming increasingly popular. The reason for this popularity is that the process works. Parents who participate in making decisions and who feel their concerns are heard are more likely to comply with an agreement than if decisions are dictated by the court. This encourages parents to work together, which is good for the children. Research has proven repeatedly that children make a better adjustment to divorce when they know their parents communicate and work together for their best interest as opposed to those parents who do not talk to each other and cannot settle their differences.

Some people still think of mediation as a fad though it is becoming more frequently used by the courts for settling disputes. For others, mediation is seen as a viable alternative to custody litigation and may someday revolutionized how courts decide custody (Warshak, 1992). The process is not a panacea for all the ills that trouble divorce families and their children. For example, there is serious question about whether mediation should be used with a couple that has a history of physical abuse. Some mediators argue that a victimized parent can never be on equal footing with an offender. There is a risk that mediation may give the offender an opportunity to continue exploiting the victim. Any agreement is looked on with suspicion because of the question of whether the victim of abuse was intimidated or entered an honest agreement. This and other issues need further research.

Working with a Counselor

There are family or personal problems that mediation is not intended to solve. Someone who has a mental disorder, is abusing drugs, or is physically abusive will require a more intense therapeutic intervention with a counselor, social worker, psychologists, or psychiatrist. Mediation is not expected to solve these issues.

Deciding Whether You Need Counseling

You may wonder whether or not you would benefit from counseling. A little guidance should help. Most people start counseling to get relief from psychological or emotional pain. Everyone has days where they feel depressed, on edge, or anxious. Having these feelings does not mean you need therapy. Therapy is helpful when, for whatever reason, you do not bounce back or recover from your psychological pain or your persistent pain interferes with your daily functioning. You have good reason for getting professional help when you are missing work, no longer enjoying pleasurable activities, are drinking more, have trouble controlling your anger, or are withdrawing from friends and family. (For guidelines on when to seek counseling for your child, see chapter 2.)

Your hurt and anger from the divorce should heal in time. For most people, a divorce will cause major changes in their life; however, these changes should not cause enduring problems. For some, healing is a slow process and aggravated by the ongoing relationship with the children and ex-spouse. If your feelings are not healing or you do not like how you are behaving, do not be too proud to say, "I need help." Divorce is a unique experience that has unique problems. This is especially true when you have children. There are many different reasons to consider counseling. Some of the reasons are listed below:

- You are not able to separate your ex-spousal role from your parental role. You may have reason to believe you are either an active or obsessed alienator.

- You spend too much time thinking about your divorce and having been betrayed by the system. You are becoming more, rather than less, depressed and angry.

- You are driving by your old house, hoping for a glimpse of your ex-spouse or children.

- When you are at home or work, you often think about when you can make your next phone call to your ex-spouse or the children. Your ex-spouse complains about your endless phone calls. Though you believe your phone calls are justified, you know they are causing problems, particularly with your children. You cannot seem to stop yourself from making the calls.

- Though you believe your anger and frustration are justified, others frequently criticize you for bothering your ex-spouse and the children. You may have quiet moments when you question your own behavior, wondering if you are harming your children.

- You are starting to use drugs or drink more.

- You are becoming more afraid and angry because of your ex-spouse's incessant harassment. You are questioning your ability to continue coping with the pressure. Sometimes you think you are unfairly taking your frustrations out on your children. You are afraid of losing control and becoming abusive.

- You are missing work because you don't feel like going and are withdrawing from your friends and family.

Sometimes parents have the idea, which is often reinforced by mental-health professionals, that people should seek professional help anytime they suffer a trauma or a major loss. The reasoning is that they can't help but become emotionally scarred if the crisis isn't somehow dealt with professionally. Later, if not now, the crisis will endanger their functioning and personal growth.

There is a problem with this belief. To begin with, people for thousands of years have suffered crises without getting therapy. Most seemed to get along fine, stumbling along for a while but often becoming stronger for their experience. They continued to function quite well and make tremendous contributions. I sometimes think that many mental-health professionals are a bit arrogant to think that they are the only ones qualified to help someone with a crisis. Time does help heal wounds, and let us not forget the support and love from family, friends, and religious institutions.

Trust Your Capacity to Heal from Pain

You are no different from most others who have felt the pain of rejection, the loss of a loved one, or a major disappointment. You probably didn't think you had to run for the nearest therapist or take for a drug to numb your senses. Instead, you most likely found support from a confidante or a trusted friend. And you probably reminded yourself, "I know I will feel better in time." How many times have you said this to yourself? You say it because it is true. You will feel better in time, hopefully tomorrow. In fact, I have found—and I hope you have had the same experience—which what was once a painful experience can become a peaceful and even comforting, memory.

This is a lesson you can only learn by living life. Remember how devastating it was as a teenager to breakup with your first boyfriend or girlfriend? Remember thinking that the pain would never go away unless you somehow got back together again? Now looking back on those years can draw a smile because you are at peace with the memory. Even the old songs, once a reminder of a lost love, can now be a nostalgic memory. So what's different now that you are older? Hopefully the difference is your belief in yourself, and your belief that the pain will heal. After all, your own experience should tell you that. You must learn to trust your capacity to heal.

Divorce Does Not Always Require Therapy

Not all parents or children going through a divorce need therapy. In fact, most don't.

I may sound critical of my professional peers, but I believe in people's ability to heal and care for themselves. On the other hand, there are occasions when people do need professional help: when the crisis or loss seriously impairs their daily functioning; or, for whatever reason, when a problem does not seem to be getting any better. Even though you cannot put a time limit on how long it takes to heal, there is a reasonable expectation when you should be better and back to your old self. Different cultures have different beliefs about how to cope with loss and what is a reasonable time to recover. I remember a psychiatrist from an Eastern country explaining that a person is psychotic if they continue to grieve from the loss of a spouse longer than six months. Well, that may be fine in his culture, but it is not true in most Western countries. Regardless, we must be sensitive in that different cultures don't always deal with crisis and loss in the same way.

Remember, there is no shame in getting help. What is shameful is recognizing there is a problem and doing nothing about it.

Finding the Right Therapist

If you decide you need help, schedule an appointment with a local psychologist, clinical social worker, or family therapist. There are local organizations that sponsor workshops or groups for people adjusting to their divorce. Your local help hotline or crisis center can help you find a qualified referral. Other good sources are the family court, friends who have had an experience similar to your own, or a local support or advocacy group like Parents Without Partners, ACES, or Fathers for Equal Rights.

Some therapists may be put off, but you should ask for therapists' qualifications and fees. Many parents have asked for mine. Therapists should have at least a master's degree in counseling, social work, or psychology. Most but not all states license therapists, social workers, and counselors. Psychologists are licensed in all states. Most professional therapists are not qualified or trained to work with divorced families having problems with alienation. They should have specialized training in domestic law, family therapy, conflict resolution, and mediation. They should also understand what parental alienation syndrome is and have experience testifying in your local domestic relations court.

When considering a therapist, don't hesitate to interview the person to see if he or she is qualified. Remember, you are trusting the therapist with your or your child's well being, and their services are expensive. Ask them for other qualifications: how many times they have testified in domestic court, how many years of experiences they have working with families, which psychiatrist they are working with in the event medication or a psychiatric evaluation may be needed, and what the fees are. There are no rules or specific qualifications that will assure you of the clinician's qualifications. You have to use your best judgment.

There should be chemistry between you and your therapist. Sometimes this takes awhile to establish, as with any other close relationship, so do not give up too easily. To do a good job, the counselor may have to tell you some things you won't want to hear at first. This is particularly true if you have been alienating your children. On the other hand, if your gut instinct is that the counselor is off target and consistently puts you down or makes you feel more depressed, do not think, "This guy has a Ph.D., so who am I to argue with him?" Trust your instincts and look for another therapist. There is one out there who can help you.

Counseling for Alienating Parents

Counseling is a complex process for treating alienation. The problem with counseling begins with the alienating parent refusing to believe they have a problem and need help. Rarely will the alienating parent seek counseling unless they believe they can convince the therapist to become their advocate against the other parent. When the alienator learns that the therapist cannot be used to support the alienation, the parent will usually drop out of therapy.

For those who seek help, therapy begins with helping the alienating parent to understand how his or her behavior is symptomatic of alienation. For this to occur, the therapist must work through the parent's defenses. Alienating parents believe their behavior is justified and get angry with someone that is not supportive or challenges their position. They rationalize their actions and blame the alienated parent for all the problems. They cannot see their role in contributing to any of the problems. Instead, they describe how the other parent and the system have victimized them.

A qualified therapist will get past the alienator's defenses and begin a process of helping the parent look at their own behavior and its effects on others. Then they can begin the process of changing their behavior. Most important, the therapist will not become an enabler to the alienator's cause.

As mentioned in chapter 1, counseling works well with Naïve and Active alienators but is not very effective in helping an Obsessed Alienator. This is why it is important to recognize the early symptoms of alienation and get help before the alienation gets worse.

14

When All Else Fails:
Seeking a Change in Custody

The decision to seek custody should not be made lightly. Let us assume that after much quiet contemplation, you have come up with many reasons for going to court. You are sincere in your conviction that your children are better off living with you. You probably find it hard to imagine how the court could possibly disagree with your reasoning. In your heart, you know that if you can get your message across to the court, you will triumph and custody will be yours. And maybe you are right.

However, before getting too excited about your good intentions, you need a word of caution. You cannot assume that someone who understands your arguments will necessarily agree with you. Believing that you are the more competent parent and better suited to raise your children may have little bearing on what the court believes is in the child's best interest. You have to keep this sobering fact in mind before returning to court.

If you do decide to proceed, ask your attorney's advice. He or she knows your local court and can advise you on the strength of your case. Do not take offense if your attorney tells you that your chances are slim. He or she may be giving you good advice, even if you do not like what you are being told. If you insist on proceeding with the litigation, your attorney will follow your instructions or refer you to another attorney.

Before deciding to seek custody, try to anticipate the risks for both you and your children if you proceed with your case and lose. Begin by reminding yourself that your children did not ask for the divorce. There is the risk that you will be worse off than before going to court. What will be left of your relationship with your ex-spouse and the children? Maybe the cooperation you are now getting won't be there after the litigation because your ex-spouse will become bitter and angry. Take a moment and think twice about what is good for your children before you think about what is good for you. Courts do not like to upset your children's routine or stability unless there are very good reasons.

Try mediation or counseling first to resolve any problems with your ex-spouse. Going through any litigation, whether criminal or civil, is intensely stressful and emotionally draining for everyone, including your children. It makes no difference whether you are the plaintiff or defendant. You learn from your experience to avoid litigation if at all possible. Very often, there are no winners.

Are You Acting on Your Children's Behalf or Your Own?

You may not want to admit that your reasons for seeking custody are flawed. Your reasons may have more to do with ex-spousal issues than what is best for your children. This realization can be painful and difficult to accept. There are probably many arguments that you could list that would support your belief that you should have custody. To better understand how relevant your arguments may appear before the court, complete the following exercise.

EXERCISE: WHY ARE YOU SEEKING CUSTODY?

Write down all the reasons the court should award you custody of your children. Make the list as extensive as possible. After completing your list, review each item and place an "M" next to the items that reflect the reasons the change of custody would be good for you. Examples may include not having to pay child support or spending more time with the children.

Again review your list this time placing a "C" next to the items that describe your reasons why a change of custody would be good for your children. Some examples may include "I'm home every day when my children return home from school, my neighborhood has younger children, or my children will not be exposed to drugs." Discriminating between an "M" and a "C" item is difficult and requires absolute honesty.

After completing your review of the items, you should have more "C" items than "M" items. The "C" items are the arguments that you would use to gain custody because they reflect the reasons living with you is good for your children. Typically, the court will have little interest in your "M" items even though you may have strong feelings about them. The decision to change or grant custody is determined by the court's judgment as to what is in your children's best interest and not what is good for you.

The "Best Interest of the Child" Doctrine

States have their own variation of how they define and interpret the "best interest of the child" doctrine. Though the state doctrine may be specific, judges will rely on their own interpretation of the law. Judge Leven said it well: "No one can really define 'best interest' to take in all the contingencies that may come before the court." There is no way of really defining it." He further explained "that the law places the burden on me to see to it that the child receives love, care, affection, proper parenting, and companionship [parenting time or visitation]." He is quick to tell parents, "I can't give that to your children. Since I can't, it is the parents' responsibility to do so. I expect them to do it. If they don't do it, I become extremely, extremely disappointed." Judge Leven believes there is no good definition for best interest, therefore his statement described his personal criteria for deciding custody.

It is impractical for this book to outline all the state laws and various local interpretations of the best-interest doctrine. To give you some idea of what judges are looking for prior to making their decision, I have paraphrased and elaborated on Ohio and other criteria for best interest:

- The parents' wishes regarding their children's care.
- The children's wishes and concerns about the allocation of parental rights and responsibilities as expressed to the court.
- The child's interaction and interrelationship with his parents, siblings, and any other person who may significantly affect the child's best interest.
- The child's adjustment to his home, school, and community.
- The mental and physical health of both parents.
- The parent more likely to honor and encourage parenting time, or companionship, rights approved by the court.
- Whether either parent has continuously and willfully denied the other parent his or her right to parenting time.
- Whether either parent has failed to make all child support payments, including arrears, that are required of that parent pursuant to a child support order.
- Whether either parent has been convicted of or pleaded guilty to any criminal offense involving any act that resulted in a child being abused or neglected, or whether either parent previously has been convicted of or pleaded guilty to any offense involving a victim who

at the time was a member of the family or household and who caused physical harm to the victim in the commission of the offense.

• Whether either parent has or intends to establish a residence outside this state.

You will need to consult your local attorney to learn the specific laws or criteria for your state.

Issues to Consider Before Pursuing Custody

You may feel ambivalent when you hear your children say, "I want to live with you." You may be excited by the compliment, and yet overwhelmed by the thought of the responsibility and lifestyle changes. Logistically, you may foresee many problems. You may not have a babysitter or adequate space. Living in an undesirable neighborhood for raising children could cause you concern. While you gingerly inquire about your children's reasons, you imagine how your ex-spouse will feel when he or she hears the news.

Here are several specific points to consider before you make up your mind on what to do next:

1. When you ask your children where they what to live, they may lie and say what they think you want to hear. They do not mean to be malicious. Instead, they do not want to hurt anyone's feelings. Often their stated desire to live with a parent is their way of saying, "I want Mommy and Daddy back together." This is particularly true with younger children. The children's fantasy that somehow their parents will reconcile is persistent, even with teenagers. Even when one parent has already remarried, the children often express the hope that one-day their parents will again be back together.

   Do not consider seeking a change of custody unless your children initiate the request or you have good reason to believe that remaining with their other parent seriously jeopardizes the children's welfare. If you initiate the idea to your children for a change of custody, you cannot trust that your children will be honest with you.

2. When thinking about a change of custody, you must move slowly. Remember, the best decisions are made when you have

the maximum information. If you do not have all the information needed, postpone making a decision until later. There are times when the only decision that can be made at the moment is to decide what information needs to be gathered before making a later decision. This is true when considering seeking custody of your children. You need to think about the consequences your actions will have on everyone, including yourself. If you are unsuccessful in your bid for custody, you will have spent a lot of money and risked damaging your relationship with your ex-spouse. This could be an expensive price to pay for a long shot.

3. Before announcing your intentions to your ex-spouse—or especially to your children—consult your attorney. Learn about the laws for changing custody and the workings of your local court. Remember, it is the court, and not your children that decides custody. Try to get an idea from your attorney about the likelihood of you will be successful in getting custody. In many jurisdictions, it is nearly impossible to get an involuntary change of custody, which means both your children and your ex-spouse object, unless there is a legal provision for the children to choose where they want to live or there is evidence of abuse or neglect. Otherwise, you must prove to the court that your children's best interest is served by their living with you. This usually involves you having to publicly degrade or attack your ex-spouse to support your argument. Successfully attacking your ex-spouse's capacity to adequately parent is difficult. Typically, courts are justifiably biased in the belief that your children are better off remaining with the custodial parent to preserve stability.

4. Do not make any promises to your children about changing custody. If your ex-spouse fights your attempt to gain custody, the time it takes in some jurisdictions to change custody can exceed one year. Your attorney can give you a better idea as to how long the process may take if the change of custody is contested. Even if you feel confident telling your children, "After today's hearing you will come to live with me," do not make promises you cannot keep. Often cases are continued when the court realizes that a full hearing is needed to settle the case. Even after the judge hears the testimony, it may take days or even weeks to make a decision.

Courts frequently schedule many hearings at the same time because they know that many of the scheduled cases will be settled through negotiation rather than having a full hearing. When negotiations between the attorneys fail, rather than proceeding with the hearing, another date may be scheduled. As a result, you and your children may wait, possibly for weeks or months, for another court date.

5. If possible, you should raise the question to your ex-spouse about seeking a change of custody. True, your ex-spouse may feel hurt and angry, but it is better for you to raise the issue rather than having your children do the dirty work. The issue is between you and your ex-spouse rather then between the children and their other parent. Do not have your children be the harbinger of bad news. If you are afraid to talk to your ex-spouse about a change of custody, think about how your children will feel.

6. When you hear for the first time that your ex-spouse is seeking custody, do not drill your children for answers about where they want to live and why. Keep your composure. Reassure your children of your love while making no harsh declarations about what you are planning to do. Take time to calm down and consult your attorney to learn the best course of action. The attorney will advise you what to do next.

Natasha

Natasha was a bubbly six-year-old who described how her father, Dan, would ask her where she wanted to live. Dan was concerned because he believed that Natasha's mother was neglectful. Often Natasha was filthy and unkempt. During Natasha's interview, she explained how she felt when Dad asked her where she wanted to live: "When he asks me that, I kinda feel I love my mom. I want to live with her." Natasha's statement reflects what often happens when a parent asks a child where he or she wants to live. Natasha felt uncomfortable with her father's questions. In response, she pulled away emotionally from her father and drew closer to her mother. Natasha's statement is a good example of the risk a parent takes when asking the children where they want to live. The questioner may actually provoke an alienation from the children.

Possible Circumstances Surrounding Custody Cases

Your circumstances at the time you decide to seek custody may determine the chances of your success. For example, if you are seeking custody before the divorce, your chances of success are better than if you seek a change after the divorce is final. Circumstances such as who is living with who before or after the divorce must be addressed before the court will make a decision.

Before the Divorce: You versus Your Spouse

Both you and your spouse are seeking initial custody prior to the divorce.

You each enter the court arena equally entitled to the custody of your children. You will have the opportunity to present evidence and testimony about why it is in your children's best interest to live with you. Though the criteria for best interest is not always clear, each judge will have personal beliefs about how he or she will make the decision. For this reason, as mentioned in chapter 13, it is best to hire an attorney who knows and understands the biases in your local court. Outside attorneys are often not familiar with the local judge's biases or the workings of the court. This can work against you.

After the Divorce: You versus Your Ex-Spouse and Children

You want to seek a change of custody but both your children and ex-spouse object. This is referred to as an involuntary change of custody.

Seeking a change of custody under these circumstances is difficult if not impossible. You are asking the court to grant you custody when everyone, including your children, do not want the change to occur. The burden of proof is on you to show the court that it is in the children's best interest to live with you. Many courts have a bias that children are better off staying where they are if they are doing well in school, have a wide circle of friends, and are well behaved. Changing custody means taking the risk of jeopardizing your children's good adjustment. Most often, parents seeking custody under these circumstances are motivated by ex-spousal issues and not the betterment of the children. Judges are aware of this and are sometimes suspicious of a parent's motives when they want a change of custody contrary to the wishes of the children.

Before the court will change custody, two issues will have to be addressed. First, you must prove to the court that your ex-spouse is somehow not suited to raise your children. The issue is not if you are a good parent but, instead, if the custodial parent is a bad parent. Most states do not have laws that define good parenting, but there is usually a law defining abusive or neglectful parenting. Each state or legal jurisdiction may have its own criteria for defining abuse or neglect. You will need to consult your attorney or local child protection agency to learn more about how your state defines abuse or neglect.

Courts are equally concerned about how cohabitation, homosexuality, drug and alcohol abuse, or other deviations from community standards of proper conduct will influence your children's adjustment and welfare. Though the issues are not considered abuse or neglect, they are concerns for some courts that may influence the decision for an involuntary change of custody. Jurisdictions will vary on the importance they place on these issues. For example, courts in smaller towns tend to worry more about cohabitation than courts in larger cities.

It is not enough for you to show the court that a parent's behavior may be neglectful, abusive, or contrary to community standards. You may have to demonstrate to the court how your children have been harmed by the custodial parent's alleged misconduct. For example, your ex-spouse may be a homosexual. Are you able to prove to the court that your ex-spouse's sexual orientation is harmful to your children? The fact that you believe it is harmful is not a strong enough argument to convince a court to make an involuntary change of custody, unless the court is already biased or unless the other parent behaves in an offensive manner in your children's presence. There is no supporting evidence to suggest that a homosexual parent is inherently harmful or damaging to children. Homosexuality is not contagious, and homosexuals are not sexually abusive toward children any more frequently than heterosexuals.

If you are successful in convincing the court that your ex-spouse is neglectful or abusive or behaves in a manner potentially harmful to your children, the second issue before the court is, "Who shall care for your children?" Your answer of course is, "I will." Now your task is to convince the court that you are right for the job. Unfortunately, the court may still not agree with your argument. Instead, it may require the current custodial parent to get professional help to solve personal problems before deciding on a change of custody. If the custodial parent fails to follow through with the court-ordered treatment, or if treatment is unsuccessful and the parent continues to be abusive or neglectful, the court may then grant you custody. This process can be expensive and time consuming.

You and Your Young Children versus Your Ex-Spouse

You and your children want you to seek a change of custody but your ex-spouse objects. All the children are under the age of election.

Many states have a provision in the law to allow a child at a certain age to address the court and express their preference as to where they want to live. The specific age of election is stated in the state law. The rationale for the age of election is based on the state's judgment as to when children have sufficient maturity to make a responsible choice. In recent years, legislators have been questioning whether the election law is a good idea because of the burden that this decision puts on the children. In effect, the election laws are asking the children to publicly reject one of their parents. Most would agree that this can not be good for children. Rather than election, courts still want to give the children the option to express their preference, but the court wants to reserve the right to make the decision based on the best interest doctrine. In this way, the children and parents should understand that it isn't the children who make the decision but the courts. I believe this is a better arrangement for the children. They shouldn't have to bear the burden of facing the parent that they have just publicly rejected.

As the noncustodial parent with children under the age of election, you are faced with the same issues as the parent who is seeking custody where neither the children nor the other parent want the change. You must show the court how the custodial parent has been abusive, neglectful, or behaved in a manner that is detrimental to your children's welfare. You must also show the court why it is in your children's best interest to reside with you. Only then do you have a chance for success. Generally, your chance of success is poor under these circumstances also.

You and Your Teenagers versus Your Ex-Spouse

You and your children want you to seek a change of custody but your ex-spouse objects. All the children are over the age of election.

Depending upon your children's ages, the judge will seriously consider their preference as to where they want to live. The judge may talk with your children in his chambers so they can share their feelings without feeling intimidated by their parents' and attorneys' presence. The judge will try to determine if your children have been pressured by either parent, evaluate their maturity, and try to understand their reasons for wanting to live with the chosen parent. Reasons such as "My dad lets me stay up late," "I can date whoever I want," or "My dad will buy me whatever I want," do not reflect much maturity and probably will not help to influence the court. Judges will listen for more mature motivations such as "I can tell my dad how I feel," "I love both of my parents but I want to get to know my father better," or "I'm more comfortable with my mom."

Each judge will weigh the children's motivations differently. Some will be liberal in supporting the children's choice. He or she may believe that children of a certain age are old enough to know what they want. Other judges will place greater importance on wanting to maintain stability in the children's lives, especially if they appear well adjusted.

Even in states without election, judges are usually interested in what children have to say. They will still make the decision based on the child's best interest, but they will take the children's wishes into account—especially older children, who usually have a better idea of what they want.

If you know that your children want to live with their other parent and you object, your task may be to show the court why your children's wishes should not be granted. You may need to show the court that the change of custody is not in the children's best interest. In many courts, this is difficult to accomplish. The bias is to allow the children to choose if they can demonstrate their maturity.

You and One Child versus Your Ex-Spouse and Another Child

You and one of your two children want a change of custody but your ex-spouse objects. The change of custody would require splitting the children.

Courts do not like splitting children between their two parents because of their belief that children are better off together. Parents must convince the court that splitting is best for the children and will not cause them harm. The judge may interview the children, together or separately, to learn how they feel about the proposal. If the children have the slightest reservation about living in separate homes, the court will usually deny the parent's request. The courts are biased in wanting to keep children together so they have the opportunity to have a sibling relationship.

You and Your Ex-Spouse versus the Children

You and your ex-spouse want a change of custody but the children want to remain with the original custodial parent.

Parents occasionally decide among themselves to change their children's residence without informing the court or seeking a formal change of custody. Unless someone complains, the court will not know where the children are living. In this situation, the children will remain wherever the parents want the children to live.

When both parents agree on changing custody, the court will typically support their decision. Both attorneys will document the parents' approval with the parents' signatures on a written motion before the court. The court will document the consent with the judge's signature on the motion. A formal hearing before the court is usually not necessary providing both parties agree to the change of custody and provisions for child support.

When both parents agree to a change of custody, the children usually have little, if anything, to say about the decision. If the court somehow learns of the children's opposition to their parent's request, it may order the children a guardian ad litem to assure protection of their rights and best interest.

15

What Are You To Do?

You should now know how to recognize the symptoms of alienation and have greater insight about what to do to monitor your behavior and how to respond if targeted by the Naïve and Active Alienator. What may not be clear is how to rehabilitate the severely alienated child or the Obsessed Alienator. The reason is simple. Presently, there are only theories or conjectures because there are no tested protocols for rehabilitating the severely alienated child or the Obsessed Alienator. As often happens with time, a clearer picture is starting to emerge from the hazy fog of uncertainty. Though research is still lacking, there are some trends that are starting to emerge offering hope for warring parents and the courts

Parents, attorneys, mental health professionals, and courts will each have their own perspective and strategy for what do with alienation. Deciding a strategy will depend on whether the parent is targeted by a Naïve, Active, or an Obsessed Alienator. Naïve Alienators should rarely appear in court because of alienating behavior. The most effective intervention for the Naïve Alienator is education and learning to monitor their own behavior. Strategies for the Active and Obsessed Alienator are more complicated. These parents frequent the courts and cause frustration for all because little seems to work in reducing the tensions between the parents.

Whether you are the target of the Naïve, Active, or Obsessed Alienator, there are some things to keep in mind to lessen the damage and hurt to you and your children. The foundation for understanding, preventing, and stopping alienation begins with recognizing the role of ex-spousal issues, changing boundaries, symbols, and strengthening relationships. You must keep calm and not panic before you apply what you have learned. Your children will be quick to sense that something is wrong if you get excited and lose self-control. In fact, you could cause your own alienation with your children if they see you retaliate against the other parent.

The Naïve Alienator

Remember that the Naïve Alienator is usually unaware of how their behavior or comments affects the children or the other parent. These are usually not malicious parents but if you happen to be targeted by the Naïve Alienator, don't panic. Keep your calm and trust your relationship with your children. Children learn early that their parents will say things they don't mean. They are very adept at letting something-said go in one ear and out the other. If you believe there is a problem trusting your children's reaction to the alienation, focus on strengthening the relationship rather than retaliating against the other parent. Monitor your own reactions and behaviors so you don't start your own alienating campaign. If you think it would be helpful, try talking to the other parent without making accusations or attacks. The other parent may appreciate your comments if they are made with some sensitivity.

What are you to do with an Active Alienator?

How you deal with the Active Alienator is similar to what you need to do with the Naïve Alienator. You must keep your calm, trust your relationship with your children, and resist retaliating. The difficulty you have with the Active Alienator is the parent's inability to control the rage and hurt built up inside. Now the feelings are interfering with your relationship and time spent with the children. Together, you need education and counseling to focus on the issues causing the problems. Sometimes, the Active Alienator requires individual therapy to help with their lose and grief. You can support these efforts without being punitive. Taking this tactic, both you and your children will be better off in the long run.

What is the targeted parent to do with the Obsessed Alienator?

Dealing with an Obsessed Alienator is more complex and difficult than dealing with the other two types of alienators because, at this point, the alienating parent has already had considerable success in alienating the kids against you. The kids may refuse to have anything to do with you, making it next to impossible for you to talk with them and try to repair the damage. As frustrated and angry as you feel, don't give up on your children. Find some support, either from your family, attorney, a counselor, or other parents. Be sure to do what ever you and your attorney believes is necessary to keep visits going. Even if the other parent refuses your visits, keep trying and maintain a log of your efforts. Also, it is very important that you do not violate any court orders or do anything that forces your attorney to defend your behavior. A common tactic used by some attorneys is to deflect the issues by attacking you and forcing your attorney to defend your behavior. Behave yourself so this does not happen.

The most difficult part dealing with the Obsessed Alienator is keeping your anger in control and not retaliating. Though your feelings are understandable, retaliation usually does nothing more than cause more problems. In fact, the Obsessed Alienator will frequently use your retaliation against you by pointing out to the children how you behaved and reinforcing the argument that you don't care about the kids. Again, you are put on the defensive without having any access to the children to blunt the other parent's blows. Whatever you do, you must stay focused on keeping the relationship with your children strong and not entangle them in the fight with your ex.

When you start to sense that your children are turning against you, don't delay in telling your attorney or mediator. As soon as possible, look into getting a court order to have your children seen by a therapist with the authority to report back to the court the parent's compliance to the court orders.

While your children are being seen and monitored by their own therapist, you and your former spouse should have joint sessions with a different therapist. The reason for a different therapist is to avoid any conflicts of interest or minimize the risk of one of you not trusting the therapist's objectivity. Sometimes, the therapist may also need to see extended families members who are caught up in the alienation. An important aspect of the therapy is to educate everyone about the symptoms of alienation, the effects on the children, and how to reduce the level of tension between the parents. The experienced therapist must be knowledgeable about family systems, the workings of the courts, abuse, domestic violence, parental alienation, and domestic state laws. The worse thing that can happen with the therapist is to lose objectivity and be taken in by the alienator. This often happens with inexperienced therapists or a therapist that has a personal political agenda.

The Court

Alienating and targeted parents often return to court. They are frustrated and angry because they feel helpless and are now looking to the court for help. At this point, the parents usually can no longer talk with each other without shouts of bitterness and accusations, or silence. Judges realize that it does no good to order parents to cooperate and calmly talk with each other because the orders usually fall on deaf ears. So what are the courts to do? To begin with, courts must realize that alienation is a real phenomenon and a progressive syndrome that gets worse in time without intervention. The courts must begin by identifying high-risk cases and intervene as soon as possible after a motion is filed. The longer the court takes to hear the case, the more damage will occur for the families and children. Cases that are most likely to appear in court and require quick intervention because of the high-risk of more severe alienation include:

- Complaints about visits being withheld.
- Children frequently not returned on time (later than a half-hour).
- A parent threatening to abduct the children.
- Allegations of sexual, physical, and/or mental abuse.
- Alcohol or drug abuse.
- A parent's severe mental disorder interferes with visits or the children's adjustment.
- Children's refusal to visit.
- Parents discussing adoption or allowing the children to use the stepparent's surname.

There needs to be a mechanism for the court to identify these cases and schedule a hearing as soon as possible. The court should not tolerate any unfounded delay tactics or continuances by attorneys. The case should proceed as scheduled.

In my years of experience with the court, I am frequently surprised at how often cases get resolved after I have given parents the opportunity to vent their frustrations and feelings. Many times, parents just want to feel they are respected and heard. After which, they are usually very receptive to a little education about parenting and the issues I have described in this book. About 25 percent of the parents that I see, listen to, and educate no longer contest the custody recommendations because they understand the reasons for the recommendations and have had an opportunity to ask questions to someone they perceived as impartial. Courts may be wise to find some mechanism for parents to be heard, ask questions, and receive some helpful education.

The courts should have protocols for helping parents to resolve their differences and protect the children from harm. This mechanism must be fair and monitored by the court for compliance. Some courts may use a guardian or an employee of the court to receive monthly reports and doc-ument compliance. Usually parents involved with mild cases of alienation cases can benefit from education and improved awareness about what they are doing and how it effects the children. Sometimes having the parents complete a psychological evaluation is helpful for the court to gain better insight into the dynamics of the case. In cases involved with more severe alienation, both parents should be ordered to a therapist familiar with family systems therapy. The court should compile a list of local qualified therapists who are willing to work with these families and report to the court. They should document for the court their qualifications working with high-conflict parents and an understanding of parental alienation.

With this level of intervention, the children may not need to participate in the therapy, but this should be left up to the therapist. The therapist sends monthly compliance reports to the court while maintaining the parent's confidentiality. This process can also be very helpful for high-risk parents before they introduce a shared parenting plan to the court. While this process is going on, it is important that the court not withhold visits unless there is a question about the children's safety. Withholding visits adds to the risk of reinforcing alienation because the children could believe there is really something wrong with the targeted parent.

In cases of severe alienation, where the court has identified an Obsessed Alienator, the court must act fast. Both parents need an immediate psy-chological evaluation to rule out possible psychopathology and order the child or children to therapy because, by definition, they are very confused and may be expressing hatred towards the targeted parent. While the chil-dren are in therapy for deprogramming, they may be better off staying with a neutral relative.

No research findings, aside from my own observances, support these recommendation, but reason dictates that if the child stays with the Obsessed Alienator, the parent can sabotage the counseling and efforts of the court to resolve these issues. If the child is placed against his wishes with the targeted parent, the child could be frightened and rebellious. I suspect that most courts would not be prepared to take the risk of placing a child with a parent he says he hates. Until there are controlled studies testing the validity of this tactic, most courts will not exercise this opinion.

Now What?

State legislators are still grappling with legislation that will help families, promote child support, reduce the court dockets, diminish hostility, and promote the best interest of the child. Courts look to the behavioral sciences for answers because they sincerely want to do what is best for children. Parents want a loving relationship with their children without any interference from anyone, particular from the ex-spouse. Everyone, except a few parents, wants child-support payments paid. Children want to be loved and not feel as if they are coming between their parents. I have sometimes been critical of my colleagues because of a tendency to take a stance on public issues when we don't know any more than anyone else. It is easy to hear various opinions from professed experts without any supporting research and documentation. True, new issues, like parental alienation syndrome, comes to the public's attention and requires thought. What is needed is research on the effectiveness of a various protocols for intervening with families. What is not needed is to make parental alienation a political issue with heated and sexist debates about whose at fault.

There Needs to be Hope

Many parents are unhappy because they have not seen their children in years. Courts continue to feel helpless in reconciling this problem. These parents need hope by hearing about how other parents overcame the damages of alienation and now have a viable and loving relationship with their children. And, perhaps we can learn from their success stories and identify trends that can give us new insights about new and creative interventions that stop alienation. Developing a theory or hypothesis about how to intervene begins with anecdotal experiences. If you have or want to read real success stories, visit the Internet web site www.parentalalienation.com. After all, you won't stop learning after reading this book. The web site will update you on new articles and research. Whatever you do, if an alienating parent is giving you and your children problems, for their sake, "Don't give up."

Appendix:
Custody and the Court System

"You see people come to court and you anticipate that some people are not going to tell the truth. The majority of the people do tell the truth, but they always tell the truth from their angle."

Referee Savakis

Custody Rulings Now and in the Past

To understand how domestic courts view families and divorce today, you need a bit of historical background. In the nineteenth century, fathers were typically awarded custody because of their ability to support the children financially. The children were seen as an asset to the family's survival because of their labor. After the turn of the century, mothers were granted custody based upon the "tender years" concept that she had inherent qualities making her a more suitable parent. It was believed that fathers were lacking in the inherent qualities necessary for them to be seriously considered as a custodial parent. Then and now, fathers were at a disadvantage in domestic court. There continues today a pervasive belief that children, especially the very young, will naturally do better with their mother than with their father.

Today, state laws have again changed their basic premise for granting custody. No longer is the tender years doctrine used; instead, the placement of the children is based on what is in the "best interest of the children." Now the assumption is that both parents enter the courtroom without any assumptions about a mother having an inherent advantage. Of course, this all sounds good, but the facts still show that mothers get custody between

85 and 90 percent of the time. The reason is that new laws do not change attitudes and beliefs that have been part of our culture for over one hundred years. There still is the pervasive view that mothers are better parents than fathers or they have an inherent right to be the custodial parent. Research has consistently found that children adjust equally well with either parent, except boys from about age nine to eleven, who seem to fare better with their fathers. If the research is correct, you would think more fathers would have custody, but this isn't the case. This issue will probably not get resolved for years to come. In any case, more parents are getting involved with custody litigation and competing for custody. Some degree of alienation is inevitable because both parents are trying to gain an advantage with the children. This becomes more obvious in states that allow children to choose where they want to live once they reach a certain age.

The definition of the "best interest of the child" is not always clear enough to make much sense. In Ohio, for example, one criterion for best interest is "the child's adjustment to his home, school, and community" (Ohio Judicial College, 1991). The Ohio criterion does not explain what is meant by adjustment, how adjustment is assessed, and what factors contribute to good or bad adjustment. (For more about how courts assess this and about the decision whether to return to court seeking a change in custody, see chapter 14.) Some factors, of course, are obvious. Good school grades and a happy disposition reflect better adjustment than poor grades and depression. The judge will weigh and rank each factor in order of importance. It is up to the judge's discretion to decide what factors or criteria are pertinent for determining good adjustment.

Courts are sincerely concerned about how to make the best decision while having little statistical information about what is good for the children. Common sense and sometimes prejudices are usually the judge's criterion for deciding custody.

The Custody Evaluation

Sometimes the judge or magistrate will order a custody evaluation. The evaluation is a complex process during which a psychologist gathers information about the children, parents, and anyone else involved in the case. After doing this as objectively as possible, the psychologist makes a recommendation to the court on behalf of the children's best interest. The reasoning behind the evaluation is that the more information available to the court, the better the decision.

There are many variations of how a psychologist conducts the evaluation. There is no single correct method. Common to all custody evaluations is the requirement to have a court order mandating the participation of all relevant individuals, including the parents, children, and step-parents. The court order is a requirement because the psychologist needs the mandate to represent the court rather than the parents. For this reason, neither the parents' nor children's therapist can concurrently conduct the custody evaluation and provide therapy. If the psychologist tries to maintain a dual relationship, he or she is likely to be seen by the court as biased and untrustworthy. In addition, this is considered to be unethical professional behavior because the therapist is ethically bound to serve as a patient advocate while an evaluator is to have no allegiance except to the court, the law, and the "best interest of the child." The psychologist cannot concurrently assume both roles.

Waiving Confidentiality

Before the evaluation, the psychologist should explain to you and your children that you will have to waive your rights to confidentiality. This means that there are no secrets between you, the court, and the psychologist. The test results and what you and your children said during the evaluation will be made available to the both attorneys and the court. Even your ex-spouse may read the report. If you, for any reason, have a problem with waiving your rights to confidentiality, immediately consult your attorney for advice before starting the evaluation.

Many psychologists struggle with the responsibility of providing the court with accurate information without harming the relationships among family members. This can be a difficult task because of what the children may say during their interview. In theory, the children's statements are to be made available to the court for review. However, the children are not always psychologically equipped to handle their parent's hurt or anger when they hear the children's statements for the first time in open court. When there is a risk that the children's statements will cause significant harm to their relationship with either parent, the children's testimony may be reviewed in the judges chambers with the attorneys present. A sensitive attorney will hopefully respect the children's dilemma and try to protect the their privacy. Doing so will help prevent alienation and further psychological harm to the children.

Preparing Your Children for the Custody Evaluation

It is difficult to take your children to a psychologist for a custody evaluation. You may feel guilty having to put your children through this ordeal.

The psychologist will share your concerns and will do whatever is needed to make your children feel comfortable and relaxed. They will try to avoid asserting any pressure on them to answer questions.

The psychologist's goal is to get the most accurate and honest information possible from your children in a limited time. The psychologist knows that you have a personal interest in what your children will say. Because of your self-interest, the psychologist will use various interviewing techniques to see if the children have been coached by either you or your spouse. To minimize the possibility of your children being biased and not truthful, the psychologist will ask both parents to bring in the children several times for interviews. A court order mandating the evaluation will require your cooperation with this process. Having two or more interviews will allow the psychologist to listen for consistency in your children's statements. To help the psychologist and ease your children's fears about the evaluation, you may want to consider the following recommendations.

TIPS ON PREPARING YOUR CHILDREN FOR THE CUSTODY INTERVIEWS

- Reassure your children that they will be talking to a nice man or woman and that they will do fine. They need to know they cannot fail an interview, even if they do not talk.

- Do not tell your children what to say to the psychologist during the interview because this could be perceived as an attempt to influence them.

- It is all right to be honest with your children and say that the psychologist will be talking to them about how they feel about the divorce. You do not need to say that the psychologist will ask them where they want to live. Many psychologists do not ask this question directly but will infer the answer from the children's responses to other questions. Some psychologists believe that asking the children directly about where they want to live puts them under considerable stress that should be avoided.

- Before taking your children out of school for the evaluation, let them know they will be returning to school unless it is too late. Treat this appointment like you would any other doctor's appointment.

- Before the interview, do not promise your children a treat or a trip to McDonald's after their interview. The children may perceive your offer as reward for their "good" performance during the interview. After the interview, you can suggest going to lunch before returning to school.

- Stay calm and reassuring. If you act scared or upset, your children will sense your reaction and may respond with similar feelings.

What Does the Evaluator Look For in the Parents?

There are a variety of methods psychologists use to conduct a custody evaluation. The methods for gathering information include psychological tests, private interviews, home investigations, social histories, and structured observations between family members. There are no mutually agreed upon procedures for conducting a custody evaluation. Most psychologists use a combination of interviews and testing. In recent years, there seems to be more of a reliance on interviews rather than testing alone because of concerns about the validity of test results for predicting future parenting and the children's adjustment living with a particular parent. Most courts continue to like psychological testing because of the perception that tests are more objective than clinical observations by the psychologist.

There is no professional consensus on what variables are most relevant for deciding which parent is more suitable to have custody. Research identifying specific variables for predicting a child's future adjustment after a divorce is rather limited. Often the psychologist will have in mind variables that are supported by research and variables that intuitively make sense for predicting future adjustment. Some of the variables that a psychologist may consider important for predicting your children's future adjustment and your capacity to parent may include the following:

- Are you flexible and willing to resolve differences with your ex-spouse? This will be looked at closely because the court knows that your children's adjustment depends on how well their parents communicate with each other. If your children see a reasonable degree of cooperation, the children will be more relaxed and less fearful. When children expect arguments or fights between their parents, they will learn to dread the times when their parents are together. They will also have the perfect opportunity to manipulate both of you, not out of malice, but out of immediate self-interest.
- Can you show an ability to separate your personal interest from your children's best interest? This often means separating the ex-spousal role from the parental role. An example would be encouraging your children not to visit when you are feeling angry because the support check is late. Your feelings may be justified, but this is an ex-spousal issue while the visitation is a parental issue.

- Are you willing to encourage visitation? The court will consider this extremely important. Failure to cooperate with visitation in some jurisdictions is sufficient reason to grant the other parent custody. The court will want assurance that you encourage your children's active involvement with their other parent.

- How much have you influenced your children's perceptions and feelings toward the other parent? Have you been trying to encourage a positive relationship between your children and the other parent, or have you alienated your children against the other parent to position yourself as the more loving and caring parent?

- Are you perceived by the children as the psychological parent? The psychological parent is the one whom the children perceive as the primary caretaker—the one who gets up in the middle of the night if they are sick, who comforts them if they are scared or hurt, who takes them to the doctor or sees that they wear the right coat. You cannot become the psychological parent overnight or because you have decided to seek custody. However, sometimes the psychological parent will change because of the child's age or sex.

- Are you emotionally accessible to your children? They need to feel your love. However, getting too mushy and sweet will appear phony. The evaluator will want to see if you are and see if you are affectionate without going overboard.

- Are you able to control how you express your anger? Your children should not be afraid of you when you are angry. Many courts will not consider you fit for custody if the judge believes you have been violent in your children's presence. The court may even limit your visitation to daytime hours with supervision.

- If your children have special medical, educational, or emotional needs, do you deny those needs or do you follow up with needed treatment or remedial education?

- Will you help the children maintain their current support network of grandparents, cousins, friends, neighbors, scout leaders, doctors, teachers, and so on? The judge will typically be biased against a parent planning to move from the area without good reason, especially if the move would take the children away from their grandparents or extended family.

- How much time do you have to spend with the children? If you work all day and your ex-spouse is home to supervise the children, you will be hard pressed to convince the court why you should have custody.

- How well are you handling the current stresses in your life? Being a full-time parent and having to work is stressful and demanding. Good coping skills include willingness to accept support from your family, community agencies, schools, and friends. Poor coping methods include reliance on alcohol and drugs, displays of temper, and lack of good judgment.

- Do you and your ex-spouse have different personal values about religion, proper diet, neatness, and so on? Most psychologists will look more favorably toward the parent whose values are most consistent with the local community standards and displays a flexibility in their approach to instilling these values in their children. The psychologist is usually uncomfortable with extreme values that could cause children to feel socially awkward or embarrassed with their friends. This is particular true with older children. (Psychologists trained to conduct evaluations are taught to be unbiased and to put their personal values aside, although admittedly, some do this better than others.)

- Are you allowing your hurt and anger to heal? This is extremely important for your children's welfare. Going through a divorce is painful and frightening for both you and your children. Allowing your hurt and anger to fester can be severely detrimental to your children's welfare.

- How do you communicate your pride to your children? Can you brag about their accomplishments? Do you share your pride in your children with the evaluator? Can you show the evaluator photographs of your children? Children need to feel that you are proud of them. They need your enthusiastic love.

- How do you discipline your children? This is important in determining custody. You will be judged on whether your discipline is age appropriate, not excessive, and effective. Age-appropriate discipline means that your child has the developmental ability to behave in the manner you want and the punishment is fitting to the crime. Some forms of punishment like uncontrolled spanking, punching your child in the face, using a belt, or burning a child's arm with a lit cigarette are never appropriate and always abusive, no matter what the child has done wrong. See chapter 8 for a more detailed discussion of discipline.

- Do you maintain rules and a predictable structure? Children need structure because they feel more secure in a home where they know the rules and boundaries. Even if your children do not like your rules, they will adjust if the rules are fair and consistently enforced.

Children should know what time they are going to eat dinner and go to bed. I am not suggesting that a parent cannot be flexible, but the family structure should be fairly predictable.

- How sensitive are you in recognizing and dealing with your children's adjustment to the divorce? Some children will actually feel relieved knowing there will be less fighting and tension around the house. Others may have more somatic or physical complaints, do worse in school, withdraw from friends, or become more argumentative.

- How sensitive are you are to your children's developmental needs? This is important to their welfare. Sometimes parents going through a divorce will push their children to grow up too fast. You may want to use your child as a confidant or encourage them to dress and act older than their years. You should resist these temptations. You may mean well, but such pressure may not be good for your children.

Bibliography

Ahrons, C. and Richard Miller. "The Effect of the Postdivorce Relationship on Paternal Involvement: A Longitudinal Analysis." *American Journal of Orthopsychiatry* 63 (3) (1993): 441–450.

American Psychiatric Association. *Diagnostic and Statistical Manual of Mental Disorders, Fourth Edition.* Washington, DC: The American Psychiatric Association Press, 1994.

Bensel, R.W., L.G. Arthur, L. Brown, and J. Riley. *Child Abuse and Neglect.* Reno, Nevada: Juvenile Justice Textbook Series, 1985.

Clawar, S.S. and B.V. Rivlin. *Children Held Hostage: Dealing with Programmed and Brainwashed Children.* Chicago, Illinois: American Bar Association, 1991.

Clinempeel, W. Glenn and N.D. Reppucci. "Joint Custody After Divorce: Major Issues and Goals for Research." *Psychology Bulletin* 91 (1982): 102–127.

Dudley, J. "Increasing Our Understanding of Divorced Fathers Who Have Infrequent Contact with Their Children." *Family Relations* 40 (1991): 279–282.

Ehrenberg, Marion F., Michael A. Hunter, and Michael R. Elterman. "Shared Parenting Agreements after Marital Separation: The Roles of Empathy and Narcissism." *Journal of Consulting and Clinical Psychology* 64 (1996): 808–818.

Emery, R. "Children in the Divorce Process." *Journal of Family Psychology* 2 (2) (1988): 141–144.

Folberg, Jay. *Joint Custody and Shared Parenting: Second Edition.* New York: The Guilford Press, 1991.

Gardner, Richard A. *Family Evaluation in Child Custody Mediation, Arbitration, and Litigation.* Cresskill, New Jersey: Creative Therapeutics, 1989.

Gardner, Richard A. *The Parental Alienation Syndrome: Second Edition*. Cresskill, New Jersey: Creative Therapeutics, 1992; 1998.

Gardner, Richard A. *The Parental Alienation Syndrome and the Differentiation Between Fabricated and Genuine Child Sex Abuse*. Cresskill, New Jersey: Creative Therapeutics, 1987.

Garrity, C.B. and M.A. Baris. *Caught in the Middle: Protecting Children of High Conflict Divorce*. New York: Lexington Books, 1994.

Groth, Nicholas. *Sexual Assault of Children and Adolescents*. Lexington, Massachusetts: Lexington Books, 1978.

Grych, J. and F. Fincham. "Interviews of Children of Divorce: Toward Greater Integration of Research and Action." *Psychology Bulletin* 111 (3) (1992): 434–454.

"Guideline for Child Custody Evaluations in Divorce Proceedings: Pertinent Literature." *American Psychologist* 49 (7) (1994): 677–680.

Guidubaldi, J., J.D. Perry, and B.K. Nastasi. "Assessment and Intervention for Children of Divorce: Implications of the NASP-KSU Nationwide Study." *Advances in Family Intervention, Assessment, and Theory* 4 (1987): 33–69.

Kauffman, J. and E. Zigler. "Do Abused Children Become Abusive Parents?" *American Journal of Orthopsychiatry* 57 (2) (1986): 186–192.

Kelly, J. "Longer-Term Adjustment in Children of Divorce: Converging Findings and Implications for Practice." *Journal of Family Psychology* 2 (2) (1988): 119–139.

Kock, M. and C. Lowery. "Visitation and the Noncustodial Father." *Journal of Divorce* 8 (2) (1984): 47–64.Ohio Senate Bill 3 (1991) Columbus, Ohio.

Rand, Deirdre Conway. "The Spectrum of Parental Alienation Syndrome (Part 1)." *American Journal of Forensic Psychology* 13 (3) (1997): 23–53.

Rand, Deirdre Conway. "The Spectrum of Parental Alienation Syndrome (Part 2)." *American Journal of Forensic Psychology* 15 (4) (1997): 39–92.

Warshak, Richard. *The Custody Revolution: The Father Factor and the Motherhood Mystique*. New York: Poseidon Press, 1992.

Wolchik, S.A., S.A. Braver, and I.N. Sandler. "Maternal Versus Joint Custody: Children's Postseparation Experience and Adjustment." *Journal of Clinical Child Psychology* 14 (1985): 5–10.

Index